GENDER PERSPECTIVES IN NINETEENTH-CENTURY IRELAND

Gender Perspectives in Nineteenth-Century Ireland

Public and Private Spheres

EDITED BY

Margaret Kelleher & James H. Murphy

IRISH ACADEMIC PRESS

This book was set in 10.5 on 12 point Bembo for
IRISH ACADEMIC PRESS
44, Northumberland Road, Ballsbridge, Dublin 4
and in North America for
IRISH ACADEMIC PRESS
5804 NE Hassalo St, Portland, Oregon 97213

A catalogue record for this title
is available from the British Library.

ISBN 0–7165–2590–9

Printed in Ireland
by ColourBooks, Dublin

Foreword

MARY CULLEN

Gender is a concept with potential to bring about far-reaching change in how we interpret the past. It is very encouraging that the Society for the Study of Nineteenth-Century Ireland should have devoted a conference to gender issues. In this foreword to a selection of the papers presented at that conference, I would like to consider briefly three aspects of the use of gender analysis in history. The first is how the concept of 'gender' developed as a category of historical analysis. The second concerns its relevance to men as well as women, and to the concept of 'separate spheres'. The third relates to the use of the words 'gender' and 'patriarchy'.

The work of historians of the new wave of women's history, which began some decades ago, has progressed through a number of stages. The initial stage, a step bigger than perhaps we recognise, was to see and to say that women are invisible in the conventional history books. I, for one, can remember studying and later teaching history for years, uneasily aware that there was something wrong about the absence of women but unsure what to do about it. It was only when feminists began openly to challenge the invisibility of women, and to follow this by turning to the historical sources to find out for themselves what women had done, that many of us began to act on that uneasiness.

Gerda Lerner has given now well-known names to the early stages in the recovery of women's past: 'compensatory' history, which looks for the 'great' individual women who have 'achieved' in the way men who are deemed 'great' have achieved; and 'contribution' history, which researches the part played by women in the political, intellectual and social life of their societies, and their status within these.[1] As Lerner points out, both compensatory and contribution history give us significant information about women in the past, and undermine the view that history has been shaped solely by males. However, both still tend to deal with the areas of human activity defined as the important ones by conventional history, written as if men were the only active agents of change in human societies.

The next stage has been to try to research the past from the perspective of how women themselves experienced it, distinguishing women's actual experience from establishment prescriptions of what they *should* have experienced. There have always been plenty of these prescriptions, and the historian needs to be wary of accepting them as evidence of what women actually did. Another source to be handled with caution is male assessments of female contributions to men's (*sic*) work.

1 Gerda Lerner, *The Majority finds its Past: Placing Women in History* (Oxford, 1979), pp. 145–67.

Once women's experience moved centre stage and information began to accumulate, new vistas emerged and with them new interpretations. The concept of gender grew from the convergence of two apparently contradictory findings. On the one hand was the enormous variation in the historical experience of women, who have comprised half or more of the population of every race, colour and nationality. There was no simple, universal women's experience or women's history. On the other hand there was a linking thread running through all of the stories. In the history of society after society, to be born a female or a male had different political, social and economic consequences for an individual's life. The life and opportunities of the daughter of an aristocratic family in the middle ages, and those of a woman living in the slums of late nineteenth-century Dublin, were light years apart in many ways, but each woman's life and her set of opportunities were influenced by her sex and, as a consequence, were different to those of her father, brother or husband. Across time and place, an individual's sex invariably carried political, social and economic consequences that could not be explained by a simple biological determinism. Such consequences varied from place to place and changed over time, they were the subject of debate and struggle, but they were a factor in individuals' lives as real as their class, race, colour, creed, or education. They shared a common characteristic in seeking to direct power and control of resources to males, curtail female autonomy and define women's role in society in terms of relationship and service to men.

The word 'gender' was brought into use to name the social roles created and prescribed for women and men. Another way of putting it is that gender analysis emerged from the growing understanding of the complex role of sex in history. Sexuality and sexual practices are obviously an important part of the history of the relationships between men and women. They are not, however, the sum total of that history nor are they themselves immutable and unchanging over time and place, fixed for all eternity by some 'biological' programming. Neither are the social relationships which societies create for men and women, and which they enforce in various ways at different times, through combinations of laws, regulations, customs, education and exhortation.

Gender then concerns social relationships between women and men, and also between different groups of men and different groups of women. As a category of historical analysis it interacts with other analyses such as class, colour, religion, ethnicity, age and nationality. The convergence of all of these locates an individual or group in its historical context. Feminist historians thus argue that conventional history, written for the most part without reference to gender, overlooks one central aspect of human experience, and is correspondingly diminished and incomplete.

It is worth considering some of the implications of the absence of gender analysis from history as it has generally been written. It is not just that women have been invisible in the history books. While men have indeed been visible, this has been a partial visibility that has obscured as much as it revealed. We are used to saying that conventional history has been the story of men's activities.

More accurately, it has been the story of the 'public' activities of a few élite males. Historians have analysed and assessed the contribution of 'great' men, political and military leaders, outstanding intellectuals and artists, with no reference to the fact that, for the most part, the freedom they enjoyed to devote themselves to their public work was built on women's domestic work. History has usually been written as if the 'separate' spheres of male and female, the 'public' and the 'private', ran forever on parallel, untouching tracks, and as if only the 'public' had significance in the story of society. Gender analysis shows that, on the contrary, male and female roles have been intermeshed and interdependent. The male role has depended on the female role being defined in terms of relationship and duties to men, and on the centrality of the wife-mother who carries the responsibility for the care of the family home and the daily servicing of the physical and emotional needs of husband and children. Historically, female dissenters have argued for both recognition of and status for 'women's work', and for women's freedom to work in both the public and private spheres.

Conventional history has seldom noted, let alone analysed, the historical evidence of women rejecting and resisting imposed gender roles. For example, the political campaigns of the nineteenth and early twentieth-century Irish women's emancipation movement, which succeeded in removing many of the civil and political disabilities of Irish women, and which was itself part of a highly visible international movement, has remained completely unknown to the general public and to generations of history students. It has only recently come under serious historical scrutiny with the new wave of women's history, and has still to find its way into most histories of Irish society. If conventional history accorded serious attention to feminist political activism, this would inevitably focus attention on the structures of society that gave rise to such activism. This in turn would focus attention on male as well as female gender roles. Women's demands to enter the public sphere, however, have always carried the threat of a fundamental revolution in existing sex roles, male as well as female, and hence in the whole status quo. At the height of the campaign to win the parliamentary vote for women, in the years before the first world war, the response of John Dillon, deputy leader of the Irish Parliamentary Party, was both typical and revealing. Women's suffrage, he said, would 'be the ruin of our western civilisation'. Bearing in mind that history is a dialogue between the present and the past, it is perhaps not so surprising that conventional historians have been so slow in giving serious attention to feminist campaigns. This is not to suggest that the omission is necessarily conscious or deliberate, but that it is part of a long-standing conditioned pattern of defending patriarchy by silencing and ignoring feminist challenges.[2]

The blindness of historians to gender roles and to women's historical experience has deprived both women and men of important elements of their past. Today

2 Hanna Sheehy Skeffington, 'Reminiscences of an Irish suffragette' in Andrée Sheehy Skeffington and Rosemary Owens, *Votes for Women: Irish Women's Struggle for the Vote* (Dublin, 1975), p. 13.

it continues to remove debate about feminism from its historical context, and correspondingly weakens contributions on all sides. Women's history and the concept of gender have both developed from feminism's endeavour to locate itself in its historical context. Yet both feminism and women's history face major problems in trying to articulate perceptions of the world as it has been, as it now is, and as how it might be in the future, while using paradigms and philosophies which reflect the experience of males. Most historians, male and female, feminist and non-feminist alike, have been socialised within these world views and using these systems of thought. For feminists they present an on-going challenge, and for non-feminists they make the challenge difficult even to perceive.

It is important that we try to hold on to the new knowledge and insights that have been gained, and establish them as a foothold from which we can push further. The foothold is precarious and could easily be lost. For example, some historians (and others) object to the word 'patriarchy', because they see it as expressing a view of relationships between men and women as an eternal, unchanging oppression of all women by all men. Such a reductionist view is clearly wrong both historically and today, and it should indeed be challenged. But the word 'patriarchy', used to mean the organisation of a society around sex-role stereotypes which see men as dominant over and more important than women, names a historical reality. Societies have been so organised, and successive generations have been taught and socialised to accept patriarchal thinking and patriarchal structures as a natural and inevitable result of male and female human 'nature'. Whatever word we use, to grasp this historical reality is important for our understanding both of the past and of the world we live in today.

There are problems also with the word 'gender'. Its grammatical derivation means that it can easily be misunderstood as simply a synonym for sex, or, more often, the female sex. In this slippage its meaning as the way in which societies construct and maintain social relationships between the sexes can get lost. This in turn blunts the edge of gender analysis. As with patriarchy, the essential issue is not which word we use to name a phenomenon or idea. The essential issue is that we do use some word and that we do not lose the hardly-won sighting of the phenomenon or the development of the idea.

Women's history and gender analysis have already restored to women today some of their lost history, its activity and diversity, contribution and dissent. They have begun to reveal the role played by relationships between and within the sexes in the history of societies, and have begun to explore how those relationships operated in the lives of women and men. The more we understand how gender, the social construction of sex, operated in the past, the better equipped we are to understand how it operates today. The studies in this book, offering a variety of disciplinary perspectives, are a welcome contribution to furthering this understanding in the context of nineteenth-century Ireland.

Contents

Preface

This collection of essays originated at a conference on Gender and Nineteenth-Century Ireland, held in All Hallows College in April of 1995, the third conference organised by the Society for the Study of Nineteenth-Century Ireland. Our special thanks to all who contributed papers at this conference and to the hospitality provided by All Hallows College.

The work of the Society for the Study of Nineteenth-Century Ireland testifies to the widespread interest in nineteenth-century Ireland and continues to provide a forum for the discussion of new perspectives. This volume owes much to the support, both financial and intellectual, provided by the society; our thanks go to its members and, in particular, fellow executive officers Richard Hayes and Leon Litvack. We also acknowledge the support given to the society and to the production of this volume by Dr Mary Cullen, Dr Peter Denman, Ms Niamh O'Sullivan and Dr Margaret MacCurtain. The excellent work by Chris Morash and Richard Hayes in producing *'Fearful Realities': New Perspectives on the Famine* (Dublin: Irish Academic Press, 1996), the proceedings of an earlier Society for the Study of Nineteenth-Century Ireland conference, provided a model for which we are most grateful. To our contributors, heartfelt thanks for responding promptly and enthusiastically to our many requests.

The Catholic University of America archives kindly provided permission for the citation of material from their Fenian Brotherhood records in Toby Joyce's article; acknowledgement is also due to the *Irish Studies Review* in which an earlier version of Colin Graham's article appeared.

Our thanks to Michael Adams and the staff at Irish Academic Press for their smooth and professional delivery of this project.

Finally, we record our gratitude to the School of Irish Studies Foundation for financial support in preparing this volume for publication. It is with great sadness that we pay tribute to the late Dr Sean White, Dean of the School of Irish Studies, whose support for this project, as for so many Irish studies, will be long remembered.

MARGARET KELLEHER, *St Patrick's College, Maynooth*
JAMES H. MURPHY, *All Hallows College, Dublin*

Gender Perspectives in Nineteenth-Century: An Introduction

MARGARET KELLEHER

Private *virtues* are public benefits: if each cell were content in his cell, there could be no grumbling hive; and if each cell were complete, the whole fabric must be perfect.

Maria Edgeworth, *Letters to Literary Ladies* (1795).

After marriage, *home* is the abiding place of woman, the natural centre and seat of all her occupations, the cause of all her anxieties, the object of all her solicitude, and it is a deranged state of society that encourages her to seek employment beyond its precincts.

Patrick J. Keenan, *Report of Commissioners of National Education in Ireland* (1855).

Gender as a category for analysis may appear a recent preoccupation; its absence, until recent years, from studies of nineteenth-century Ireland might lead readers to infer that the questions it raises regarding the construction of identity are separate from that period. Yet central to literary, social and political writings of the nineteenth century are arguments regarding men and women's 'proper sphere': the fierce opposition of Patrick Keenan, school inspector, to the employment of married women illustrates just one of many such debates. Attempts like Keenan's to delineate women's 'place' and, by implication, men's 'place' through the doctrine of 'separate spheres', and the related separation of private and public realms, received strenuous support and significant opposition throughout the century.

While analogous debates in, for example, nineteenth-century America have received much scrutiny, the specific nature of Irish discourses on gender has remained obscure.[1] The path-breaking work on Irish women's history, in recent years, provides some key insights; yet, as Mary Cullen reminds us in her foreword to this volume, gender history is not a synonym for women's history. Alongside the continuing recovery of women's past, and facilitated by this work, the historical relations within and between the sexes deserve closer attention.

To this end, the Society for the Study of Nineteenth-Century Ireland chose the subject of gender in nineteenth-century Ireland as the central theme of its third conference, held in All Hallows College, Dublin, in the spring of 1995.

1 See, for example, Joan W. Scott, 'Gender: A Useful Category of Historical Analysis' in *American Historical Review*, xci (December, 1986), pp. 1053–75 and Linda K. Kerber, 'Separate Spheres, Female Worlds, Woman's Place: The Rhetoric of Women's History' in *Journal of American History*, lxxv, 1 (1988), pp. 9–39.

Scholars from various disciplines, sociological, educational, literary, historical and theological, gathered to discuss the potential of gender studies to re-evaluate not only female but also male history, together with the interconnections of these histories. The essays in this volume, arising out of the conference, unpack the ideology of gender and examine its operations in various ways; significantly, not alone in the domestic or family sphere – the terrain to which gender history is sometimes regrettably limited – but expanding the field of gender studies to include the history of education, social and religious institutions, and political events.

This expansion is especially apparent in the volume's first section, 'Gendered Re/visions', in which some of the dominant discourses and central events of nineteenth-century Ireland are reread from a gendered perspective. Timothy P. Foley's article provides a unique study of gender and political economy – traditionally the 'sovereign discourse of the public sphere, the quintessentially male space' – through a detailed examination of the debate surrounding women's employment which unfolded in the 1860s, the repercussions of this critique extending beyond the doctrine of spheres to the very basis of political economy itself. The dimensions of gender in nineteenth-century schooling, including significant differences in access to education, form the subject of John Logan's study; as he illustrates, prevailing notions of 'separate though complementary spheres' operated throughout curriculums of instruction of this period. In David Fitzpatrick's work on women and the Great Famine, gender's role as a category of historical analysis takes quite a different form. The supposition that women, as a group, were more vulnerable to famine or subject to large-scale discrimination, is challenged by recently-uncovered data, made available by the National Famine Research Project, regarding famine mortality, relief and emigration. In the course of his analysis, Fitzpatrick suggests an important extension to existing work on gender as a determinant of 'entitlements', to include not only women and men's role as workers or producers but also their non-monetary assets and services, as, for example, household managers and reproducers. In contrast to the 'cult of womanhood' challenged and redefined in the context of famine, Toby Joyce's work on the Fenians, which concludes this section, examines the 'cult of manhood' prevalent at the time. Linked to 'respectability', the 'spirit of manhood' proved a potent weapon in generating recruits from men of the middle and lower middle classes, to Ireland's 'trained and marshalled manhood'.

The revision of historical perspectives provided by the first section is continued in the second, with a specific focus on literature of the post-Union period. Siobhán Kilfeather's 'Sex and Sensation in the Nineteenth-Century Novel' re-examines the sensation novel of the nineteenth century as a central means through which the 'complexities of desire' were articulated. The novel's 'special ability to incorporate conflicting discourses' renders it not only, as Kilfeather demonstrates, a particularly 'significant source of information about sexuality' but also a key indicator of the conflicting political discourses of its time. Thus, Colin Graham's essay on 'History, Gender and the Colonial Moment' concerns Maria Edgeworth's *Castle Rackrent*, a novel 'placed precariously on the moment of Union'. Using

Homi Bhabha's theory of 'sly civility', Graham's reading of Edgeworth's 'textual tactics' uncovers the doubleness of colonial discourse, the cracks beneath the surface, in this 'slyly civil' narrative. The literary and historical contexts for Edgeworth's writings gain a further dimension in Clíona Ó Gallchoir's reading of *Letters for Literary Ladies* (1795) as a text grounded in the novelist's position as a woman writing in a post-Revolutionary culture. The recurring debate regarding the relations of public and private takes an interesting shape in this narrative, encapsulated in the extract quoted above; Ó Gallchoir shows how Edgeworth, refusing the hierarchy of metaphorical identification, turned to a metonymic system of representation in which the public sphere becomes 'no more than the sum of its domestic parts'. The narrative strategies employed by Edgeworth, in comparison with those of her contemporary Lady Morgan, form the subject of Anne Fogarty's essay, 'Imperfect Concord', which completes the section. Here Fogarty demonstrates how the novelists' attempts to write totalising fictions were 'countermanded by the contradictions and conflicts in Irish society which their work exposes' and by the 'spectral Irelands' of the past continually haunting their 'hybrid' texts.

The doubleness of discourse regarding Ireland in the early nineteenth century, as a country progressing into the future yet haunted by its past, reappears in travel writings, a genre studied in the third section of this volume. Anne Plumptre, 'An Independent Traveller', novelist and translator, and the author of a travel narrative concerning Ireland, published in 1817, is the subject of Glenn Hooper's essay. Plumptre, Hooper suggests, may be viewed as a proto-feminist writer, 'indifferent to contemporary discourses of femininity', while her treatment of Ireland contains an intriguing ambivalence: a country to be discovered but also the means through which the writer's own authority may be asserted. Both Hooper's work, and the succeeding essay by John McAuliffe on Irish travel writing of the 1840s, provide important applications of earlier theories of travel writing by Mary Louise Pratt and Sara Mills to the case of Ireland. The writings of Englishwomen Lady Henrietta Chatterton and Mrs Frederic West, with American woman Asenath Nicholson, employ prevailing conventions of sentimental travel writing yet also demonstrate distinctive features. Assertions relating to their individual presence and personal perspective enabled female writers to resist the 'all-seeing' role of male contemporaries, yet, as McAuliffe argues, such strategies also undermined their authority as commentators on Irish society. Later in the century, the genre of Irish travel writing was to be significantly extended by the writings of Irishwomen abroad, including Isabella Croke (1825–88), subject of Mary Ellen Doona's essay. Croke's diary of her experiences during the Crimean War (1854–56) provides, as Doona conveys, a unique testimony to the conflicts and philanthropic operations of the time.

The complex intersections of private and public spheres within nineteenth-century institutional life form the subject of the fourth section. In Oonagh Walsh's study of the Connaught District Lunatic Asylum, the first public institution established for the care of the insane in the west of Ireland, the importance of

lunacy with, in a majority of cases, male insanity attributed to physical causes and women's insanity more likely to be attributed to moral causes. Within the asylum, gender assumptions influenced where patients were housed and, consequently, during the famine, their chances of surviving fever and disease. Gender as a shaping force in men's history is a central theme of Brian Griffin's work on the Royal Irish Constabulary and Dublin Metropolitan Police, in which he explores the influence of public and institutional life on the male domestic sphere – still a rare subject of enquiry. Membership of the police forces, Griffin demonstrates, controlled individuals' identities as husbands, fathers and lovers, with codes of rules and regulations extending to the most private sphere. All three of the studies in this section make available original historical research, contributing valuable new information and perspectives regarding nineteenth-century Ireland. Thus, Gráinne Blair's study of the Salvation Army Rescue Network, which completes this section, uses unpublished Salvation Army records to trace the histories and experiences of the 233 Irish women who used the Army rescue network between 1886 and 1892.

The fifth and last section expands, and rewrites, what is known regarding the writings of later nineteenth-century Ireland, and the intersections of gender, class and nationality which occur within these narratives. Christina Hunt Mahony's essay on 'Women's Education, Edward Dowden and the University Curriculum in English Literature' focuses on a little-known episode: the Dublin Afternoon Lectures on Literature and the Arts, held between 1863 and 1868, geared towards gentlewomen and male civil servants. Despite their 'extra-mural' nature, these lectures were to play an important part in the continuum of educational reform, serving as a proving ground for early canon formation in the university curriculum of English literature. The suggestion that the nineteenth century constituted a period of silence for women writers is fatally undermined by Anne Colman's work on nineteenth-century women writers. In the course of her essay, she estimates that some five hundred women were writing and publishing, throughout all genres, between 1800 and 1900. More specifically, the women of the *Nation* are discussed in Jan Cannavan's essay on 'Romantic Revolutionary Irishwomen: Women, Young Ireland and 1848'. Examining prose pieces and poems written by women during the 1840s, together with the responses of men, Cannavan situates these writings in the context of evolving debates regarding 'equality' and 'difference'. Finally, James H. Murphy's essay on the women novelists of the *Irish Monthly* continues the recovery of lesser-known writers of the period. In contrasting their fiction with that of George Moore, Murphy also uncovers the centrality of class concerns and the desire for Victorian respectability which characterised these writers, made clearly manifest in the subject-matter of their writings.

Taken as a whole, these essays challenge in many ways the accuracy and utility of the concept of 'separate spheres' to describe nineteenth-century Ireland. Interconnectedness, rather than separateness, is frequently evident: the domestic realm influenced by and itself shaping the public domain; male and female roles, in Mary Cullen's words, 'intermeshed and interdependent'. Yet the doctrine of

realm influenced by and itself shaping the public domain; male and female roles, in Mary Cullen's words, 'intermeshed and interdependent'. Yet the doctrine of spheres, while a cultural and rhetorical construction, was, as these essays also attest, no less powerful for its fictive basis. In a century of complex and changing power relations, key conflicts, negotiations and resolutions occurred along and between gender lines. From a variety of perspectives and disciplines, the contributors to this volume examine the operations of gender in nineteenth-century Ireland, deepening, in crucial ways, our understanding of the past and its legacies for the present.

I

Gendered Re/visions: Nineteenth-Century History

Public Sphere and Domestic Circle: Gender and Political Economy in Nineteenth-Century Ireland

TIMOTHY P. FOLEY

There was an orchestrated attempt in the nineteenth century to assimilate Ireland to England by, in effect, changing the perceived national character of the Irish to a robust, hard-headed, progressive, modern, in a word, masculine mode. The conductor of the orchestra was Archbishop Richard Whately of Dublin and his chosen instrument was a particularly swashbuckling macho version of the 'science' of political economy. In the nineteenth century, political economy was undoubtedly the sovereign discourse of the public sphere, the quintessentially male space, in the modern industrial Great Britain. It was perceived as a natural science, its laws the laws of nature, which were not only seen as given and unchanging, but as virtually unchangeable. Like the laws of nature, they were seen as stern and unbending and utterly ruthless in their application. In the harsh climate of the competitive public sphere in modern industrial society, only the fittest survived. The rational, egotistic economic agent, the *homo economicus*, prudently fingering his felicity calculus, was stereotypically a white, male, heterosexual, Protestant Englishman.

Women, by nature sensitive, altruistic, self-giving, in the words of Charles Kingsley, 'born for others', virtually Christlike in their self-abnegation, were unfitted to the outdoor rigours of the public sphere and so needed the 'protection' afforded by the enclosing domestic circle, though this fortress was increasingly seen by many women as a prison. Women were the keepers of tradition, the exemplars of morality as traditionally defined, the disinfecting element in a morally dissolute society. The Irish national character was represented as feminine and as such unsuited to modern life and Whately's project was no less than a regendering of Ireland. In the economic arena, in the high-noon of *laissez-faire* ideology, one of the few concessions made to the uncompetitive was the doctrine of the 'infant industry'. Protectionism was sometimes allowed to operate in the specific, strategic context of enabling 'backward', agricultural countries to modernise. Clearly this exception was allowed by appealing to an Athenian rather than to a Spartan theory of child-rearing, where God, in his mercy, tempered the wind to the shorn lamb. Operating with the same stereotypes of national character, Irish nationalists argued that the lady was not for turning, that Ireland, in effect, was a 'local' exception to universalist economic laws, was by nature more domestic and feminine, and being both 'young' and female was in double need of protection from the harsh winds of free trade and *laissez-faire*. The politically unacceptable face of this approach was the inevitable corollary that Ireland was, in her antipathy to cold modernity, low in the evolutionary scale. The opportunity cost of an identity based on the domestic, local, and rural, which valorised the warm, affective, co-operative, and generally selfless feminine virtues, was the devaluing of the competitive, masculine 'virtue' of selfishness, the supposed *sine qua non* of economic progress. National character had to be sacrificed on the altar of modernity, for many, and not only Whately, a sacrifice worth the making. Or Ireland could retain her national character, but the price to be paid was historical peripherality, often characterised by the image of time as either standing still or moving endlessly in circles. Whately's effort to regender Ireland in the interests of modernity, though it ultimately failed, was certainly progressive in rescuing the Irish from the ontological inferiority often previously ascribed to them and making them available for the category of mere historical backwardness to which the new evolutionary theory would consign them.

Arnold's Celticism celebrated Ireland's femininity, but in the interest not of autonomy but of union, the ideal marriage partner for the solid, rational, if prosaic, John Bull. In the Arnoldian scenario, hegemony was to be achieved through the cultural and aesthetic rather than rational discourse; a rhetoric of interests was replaced by one of affections. Political economy gave way to poetry, rational discourse to the language of seduction, the masculine to the feminine. But by figuring Ireland as female, by virtue of the dominant ideologies of gender of the day, Arnold inevitably presented Ireland as unequal to England. This 'feminisation' of ideology could be said to have begun in the traumatic experience of the Great Famine and in the crucial encounter between gender and political economy which was staged in Ireland in the early years of the 1860s. Both of these events, in their different, if complementary, ways, challenged the universalist claims and pretensions to ideological neutrality of political economy as had frequently been done in the name of class. But, to adapt the words of Robert Lowe, it could be argued that the Great Famine starkly demonstrated that political economy had a nation;[1] in like manner the challenge of gender in the form of a sharply-focused debate on the employment of women, revealed that political economy also had a gender. This feminisation manifested itself in many ways apart from Arnold's Celticism: in the moral critique of political economy, representing a trespassing of the 'feminine' into this quintessentially male discourse, and in the emphasis on the family as against the individual as the basic unit of society, thus changing the focus from the public arena to the household, from the site of production to that of consumption, coinciding, in Britain, with a radical paradigmatic shift from economic analysis based on a labour or cost-of-production theory of value to one based on individual utility. But Ireland, young and feminine, was unsuited to free competition, and Whately's modernising objective that she should grow up and become a man no longer seemed feasible. Arnold decided to accept and indeed celebrate Irish national character rather than change it after the fashion

1 See Thomas A. Boylan and Timothy P. Foley, '"A Nation Perishing of Political Economy"?' in Chris Morash and Richard Hayes (eds.), *'Fearful Realities': New Perspectives on the Famine* (Dublin, 1996), pp. 138–50.

of the archbishop. In like manner, the debate about the employment of women in the 1860s saw a modernising *laissez-faire* ideology, advocating the radical throwing-open of the labour market to women, accused of flying in the face of the 'nature' of woman. But, seen in class terms, by this time *laissez-faire* was frequently condemned as injurious to the interests of workers and the lower classes in general, including, of course, the women members of these classes. So, the 'progressive' case for the emancipation of women from enforced domesticity, and their integration into the labour market, was made in terms of an ideology that stood accused, especially after the Great Famine, of grinding the faces of the poor. Indeed, one of the central figures in the debate, Arthur Houston, advocating a free labour market for women, condemned what he called the 'tyranny of trades' unions'.[2] Their opponents valued women so highly that they invoked the very doctrines of morality to keep women, forcibly if necessary, in the home for their own good, to protect their sensitive natures against the predacity of the market-place. It was, ironically, the hard, masculinist version of political economy which allowed women to enter the labour market; the morally sensitive, feminised version confined them to the home.

Central to Victorian ideologies concerning gender difference were essentialist notions of male and female natures, biologically or, occasionally, mystically determined. One of the few tasks retained by the Almighty, after Darwin, was the allocation of stations on the basis of class and of spheres on the basis of gender. The divine ordination of the doctrine of spheres decreed that men occupied the public sphere of power and women the domestic sphere (or circle, as it was often called). Women, lacking power of a vulgarly palpable kind, were held to wield 'secret influence' by their moral and religious pre-eminence and other more-or-less occult powers. This 'consoling fantasy of power', as it has been called,[3] like the 'greater delicacy and spirituality' which Arnold found in the 'feminine' Celts,[4] served to distance and disqualify them from political power. Rocking the cradle and ruling the world were two profoundly unconnected activities. The medicalisation of sexual discourse, though apparently modernising, served mainly to confirm traditional moral views that a woman's place was in the home.[5] People were located in the different spheres and stations according to the 'natures' which God, or his secular equivalents, had been so good as to give them. They behaved according to the sphere or station they found themselves in and it was a serious transgression to act above or below one's station, or to move into another sphere. In 1855, Patrick J. Keenan, one of the great Irish schools' inspectors, writing on the 'exceedingly small' number of married women teachers, maintained that

> after marriage, *home* is the abiding place of woman, the natural centre and seat
> of all her occupations, the cause of all her anxieties, the object of all her

2 Arthur Houston, *The Emancipation of Woman from Existing Industrial Disabilities: Considered in Its Economic Aspect* (London and Dublin, 1862), p. 7.   3 Penny Boumelha, *Thomas Hardy and Women: Sexual Ideology and Narrative Form* (Sussex and New Jersey, 1982), p. 21. 4 Matthew Arnold, *On the Study of Celtic Literature and Other Essays* (London and Toronto, 1910), pp. 5, 85.   5 Boumelha, *Thomas Hardy*, p. 14.

solicitude, and it is a deranged state of society that encourages her to seek employment beyond its precincts.[6]

Indeed it was appropriate that women, naturally caring and benevolent, should be allowed to enter the public sphere mainly for the performance of charitable works. Home was seen as an oasis of selflessness, self-denial, community, indeed of virtue as traditionally understood. Women, as guardians and transmitters of tradition and morality, were held to be naturally moral and self-sacrificing, whereas men had to struggle (sometimes without success) to be virtuous. Women were vital to the moral health of society, like Barbara Friechie who 'raised up the flag the men hauled down'.[7] According to the Catholic periodical, the *Dublin Review*, 'The very soul and secret of a nation's strength is its sound morality: without it all greatness is hollow and all progression unsatisfactory; and national morality must originate in, and radiate from the homes of the poor'.[8] Women were the repositories of a traditional morality of sympathy and benevolence which it was no longer possible to practice in the competitive arena of bourgeois society. Men had their interests; women had their duties. Women were agents of sociability in this society, as against the cold civility of the public arena, what Kant called its 'unsocial sociability'. But there were fears that the 'morality' of the market-place might trespass into the sphere of personal relations, as in, for instance, Shaw's notion of marriage as legalised prostitution or George Moore's concept of the 'marriage mart'. But there was anxiety also concerning moral migration in the opposite direction. Archbishop Richard Whately of Dublin felt that an excess of the 'feminine', of altruism and sympathy, in the public domain, was economically and politically disabling, even subversive. It was, he claimed, 'a mistake to suppose that religion or morals alone would be sufficient to save a people from revolution. No; they would not be sufficient, if a proper idea of Political Economy was not cultivated by that people'.[9]

Political economy operated with the central notion of the *homo economicus*, the rational, self-interested individual actor, in true utilitarian fashion, maximising his utilities and minimising his disutilities. However, in classical political economy the concept of class operated as a counterbalance to the excesses of individualism and radically problematised it. Neo-classical theory neatly solved the problem by evicting the notion of class entirely from the discipline. It was, according to Houston, the 'glory of Political Economy to have shown that the true and ultimate interest of the community is inseparably bound up with that of the individual'.[10] But for many people in Ireland the Great Famine seemed to prove

---

6 Patrick J. Keenan, *Appendix to Twenty-Second Report of Commissioners of National Education in Ireland* (1855), Appendix G, p. 97.   7 John Greenleaf Whittier, 'Barbara Frietchie' in *The Poetical Works*, edited by W. Garrett Horder (London, 1898), p. 374.   8 'The Employment of Women' in *Dublin Review*, 52 (1862–3), p. 17.   9 Richard Whately, 'Report of the Address on the Conclusion of the First Session of the Dublin Statistical Society' in *Transactions of the Dublin Statistical Society*, 1 (1847–9), p. 5.   10 Houston, *Emancipation of Woman*, p. 6.

definitively that there was no easy coincidence of interests between individuals and the community at large. In any case individualism was held to have been unnatural for the Irish: the manly independence of the English character produced the *homo economicus* and the industrial revolution, while its Irish counterpart was more feminine and associative and seen to be more suited to agricultural pursuits. The post-famine moral critique of political economy was centrally a critique of individualism and utilitarianism and it was conducted overwhelmingly in the name of the family.

In 1859 William Neilson Hancock, once the most powerful advocate of unbridled individualism, read a paper to the Dublin Statistical Society entitled, 'The Family and not the Individual the True Unit to Be Considered in Social Questions;With Some Applications of this Theory to Poor Laws, the Employment of Women, and the Enlistment of Soldiers'.[11] In fact, beginning in 1855, Hancock published several papers, on a wide range of issues, defending the 'family system'. However, it was the issue of the employment of women which played the central role in Irish opposition to individualism. This debate had obvious repercussions for what was then usually called the 'woman question', but it had also profound consequences for the very discourse of political economy itself.

In August 1861 the National Association for the Promotion of Social Science, usually called the Social Science Congress, met in Dublin, and several important papers on the employment of women were presented to it. The topic had first been broached, in 1857, in the pages of the *English Woman's Journal* and it was brought before the Association in November 1859. Around this time discussion of the question had also begun in France. The Society for Promoting the Employment of Women, later to be re-titled 'Educated Women', was founded in this period and affiliated to the Association. At the Dublin meeting no fewer than ten papers on the topic were read to the Social Economy Department of the Congress.[12] As a result of this meeting an Irish branch of the Society for Promoting the Employment of Educated Women was founded. Consciousness of gender was raised to such an extent that women (or, at least, 'ladies') were allowed to become

11 Proceedings in *Journal of the Statistical and Social Inquiry Society of Ireland*, 2 (1857–60), p. 396. This paper was not published.   12 Two papers were printed in full in the *Transactions of the National Association for the Promotion of Social Science*: Bessie R. Parkes, 'The Condition of Working Women in England and France' in George W. Hastings (ed.), *Transactions 1861* (London, 1862), pp. 632–40 and Anne Jellicoe, 'The Condition of Young Women Employed in Manufactories in Dublin' in *Transactions 1861*, pp. 640–5. The following papers were also given but only brief summaries of most of them were published, together with a short account of the discussion (pp. 685–7): Mrs Catherine Brougham, 'Women's Work among the Female Peasantry of Ireland'; Jane Crowe, 'Report of the Society for Promoting the Employment of Women'; Emily Faithfull, 'Female Compositors'; Jessie Boucherett, 'Local Societies for Promoting the Employment of Women'; A. Overend, 'Remunerative Employment for Educated Women'; Maria S. Rye, 'The Emigration of Educated Women: Its Necessity, Practicability, and Advantage'; Mrs Bayley, 'On the Employment of Women'; Daniel Sheriff, 'The Advantages Derived from Embroidery by the Employment of Women in the North of Ireland'. These contributions are listed in *Transactions 1861*, p. 680.

associate members of the Statistical Society. Not unconnected events were the extension of the objects of the Society to 'all questions of Social Science', the change of name to the Statistical and Social Inquiry Society of Ireland, and increased discussion on co-operation, all seen as 'feminine' alternatives to the 'masculine' discipline of political economy and the manly strife of competition.

It was perfectly predictable that when Hancock began to relate morality to political economy, early in 1855, he should immediately turn his attention to the role of women in society. It was also inevitable that he should sternly defend traditional teaching on the question, the 'spontaneous and universal recognition of the principle that women ought naturally to be supported by men'.[13] The 'natural way of rearing children' was as 'members of a family, with a mother to cherish and a father to control'.[14] Five years later Hancock wrote that 'women are, and must in general be, supported by men, their employment being absorbed in the domestic work, on which so much of the health, comfort, and moral well being of society depends', and argued that the 'domestic employment of women is a necessary consequence of the great fundamental law of our nature – the division of mankind into families'.[15]

On 24 December 1861 Edward Gibson read a paper to the Statistical Society entitled, 'Employment of Women in Ireland'.[16] He began by assuming the 'advisability of not limiting educated women to obtaining subsistence by the one overstocked profession of governess; and also that the sex of a woman, though it may be a misfortune, is not a crime'.[17] A main object of Gibson's paper, in which he advocated that the 'labour market should be thrown open to all comers',[18] was to give an account of what the new branch of the Society for Promoting the Employment of Educated Women was doing. It had just issued its first quarterly report, and it was in 'good working order'. Gibson reminded his audience

> that the movement had been hitherto altogether confined to England; that it was little known, and less liked in Ireland; and that in Ireland, probably more than in any other country, sympathetic associations and prejudices regard with greater favour and compassion a starving than a struggling woman. We worship those we martyr; those who decline the privilege we ridicule.[19]

With regard to the title of the Society, Gibson remarked that

> [i]t might have been well if the word 'educated' had been left out of the title, as it apparently narrows too much the sphere of its usefulness; but a ready excuse

---

13 William Neilson Hancock, 'The Workhouse as a Mode of Relief for Widows and Orphans' in *Journal of the Statistical and Social Inquiry Society of Ireland*, 1 (1855–6), p. 85. 14 Ibid., p. 86. 15 William Neilson Hancock, 'The Effects of Employment of Women' in *Journal of the Statistical and Social Inquiry Society of Ireland*, 2 (1857–60), p. 439. 16 Edward Gibson, 'Employment of Women in Ireland' in *Journal of the Statistical and Social Inquiry Society of Ireland*, 3 (1861–3), pp. 138–43. 17 Ibid., p. 138. 18 Ibid., p. 142. 19 Ibid., pp. 138–9.

for the assumption of this special character may be found in the peculiarly wretched condition of that class.[20]

In 1862 Arthur Houston, the Whately Professor of Political Economy at Trinity College Dublin, published what was certainly the most important document in this whole controversy, *The Emancipation of Woman from Existing Industrial Disabilities: Considered in Its Economic Aspect.* This was a (presumably expanded) Whately lecture, in which it was intended to apply abstract principles to 'questions of immediate practical interest'. According to Houston, the 'principle which I chiefly seek to illustrate today is that of Unrestricted Competition – the problem to the solution of which I mean to summon its aid, is that of the employment of Women'.[21] An unintended consequence of Houston's theorising was that for many commentators, far from the abstract principle solving the practical problem, the practical problem dissolved the abstract principle.

According to Houston, the doctrine of the harmony of interests was now firmly established in international trade, but not so fully in the case of individual producers:

> We still, partly by the influence of positive law, but much more by the tyranny of trades unions and the force of public opinion, countenance a distribution of employments founded on the obsolete principle of protecting the interests of one class of producers at the expense of those of all other classes of society, consumers and producers alike.[22]

Many instances could be adduced, but

> by far the most striking is that of the arbitrary exclusion of one sex from certain species of employments, for which it cannot be denied that they are naturally qualified, more or less; since, if not qualified, there could be no necessity to exclude, by force of law or opinion, those who would be sufficiently excluded already by the insurmountable barrier of incapacity.[23]

Houston was clearly aware of how daring his project was:

> I trust no one will be deterred from giving the subject a calm consideration, on account of the novelty of such a proposal as that of placing both sexes on a level as to the right of entrance into professions and trades. It is always difficult to estimate how much of the repugnance felt towards a change arises from the fact that we have been all our lives accustomed to see an opposite state of things prevail, and so have come to look upon that state as in some way natural and normal. We see every day how much our opinions are the creatures of custom.[24]

---

20 Ibid., p. 140. **21** Houston, *Emancipation of Woman*, p. 5. **22** Ibid., pp. 6–7. **23** Ibid., pp. 7–8. **24** Ibid., p. 8.

Sometime later he again felt the need to apologise: 'Trusting I have now said enough to calm the alarm which a hypothesis so novel is calculated to excite, I will offer no further apology for bringing this question under your notice'.[25]

Houston stated that the most common objection to the 'unfettered choice of occupations' was that it would take women out of their 'proper sphere', which some people, such as Charles Kingsley, would define as the 'southern and western hemispheres'. Houston then asked the question: what *was* a woman's proper sphere, and went on to argue in favour of its cultural relativity: 'it has been defined in different modes at different times, and in different places'. It was a 'perpetual state of pupilage in the Roman social system and it is not much better under our own'.[26] He then quoted from a work, written by a woman to instruct her sisters, called *My Life and What I Should Do with It*. Here a woman's mission was defined as follows:

> A true womanly life is lived for others. Not for things, as a man's may be, who is engaged in any productive labour or trading; not for mind, as a studious man's may be; not for the increase of knowledge, for the discovery of truth, nor for art; not for the human race in their collective masses – nations, churches, colleges – but for others as individuals.[27]

Houston added lyrically:

> If true, this is a melancholy fact. No desire of independence, no patriotism, no devotion to art, to the sacred cause of truth, or to the ennobling pursuit of knowledge must enter into the hearts of over one-half of the species! Every particle of individuality the ultimate crystal from which every regular form of civilization must be developed – is to be sunk in the pursuit of the advantage of 'others as individuals'.[28]

He claimed that though this was dismal,

> it is plausible, and is tinged with a certain awe of religious romance, that commends itself with peculiar force to a certain order of minds. It is nothing but a gratuitous assumption, however, and all the more dangerous on account of the garb of pious self-denial with which it is clothed.[29]

Houston then proceeded to deliver a scathing attack on what he called the 'self-immolation' which society had imposed on women in a passage which deserves to be quoted in full:

> It is no doubt true that we should all be prepared, when necessary, to make great sacrifices of our feelings and our interests, in order to promote the welfare

25 Ibid., p. 14.   **26** Ibid., p. 9.   **27** Quoted in ibid., p. 10.   **28** Ibid.   **29** Ibid.

of our fellow-creatures. But that any one portion of humanity should be called on more particularly than another to perform this self-immolation, is, it seems to me, a most absurd and abominable doctrine. It is one of which those who are summoned to make the sacrifice must feel the injustice, and at which they must repine, unless where the vanity of martyrdom – not so uncommon a species of vanity as might be supposed – buoys them up under the trial. It is a doctrine, also, which can have no other effect on the remainder of humanity than to feel their arrogance, and minister to their selfishness. Self-sacrifice, to be beneficial, must be a mutual duty. Like a compromise, when the concession is confined to one party, where, as a countryman of ours is reported to have said, 'the reciprocity is all on one side', it can never be extorted except by force from fear, or from ignorance by fraud. It is precisely the same fallacy that underlay the doctrine of absolute monarchy ... and that underlies that of sacerdotal supremacy, in the east and elsewhere.[30]

The question of a woman's proper sphere had, according to Houston, been answered by a woman, the wife of John Stuart Mill.[31] The proper sphere of any rational being was 'the highest which that being is capable of filling'.[32]

Houston, however, tempered his daring with caution, for he did not undertake to recommend that 'all barriers to the employment of women should be broken down. I merely take this as the simplest hypothesis on which to argue'.[33] He justified his ultimate failure of nerve on the basis that he was dealing merely with the economic aspects of the problem. All women would not, he felt, immediately thrust themselves into jobs now undertaken by men:

> My own opinion is, that there are certain branches of almost every calling for which, by physical strength and natural inclination, each sex is peculiarly qualified. Into these, if competition were free, each would naturally fall. To take the learned professions, for instance; it can, I think, scarcely be doubted that there are certain branches of the medical profession which might, with propriety and advantage, be confided to females.[34]

He referred to the success of the all-female printinghouse, the Victoria Press, which had been established and conducted by one of the main speakers at the Dublin meeting of the Social Science Congress, Emily Faithfull. But, he added, it was not in the least likely that women 'would be at all satisfied to sacrifice their own natural tastes and feelings so far as to become barristers or surgeons'.[35] Clearly, Houston did not challenge the ruling ideology of gender which, in strict binary fashion, distinguished, mainly on the basis of biology, innately differing male and female natures. His study, he tells us, concerns

30 Ibid., p. 11.   **31** Ibid.   **32** Ibid., p. 12.   **33** Ibid., p. 13.   **34** Ibid, p. 14.   **35** Ibid.

the destinies of those who are, by their physical inferiority, incapable of asserting
their own rights – whose sufferings, though providentially lightened by an
habitual resignation, are doubtless aggravated by their constitutional sensibility.
It concerns the destinies of a class which needs all the safeguards that consciousness of independence can supply, to protect them from moral dangers. Lastly, it
concerns the destinies of a class whose *actual* condition, in certain ranks, is very
far from what any one having the interests of our common humanity at heart
can contemplate without compassion.[36]

When Houston periodically became aware of the more radical and decon-
structionist possibilities of his argument, he reiterated the merely economic nature
of his analysis. Political economy modestly treated of the production and distribution of wealth, explaining what agencies tended to 'increase or diminish
production', and to 'cause equality or disparity among the shares into which the
produce is distributed'.[37] From the standpoint of economic efficiency, Houston
advocated a policy of free trade in labour, though almost universally

the free circulation of labour from employment to employment was rigidly
restrained by the regulations of guilds and other trading corporations in Europe,
for the benefit of the productive classes, and regardless of the interest of consumers.[38]

The best system, he claimed, was that all should be free to choose, for there were
no means by which the capacity of an individual could, as a rule, be estimated *a
priori*. Success in any occupation was the 'true touchstone of merit'. To achieve
the maximum 'public welfare', he argued, '[p]erfect freedom of competition,
unrestrained by customary or legal limitations' was 'the *régime* best calculated to
effect this object'.[39]

In Houston's opinion, it was generally admitted that in society as it was then
constituted, there was 'something anomalous in the position of the female section
of the community'. Even the charges of frivolity frequently brought against those
born in 'the more favoured ranks', if they were true, could be 'sufficiently
accounted for by the fact that almost every avenue to distinction or influence is
sedulously closed against them'.[40] An indication of the anomalous social position
of women was the very existence of associations established for the purpose of
providing employment for educated women, when this was unnecessary in the
case of educated men. The following were the usual explanations given:

One is the fact that, partly owing to the proportion of females born being
greater than that of males, partly owing to their greater longevity, and partly
to their greater disinclination to emigrate, the female population in these islands
now exceeds the male by more than half a million.[41]

36 Ibid., pp. 14–5.   37 Ibid., p. 17.   38 Ibid., p. 24.   39 Ibid., p. 26.   40 Ibid.,
pp. 26–7.   41 Ibid., p. 27.

On the widely discussed question of the alleged 'superabundance' of women, Houston asked if the 'sole cause of the deficiency of employment be the redundancy of women, why does it not affect all classes alike'? If the pressure of employment could 'arise exclusively from the superabundance of female labour', why, he asked, was this pressure not felt in the lowest ranks? Clearly, he replied, 'because in them nearly all employments are open equally to both sexes'. Discrimination took place in the higher classes, where it was 'true that, certain occupations being closed by the laws and usages of society against female competition, the remainder are overstocked'. This was the 'true cause of the surplus female labour, though aggravated by the disproportion between the female and the male population'.[42]

Houston went on to consider, and swiftly reject, the commonplace that over-educated women would scorn existing employment. The reason why we did not hear any complaints of the male sex being over-educated, was because it made men more valuable members of society. The error was, 'not in educating too much, but in refusing the means of turning this knowledge to account'. But what, then, was to be done with 'these intelligent but superfluous females'? The answer of the Reverend Charles Kingsley was simple: '"Emigrate". Westward ho! is the motto inscribed on his banner'.[43] Houston rejected the solution of female emigration, for redundant females were in the middle and upper classes and the colonies needed women for agriculture. The only answer was 'to break down the barriers which impede the entrance into suitable employments at home'.[44] This would also increase the proportion of employed to unemployed, so the unemployed would be less of a burden:

> Many women who are now supported at the expense of others, or on private property of their own, would, if a pleasant, profitable, or honourable career were opened to them, embark in it joyfully, instead of passing their lives, as at present they do, in a process as nearly allied as possible to vegetation.[45]

Houston proceeded to consider the effect of his daring policy on population. The progress of a nation depended on the proportion between wealth and population and the advance of population in civilised countries was chiefly controlled by the 'prudential check': when it was strong, the standard of living was high and vice versa. Houston argued 'that the removal of the industrial disabilities under which women now labour would call the prudential check into more active operation, and thus conduce still more to the material well-being of the nation'.[46] In nineteenth-century Ireland, as elsewhere, marriage was almost the only desirable, if not always available, vocation for women. According to Houston,

> It will, I suppose, be readily admitted that, as society is at present constituted, marriage, in most instances, improves the position of the woman. If not the

42 Ibid., pp. 28–9.   43 Ibid., p. 30.   44 Ibid., p. 34.   45 Ibid., p. 35.   46 Ibid., p. 36.

child of parents rich enough to give her a fortune, finding herself debarred from almost every means of obtaining, by her own exertions, anything but a precarious competence, she naturally looks to matrimony as the means to escape from the difficulties of the future. Again, even if happily born in a higher rank, she finds all the avenues which lead to social eminence closed against her, and sees, in a union with some person of her own class, but of a more favoured sex, the sole chance of being enabled to exercise her legitimate influence in society.[47]

In most instances the time when a woman married was dependent on the inclination of a man. It was a matter of prudence for a man to abstain from contracting a marriage, but a matter of prudence for a woman to 'hasten' to contract it. So it was the prudence of the male, and not of the female population, which formed the prudential check to marriage, and on which the material well-being of all 'old' countries so much depended. But

> if the revolution we are considering were accomplished, all this would be altered. The road to affluence or to eminence would no longer lie through matrimony alone. A woman would then have to consult her inclinations merely, since she could secure her independence and her position irrespective of her union with a husband. So far as the female is concerned, therefore, the operation of the prudential check would be strengthened. But, on the other hand, there would be no longer the same necessity for forethought on the part of the other sex. When, by marriage, he would unite himself with one capable of contributing a considerable quota to the support of the household, there would be less to deter him from embarking in the partnership, through fear of sacrificing his material comforts, and compromising his position in society.[48]

Unlike her lowly sisters, the woman of a higher class would not neglect home and family. She might, in some cases, be able to 'devote a portion of her time to industrial occupation; but in a majority of instances she would find the management of her household sufficient to employ it all'.[49]

How would the application of *laissez-faire* to the labour market effect the distribution of produce? Would the increase in women's income be at the expense of the already employed? According to Houston, in the present market, with restricted entry, wages were kept up artificially 'to the permanent injury of other classes'. There would be a fall in wages for a time, but increased profits would bring in more capital and wages would eventually go up again.[50]

At a meeting of the Statistical Society in June 1866, Houston again returned to the subject of the employment of women. The purpose of his paper was 'to submit to the test of experience the conclusions at which we have arrived by the path of abstract reasoning'. He again addressed the central topic of a woman's proper sphere and concluded that unless the

47 Ibid., pp. 36–7.   **48** Ibid., p. 38.   **49** Ibid., p. 39.   **50** Ibid., p. 42.

domestic circle affords the highest occupation of which women are capable, which in a great many cases is little more elevated than that laid out for them by the cynical Iago, the domestic circle is not the proper sphere for women. But, furthermore, even granting it to be so, a difficulty arises from the fact that a great many women never get into that sphere at all, and a still larger number are twenty, thirty, or even forty years excluded from it.[51]

What, he asked, was to be done with these women? Because they were not in their proper sphere were they to be excluded from all spheres? This, he said, was the 'absurd' position taken up by Hancock, who advised, in the words of Houston,

> that after a certain age ladies who had failed to effect an entrance into the domestic circle through the gate of matrimony, should be provided for at the public expense, in asylums presided over by matrons of mature years and approved experience.[52]

This, Houston claimed, was a logical solution to the problem, but permitting women to compete in the labour market was more consonant with 'common sense'. A general approval for his conclusion should not prevent one from noting weaknesses in Houston's argumentation. He held that political economy, and the policy doctrine of *laissez-faire*, had unimpeachable scientific credentials and that, despite manifest differences, they shared one crucial area of agreement with 'common sense': both forms of knowledge were outside ideology. But, of course, the doctrine of the spheres was an intrinsic part of the dominant Victorian concept of common sense. Houston, however, did point out a serious contradiction in the reasoning of Hancock and his kind. While it protested against women entering the professions of law, medicine, and divinity, society had not forbidden them to become novelists, poets, painters, musicians, or teachers. In thus 'admitting necessary exceptions to its favourite theory', society had 'sacrificed its logic at the shrine of expediency'. The theory, he concluded, 'of a proper sphere for women cannot be maintained in principle, and is not maintained in practice'.[53]

Houston then considered briefly the objection to women working based on the necessity 'of preserving that delicacy and refinement which constitute so great a charm in the sex'. If this risk existed, it was worth taking, as the possibility of a life of penury was too great a price to pay for such adornments.[54] But even those women 'blessed with means', were often scarcely less unhappy, for useful occupation was 'absolutely essential to health of body and mind'.[55]

Faced with this intractable dilemma, Hancock relented on *laissez-faire* in order to defend the doctrine of the gender-based separation of public and private

---

51 [Arthur] Houston, 'The Extension of the Field for the Employment of Women' in *Journal of the Statistical and Social Inquiry Society of Ireland*, 4 (1864–8), p. 345. A discussion followed Houston's lecture to which Hancock, among others, contributed and to which Houston then replied. A report of this item, entitled 'Discussion', was appended to Houston's published paper.   52 Ibid., p. 346.   53 Ibid.   54 Ibid.   55 Ibid., p. 347.

spheres. He accused Houston of ignoring the 'family system' and the 'proper and natural division of labour'.[56] Domestic economy was a woman's proper study, political economy that of a man. Houston closed the debate which followed his paper by repudiating any intention of ignoring the 'family relation' but significantly hedged his bets by 'neither admitting nor denying that the family system should be made the basis of society'. He thought that any woman 'of right feeling' would refuse to become 'a burthen either on the public or her male relatives, so long as she felt she had the ability to earn an honourable independence'.[57] This was in reply to Hancock's statement that he feared that 'the existing agitation for a more extended employment of women's labour arose from a selfish desire on the part of men to be relieved from the duty of supporting their female relatives'.[58]

In its review of Houston's book, *The Emancipation of Woman*, the London-based *Dublin Review*, was shocked to find

> the professor of political economy in one of the universities of this kingdom, indorsing to the full the pernicious and anti-Christian craze of Mr J. S. Mill, for which that very eminent thinker was indebted to his wife, who was doubtless a most amiable lady, but not a very deep philosopher. Professor Houston of Trinity College, Dublin ... startles us with gravely advancing theories which we never expected to see emanating from a learned and Christian university. 'Emancipation of Women,' – startling heading! What is the slavery in which our fair friends are?[59]

Instead, the review continued, of opening up 'useful occupations and charitable callings to engage them in becoming industry', professors and social science meetings 'at once fall a talking about emancipation and college degrees, people at present being, of course, wiser than the old-fashioned teaching of religion'. Did the professor propose that women should,

> like the Amazons of old, take up arms in their countries' cause, and stand in the ridges of grim war? Will he organize a female police force who will patrol and keep in order our streets by night? Will he send our fair friends on the stormy ocean, and have young sailor girls rocked to sleep on the high and giddy mast? And does he suppose that if men do all the hard stern work, they will have women directing and ruling their toil?[60]

The writer consigned Houston to the company of 'shallow philosophers' of 'this wonderful nineteenth century' who were 'forgetting the nature of the men and women for whom they are devising wise things'. They might 'improve the human race; they will never radically change it'.[61] Men were needed to help 'ladies', especially to provide them with business acumen. Indeed, it was 'a poor way to

56 Ibid., p. 352.   57 Ibid., p. 353.   58 Ibid., p. 352.   59 'The Employment of Women', in *Dublin Review*, 52 (1862–3), p. 38.   60 Ibid., p. 39.   61 Ibid., pp. 39–40.

discharge our duties to the female dependent portion of our population, to leave remedies to their own efforts, and then, if a mistake be made, to laugh at the incompetence of ladies'.[62]

The whole debate about the employment of women was fraught with contradictions. The progressive case for freeing the labour market was made in terms of what was increasingly seen as the reactionary doctrine of *laissez-faire*, a policy seen to militate structurally against the interests of the lower classes, including, of course, the women members of those classes. But this is not surprising as the debate almost exclusively concerned itself with the condition of women of the middle and upper orders. At one level, it was a very unsisterly victory for ladies over women; at another, by attempting to establish, in however qualified a fashion, the principle of equal access to employment, a definitive discursive battle was won for all women. It would be a century before the seeds planted by Houston and others would begin to bear full fruit. Houston, in the end, did not confront the notion of separate spheres; he sought only to liberalise it, for he operated within the problematic of given male and female 'natures' which underpinned the moral principle of the double standard and indeed the doctrine of the spheres itself. On the other hand, the progressive moral critique of political economy, which was to lead, in Ireland and elsewhere, to a historicisation of the discipline, did not result in any critique of gender-based spheres of action, and continued to keep women virtually under house-arrest. However, for the efficient working, reproduction, and growth of capitalism, for the servicing of labour and the investment in human capital, the unpaid labour of women in the home was vital. The values of individual greed and selfishness were crucial to success in the market-place, but a traditional morality of self-abnegation and self-sacrifice was demanded of women in the home. The future of capitalism depended on the unselfishness of parents, especially of mothers, in relation to their children, an investment in human capital for which there was little or no economic return. Women needed no economic inducement to acting morally, for it was 'natural' and virtue was, quite literally, its own reward. They acted for love, men principally for money.

The moral double standard and the doctrine of the spheres were central tenets of political economy, bourgeois society's official self-knowledge. The relentless feminist attack on both of these concepts in the latter part of the nineteenth century was also, knowingly or unknowingly, a searing critique of political economy itself. The apparently simple question of the employment of women forced William Neilson Hancock to abandon his cherished doctrine of *laissez-faire*. It could be argued that bourgeois society was so ordered that it was structurally unable to provide full emancipation for women, and that a critique of its 'science' was a necessary condition for the achievement of that goal.[63]

---

62 Ibid., p. 40.   63 For a contextualisation of the material dealt with in this essay, see '"Next to Godliness": Political Economy, Ireland, and Ideology', in Thomas A. Boylan and Timothy P. Foley, *Political Economy and Colonial Ireland: The Propagation and Ideological Function of Economic Discourse in the Nineteenth Century* (London and New York, 1992), pp. 116–60.

The Dimensions of Gender in Nineteenth-Century Schooling

JOHN LOGAN

At the beginning of the nineteenth century only a small minority of children attended school. In the course of the century the demand for instruction increased, a diverse group of individuals and agencies established schools and a period of schooling became part of the upbringing of most people. Rates of enrolment and attendance varied widely, however, and prior to the compulsory attendance legislation of the 1890s and 1920s, those differences may be accounted for by the belief held by both the suppliers of schooling and by those who sought to avail of it, that a population differentiated by social and economic circumstances, by age, by religion, by ability and by sex, required appropriate and diverse forms of upbringing and instruction. Depending on the characteristics of the pupil, a desired curriculum would be conveyed through an appropriate pedagogy whether in the pupil's own home or in a school. From the 1830s onwards the state sought to formalise instruction within a national school system with the aim of ensuring that, whatever the differences in the pupil population, each child would follow a standardised curriculum and emerge bearing the marks of a common culture.

In the earlier part of the century the difference in participation accounted for by sex was stark: in the 1820s and 1830s, as Figure 1 shows, the number of female pupils was less than half that of male pupils.[1] From the 1840s onwards the gap narrowed rapidly, though, by the end of the century, it still remained open, with the number of male pupils generally higher than that of females. Over the course of the century the number of young women in the population was always less than the number of young men and when that variation is controlled for, as in Figure 2, it reveals that the difference in school participation by boys and by girls was less than the raw numbers might suggest. The gap between male and female participation had closed by the 1870s and thereafter the proportion of girls at school generally equalled that of boys.

One of the most appropriate ways to observe the disparity in educational participation is through regional, in this case, county variations. They reveal that in the earlier part of the century the counties experiencing the lowest levels of participation were in the poorer and non-urbanised north and west where low female participation accounted for much of the low level of schooling. In 1824,

---

1 Pupil data derived from the decennial *Census of Ireland, 1821–1901; Second Report of the Commissioners of Irish Education Inquiry*, H.C. 1826–7 [12], xii; *Second report of the Commissioners of Public Instruction, Ireland*, (47), H.C. 1835, xxxiv.

Figure 1   The pupil population, by sex, 1821–1901

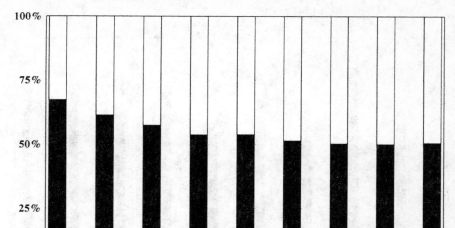

Sources: *Second Report of the Commissioners of Irish Education Inquiry*, H.C. 1826–7
[12], xii; *Second report of the Commissioners of Public Instruction, Ireland*, (47),
H.C. 1835 xxxiv; *Census of Ireland*, 1821–1901.

The pupil population was measured at ten points between 1821 and
1901. The instruments used and the conditions of enumeration varied
significantly, particularly in the period 1821–51. The inconsistencies in
the data make long term comparisons difficult but the data may be used
to indicate the relative number of female and male pupils at various
points in the century.

as Map 1 shows, counties where the participation of women was frequently half
that of boys included those in the west stretching from Leitrim to Kerry. Though
rates of participation soon improved, that east-west pattern of male-female
disparity was substantially intact in 1841 but, as Map 2 indicates, was showing
signs that it might alter: two eastern counties – Wexford and Down – were among
those where female participation was lowest. During the second half of the
century the gap between male and female participation rates lessened and the
counties where female participation had been lowest began to record rates similar
to those in the highest – scoring counties less than a generation before. By the
1860s, such divergence as did exist, plotted here in Map 3, reveals a reversal of
earlier patterns. In some of the north-Leinster counties the proportion of females

Figure 2   The pupil population, by sex, controlled for size of male and famale
population, 1821–1901

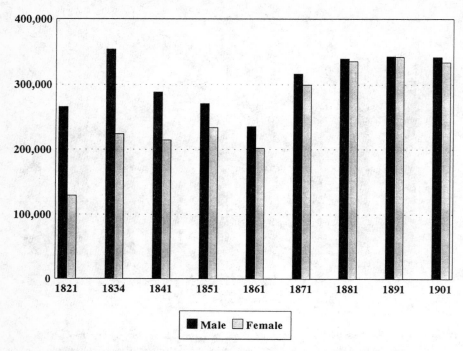

Sources: *Second Report of the Commissioners of Irish Education Inquiry*, H.C. 1826–7
[12], xii; *Second report of the Commissioners of Public Instruction, Ireland*, (47),
H.C. 1835 xxxiv; *Census of Ireland*, 1821–1901.

Through the century the average male female ratio was 95.9 : 100. For
each decennial census from 1841 to 1901 the commissioners tabulated
the population by age-cohort and sex, thus facilitating a computation
of the male female ratio in the youth population. The population under
17 was used for 1841–51 and the population under 15 for 1861–1901.
Age specific tabulations of population are not available for 1821, 1824
or 1834, for which years the mean for the period 1841–1901 was used.

attending frequently exceeded that of males, and the Ulster counties, where
previously female participation had been relatively strong, now began to display
relative disadvantage. By the end of the century, as shown in Map 4, the western
counties, where during the earlier part of the century females had shown the
lowest participation rates, now recorded the highest. Conversely, some Ulster
counties – Antrim, Derry, Tyrone – and the Leinster counties of Carlow and
Queen's, which during the earlier part of the century had the highest female

Maps 1–4 Female pupils as a percentage of male pupils, by county, 1824–1891

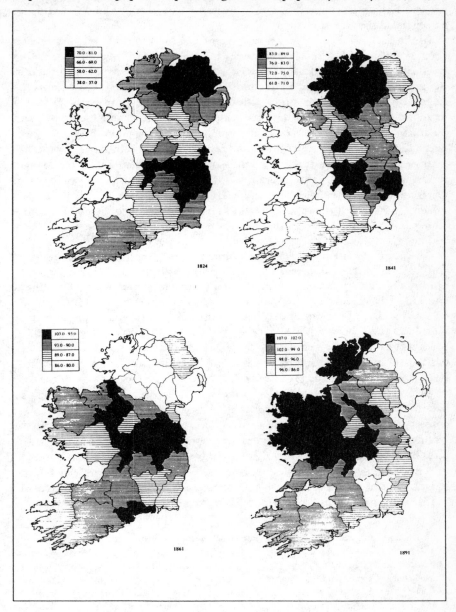

Source: *Second Report of the Commissioners of Irish Education Inquiry*, H.C. 1826–7
        [12], xii; *Second report of the Commissioners of Public Instruction, Ireland*, (47),
        H.C. 1835; xxxiv, *Census of Ireland, 1821–1901*.

participation, recorded some of the lowest. As a consequence of their initial low level of female participation, the counties of Connaught and west Munster experienced the largest growth.

In the early nineteenth century the demand for schooling may have been strongly influenced by the extent to which a region's economy reflected higher levels of commercial and administrative activities.[2] These were concentrated in the urban centres and their hinterlands and it may be that in those regions the sluggish demand for female instruction can be accounted for by the relatively low level of female participation in occupations and social activities dependent on an ability to read and write. As the supply of schooling improved, as its costs decreased and as powerful political and religious forces combined to promote increased enrolment, instruction became much less associated with urban areas and their hinterlands. Thus in the late 1830s in Ballymartin, midway between Carrickfergus and the northern shores of Lough Neagh, an ordnance survey officer reported that the supply of schools had increased recently and that more attention was being given to the education of girls, an activity that previously had been 'very limited'.[3]

The accounts of educational development given by contemporary observers and by state officials all reveal a preoccupation with the factors considered to inhibit regular attendance. Many concluded that while overall enrolment continued to increase, children left school as soon as they were of use at home or able to earn.[4] That notion has been statistically tested by David Fitzpatrick who has shown how, in the second half of the century, variations in levels of participation can be explained by the extent to which children continued to participate in the labour market: schooling had a low value in regions where child labour could still be profitable.[5] This proved to be especially so in the case of girls, and counties such as Donegal and Derry where female labour was valued had low levels of female schooling. In the post-famine decades, however, most employment opportunity lay outside the country and this was particularly so for women. Until the 1880s the illiterates in the population had been among those most likely to emigrate, but from then onwards, the reverse was the case. A period of schooling, now more widespread and cheaply available than ever before, became part of the preparation that an increasing number of girls – particularly in the western counties – made for a life in America, Britain or elsewhere.[6]

---

2 John Logan, 'Schooling and the Promotion of Literacy in Nineteenth-Century Ireland' (Ph.D. thesis, National University of Ireland, 1992), pp. 161–209.   3 Royal Irish Academy, Ordnance Survey Memoirs, box 3, VI.   4 For example, John McEvoy, *Statistical Survey of the County of Tyrone with observations on the means of improvement drawn up in the years 1801 and 1802* (Dublin, 1802), pp. 163–6; and James M'Parlan, *Statistical survey of the county of Donegal with observations on the means of improvement: drawn up in the year 1801* (Dublin, 1802), p. 77.   5 David Fitzpatrick, '"A share of the honeycomb": education, emigration and Irishwomen' in David Dickson and Mary Daly (eds), *The Origins of Popular Literacy in Ireland: Language Change and Educational Development 1700–1920* (Dublin, 1990), p. 172. 6 Ibid., pp. 180–83.

In the period prior to the widespread dissemination of the school, the household was the principal source of instruction for most children. In poorer families, tuition, if it occurred, had to be integrated into a working routine that made demands on all but the very young. Inevitably, informative accounts of home instruction are infrequent but that by Peadar Ó Laoghaire, growing up near Macroom in the 1840s, reveals some of its critical dimensions:

> During the day we worked on the little farm, such of us as were able to do any work at all. When night fell my mother lit a candle on the table, put us sitting round it, handed us the books and taught us our lessons. The teaching she gave us was much better than that given to the children who were going to school. But it was thought, naturally enough, that the teaching in the schools was better.[7]

If family circumstances permitted, a teacher might be employed and the low cost of doing so – sometimes not much more than that of board and bed – meant that many less-well-off families could employ one.[8] Generally, if a man was employed, it was for the tuition of older boys, while women taught girls and younger boys. Consequently the wealthiest households drew simultaneously on the services of a tutor and a governess and extended that sex-based division of labour, employing maids and nurses to look after younger children. At Parsonstown in 1840, for example, a nurse was caring for the infant in the family of the earl of Rosse, a governess taught a girl aged five and three boys aged seven, nine and eleven, while a tutor was responsible for a fourteen-year-old boy.[9] In a Meath rectory in the 1850s, a governess taught Alice Stopford Green and her three sisters while a tutor taught her five brothers.[10] A similar sex-based distinction applied where a teacher was employed to supplement the work of family members. For example, in the first decade of the century Gerald Griffin and his brothers were taught by a tutor in their county Limerick home, their two older sisters were taught reading by their mother, and they in turn helped with the tuition of two younger sisters. The girls, however, joined their brothers for French lessons by the tutor.[11] The use of tutors, principally for older boys and the practice of sending boys to a school, even from an early age, made household tutoring a predominately female occupation: the 1861 census – the only occasion when separate tabulations were made – recorded almost ten times as many tutors as governesses.[12] Eventually each would be replaced and in the last decades of the century an increasing

7 Peadar Ó Laoghaire, *My Own Story. A translation by Sheile O' Sullivan of Mo Scéal Féin* (Dublin, 1973), p. 17.   **8** Louis Cullen, 'Patrons, teachers and literacy in Irish: 1700–1850' in Dickson and Daly, *Popular Literacy*, pp. 16–19.   **9** Randal Parsons, *Reminiscences* (privately printed, n.d.), p. 8; (copy in Muniments Room, Birr Castle).   **10** R.B. McDowell, *Alice Stopford Greene: A Passionate Historian* (Dublin, 1967), p. 14.   **11** Ethel Mannin, *Two Studies in Integrity* (London, 1954), p. 24.   **12** *The Census of Ireland for the year 1861, part v: General Report, with appendix, county tables, summary of Ireland and index to names of places* (3204–IV), H.C. 1863, lxi, i, pp. lxii–lxix.

number of boarding and day schools offered well-off families what was variously described as 'superior', 'secondary' or 'intermediate' education as an alternative to household-based instruction.[13] They developed largely from the need to prepare for entry to higher education and to the expanding ranks of the professions, a world in which women had, as yet, a confined space. Nonetheless an increase in the numbers being employed in emerging and expanding occupations where women would attain prominence, such as nursing, teaching, and retailing, ensured that more and more women would prepare themselves by remaining in school long after the completion of elementary instruction. Such occupations became even more attractive as opportunity within post-famine agriculture diminished.[14]

As schooling became more widely available, a family would look to it to reinforce the skills and values that it wished to transmit, or in the case of new skills such a literacy or the English language, for the acquisition of knowledge absent at home. Data collected by the two great official surveys of the early nineteenth century curriculum, carried out in 1824 and 1834 respectively, corroborate the literary accounts and show that reading instruction formed its core.[15] Writing was almost as widely available, and absent only from the scriptural Sunday schools, from some of the weekday schools funded by evangelical societies and from a small number of the schools of the teacher proprietors, that is the schools officially classified as 'pay' or 'hedge' schools. For example, out of the 262 schools in Kildare and Leighlin for which there are curricular details in 1824, all but one of 183 male teachers taught writing, and of seventy-nine female teachers, all but seven taught writing.[16] Writing was thus available in most schools save for a few attended exclusively by girls. At an earlier period there may have been less emphasis on the teaching of writing to girls but by the second or third decade of the century, the tendency had lessened. Thus the largest of the philanthropic education societies, the Society for the Education of the Poor in Ireland, generally known as the Kildare Place Society, made no distinction in the time allocated to the teaching of writing for either boys or girls. In practice, however, the tendency for the girls' manual curriculum – usually needlework and household skills – to take a large portion of time and its timetabling against book-keeping for boys, meant that some girls continued to receive less writing practice.[17] The distinction remained strongest in the case of poorer girls, especially those in custodial institutions or those who were dependent on charity for their schooling. In the Killaloe parochial schools in the 1810s and 1820s, for example, boys learned

13 Anne V. O'Connor, 'Influences Affecting Girls' Secondary Education in Ireland, 1860–1910' in *Archivium Hibernicum*, 141 (1986), pp. 83–98.   14 Mary E. Daly, 'Women in the Irish Workforce from Pre-Industrial to Modern Times' in *Saothar*, 7 (1981), pp. 74–6.   15 *Second Report of the Commissioners of Irish Education Inquiry* H.C. 1826–7 [12], xii Appendix 22, and *Second Report of the Commissioners of Public Instruction* H.C. 1835 [47], xxxiv.   16 Martin Brenan, *Schools of Kildare and Leighlin, A.D. 1775–1835* (Dublin, 1935), pp. 177–612.   17 Society for the Education of the Poor of Ireland, *The Schoolmasters' Manual* (Dublin, 1825), p. 54.

catechism, reading, writing and arithmetic while girls learned catechism, reading and needlework.[18] The schools operated by the Presentation sisters at the same period also gave priority to religious instruction, needlework and reading; writing was taught in a separate class by a special teacher and only to advanced pupils.[19]

Elementary numeracy – variously described as 'ciphering', 'numbers', 'arithmetic' or 'reckoning' – was less widely available than reading and writing, and here a sex distinction was more discernible: in the early 1820s all but five of the 262 men teachers in Kildare and Leighlin taught some form of numeracy, but of seventy-nine women teachers, thirty-six did not teach it. Consequently, perhaps as many as half of the girl pupils who attended a school operated by a woman did not have arithmetic available to them. It is unclear whether the choice of school and curriculum reflected a family's capacity to pay the higher fees that numeracy tuition commanded, or the assumption that girls would not benefit greatly from it. In either instance there was a sufficient demand to ensure the continuing operation of such schools. It is also the case that, from the 1810s onwards, progressive educational agencies were providing for the numeracy instruction of girls equally with boys, though for some time it would still be regarded as a subject for older and abler minds. In the Kildare Place schools, for example, its initial lessons – the learning of numbers and simple calculation – did not begin until the upper division of the second class, by which stage many pupils would have completed their time at school.[20]

Neither class nor sex precluded the need for religious instruction and educational reformers who were part of a wider evangelical movement sought to ensure its provision for all girls and boys. As a result the supply of educational institutions increased rapidly in the 1810s and 1820s and the contributions of the urban élite who funded organisations such as the London Hibernian Society (1806), the Sunday School Society for Ireland (1809), the Kildare Place Society (1811), the Baptist Irish Society (1814) and the Irish Society (1818) did much to drive down fee levels or remove them altogether. The societies employed local teachers who in return for a salary spliced a scriptural component into a utilitarian curriculum in schools open to girls equally with boys. Many were established in regions that had previously been unable to support a teacher and it is likely that some of the poorest households owed their first educational opportunity to these mission schools. Similarly motivated, the teaching religious did much to ease the educational bottleneck in the towns and by adopting a quasi-monastic rule, female congregations such as the Presentation sisters (1775), Brigidine sisters (1807), Irish Sisters of Charity (1816) and Mercy sisters (1827), as well as male congregations such as the Christian brothers (1802), Patrician brothers (1808), Franciscan brothers (1818) and Presentation brothers (1827), established schools whose regulations and curriculum reinforced a sexual division.[21]

---

18 'An account of parochial schools in the diocese of Killaloe (National Library of Ireland, MS 17, 947).   **19** [Presentation Sisters], *A Directory for the Religious of the Presentation Order According to the Practices of the Parent House Founded in the Year 1775* (Cork, n.d.), p. 34.   **20** *Schoolmasters' Manual*, p. 10.   **21** For examples, see [Christian Brothers], *A Manual of*

By the 1820s the state had adopted the project of universal schooling, believing that citizenship – something that might be exercised differently by men or women, rich or poor, but which demanded obligations from all – could be effectively promoted through a centrally regulated school system. As a consequence it increased its subsidy for approved local educational initiatives and in 1831 appointed a commission to oversee the process. The prospect of a state dominated by an Anglican élite regulating the education of their flocks may have dismayed many Catholic clergymen, but those fears were allayed when it became clear that the government wished instruction in a child's own religion to be part of the compulsory curriculum.[22] For their part, Anglican clergymen were hostile towards a school system that would no longer allow them, as ministers in the established church, a supervisory and controlling role and they were opposed to a curriculum where religion would be taught separately from other subjects. However, for the vast majority of the Catholic clergy – and eventually for their Protestant counterparts – national schools would not only prove to be acceptable, they would also be necessary, for it had become clear that the spiralling demand for schooling would create a burden beyond the resources of most parishes.[23] Thus the national school became part of the pastoral apparatus of the Catholic church, and the mission of the parochial clergyman operated 'with close support from what more and more was his school'.[24] The national school was quickly adopted as the principal conduit for the cathecesis of the young, girls equally with boys. Religious instruction became an important reason for attending – in some cases the only reason – and it was frequently the case that schooling began only when the need to prepare for communion arose and ended with the completion of instruction for confirmation.[25] It may be one of the deeper ironies of nineteenth-century education that it was the abundant funding of the national school system by the state that allowed the church to construct an apparatus with which it would successfully complete its devotional revolution.

From their inauguration the commissioners for national education were conscious of a popular demand for a continuing availability of the curriculum that had been offered by the teacher proprietors. As a result, the national schools followed the practice of their precursors and set reading and writing at the centre of the curriculum. However, by introducing numbers in the first days of schooling, they gave arithmetic a priority that it may not have had previously. The commissioners also argued that if literacy and numeracy had been taught in the schools

School Government: – Being a Complete Analysis of the System of Education Pursued in the Christian Schools, Designed for the Junior Members of the Society (Dublin, 1845); [Irish Sisters of Charity], *School Government Book* (Dublin, n.d.).   **22** Donald H. Akenson, *The Irish Education Experiment: The National System of Education in the Nineteenth Century* (London and Toronto, 1970), pp. 160 and 225–74.   **23** Mary Daly, 'The Development of the National School System, 1831–40' in Art Cosgrove and Donal McCartney (eds), *Studies in Irish History Presented to R. Dudley Edwards* (Dublin, 1979), pp. 150–63.   **24** Patrick Corish, *The Irish Catholic Experience: A Historical Survey* (Dublin, 1985), p. 178.   **25** For example, see Cork Archives Council, MS U. 60.4.

of the teacher proprietors primarily as a set of simple psycho-motor skills, such would not be the practice in their schools. They proposed that in the 'new system' reading lessons would be used 'to convey information', that writing lessons would be used for 'fixing instruction on the memory' and that arithmetic, instead of being taught by unexplained rules, would be the means of training the mind 'to accuracy of thinking and reasoning'.[26] Thus the commissioners drew a sharp distinction between defining characteristics of the old and the new and sought to exclude what they regarded as the most objectionable aspect of past practice, an unregulated flow of ideas and information. The national school would instead be used to promote a stipulated body of knowledge and the commissioners believed that a carefully designed set of readers in the hands of good teachers, constantly supervised, would ensure its transmission.

The first reader was published in 1831 and almost every year thereafter the commissioners added to a list which by 1850 had forty-one titles. The readers maintained the didactic tradition of the voluntary societies and the religious congregations and conveyed a world view that emphasised respectful deference to hierarchy, the justness of a divinely sanctioned social structure and the appropriateness of the modest rewards that accrued to honest labour.[27] That view was typically illustrated with domestically situated tales from the everyday life of a hard-working and honest labouring man, supported by a thrifty and inventive wife, and the message was reinforced by the regular appearance of their opposites: a squalid, complaining cottier whose downfall is hastened by the extravagances of a slovenly spouse.[28] The message in those homely tales was made explicit and given a rationale in advance by texts of domestic and political economy, history and scripture. In that regard a reader published in 1846 calmly rendered the assumption of a separate and subordinate female sphere by declaring that it would teach her 'to know her place and her functions; to make her content with the one and willing to fulfil the other ... to render her more useful, more humble, and more happy'.[29]

The notion of separate though complementary spheres had a powerful manifestation in a curriculum of manual instruction. The commissioners had granted aid to two agricultural schools in 1832 and in 1838 established a model farm at Glasnevin for the training of agriculturists and for the teachers attending the central training institute. Soon after they established a number of model agricultural schools and they funded farms attached to ordinary national schools. During the 1830s needlework became a subject in the training of women teachers and it was expected that they would teach it to their girl pupils. It was made

26 *Second Report of the Commissioners of National Education in Ireland, for the Year Ending 31st March 1835*, H.C. 1835 [300], xxxv, p. 7.   **27** J. M. Goldstrom, *The Social Content of Education 1808–1870: A Study of the Working Class School Reader in England and Ireland* (Shannon, 1972), pp. 52–90.   **28** Commissioners of National Education in Ireland, *Agricultural Class Book; or, How Best to Cultivate a Small Farm and Garden: Together with Hints on Domestic Economy* (Dublin, 1848), p. 113; and *Third Book of Lessons for the Use of Irish National Schools* (Dublin, 1835), pp. 215–20.   **29** Commissioners of National Education in Ireland, *A Reading Book for the Use of Female Schools* (Dublin, 1846), p. 7.

compulsory for older girls and in schools employing only male teachers the regulations allowed for the employment of a female 'work mistress'. In 1847 the female manual curriculum was extended to include instruction in cookery and cottage economy, and the following year the commissioners published *The Agricultural Class Book,* a theoretical introduction to farming for boys with sections on kitchen management for girls. In 1867 they published a new agricultural textbook as a reader for ordinary literary classes, thereby introducing the study of agriculture and domestic economy to pupils who otherwise might not have been inclined to study it. At the same time the commissioners decided that all male teachers in training would be examined in agriculture and that the weighting of the marks allocated to it in their grading examinations should be increased.[30]

In addition to the provision of agriculture and needlework, the manual curriculum was promoted through a number of special subjects. For example, the argument that drawing would promote industrial skills prompted the commissioners to appoint a drawing teacher at the central model school in 1847 and from then on all male teachers in training took a drawing course.[31] Navigation and commercial fishing were introduced in 1858 in the model schools of the port towns and shortly afterwards navigation became an optional subject, eligible for a special grant when taught by a teacher who had passed a special examination. In 1883 handicraft was introduced as a subject for male teachers at the central model school and two years later the commissioners sanctioned it as an extra subject for boys in fifth and sixth standard. A vigorous burst of innovation and specialisation in the 1880s and 1890s led to further demarcation of new subject areas in technical and manual instruction. For example, needlework and domestic economy – between them the basis of the female manual instruction curriculum – now spawned sewing, dressmaking, cookery, poultry management, laundry work, dairy management and spinning. In such ways did the commissioners set out to achieve the aim that their schools would have a central role in the development of the country's resources: its youth would be systematically initiated into appropriate and consequently separate occupations.

In the early decades of the century the predominately male profile of the pupil population may account for the pervasiveness of male teachers. In any case the low levels of participation by females in schooling would have confined the pool from which female teachers might be drawn. Though data are incomplete they reveal an occupation which at that time was overwhelmingly male: in the mid 1820s women constituted approximately 22 per cent of teachers.[32] While men often taught boys and girls of all ages, women did so less frequently though they were the favoured teachers of infants, whether boys or girls. The educational reformers in the voluntary societies believed that a school segregated on the basis of sex

---

30 *Thirty-sixth Report of the Commissioners of National Education in Ireland for the Year 1870*, [C 360] xxxiii (1871), pp. 25–6, and *Fifty-eight Report of the Commissioners of National Education in Ireland for the Year 1891*, [C 6788] lviii (1892), p. 37.   31 *Fourteenth report of the Commissioners of National Education in Ireland for the Year 1847*, [832] H.C. 1847–8 xxix, p. 226.   32 See note to Figure 3.

was the ideal but readily accepted that it might not be attainable where the
demand for schooling was low and the provision of a separate male and female
teacher costly.[33] It may be then that the increasing number of girls in the pupil
population accounts, in part, for the feminisation of the teaching force. By the
1840s, from which time the decennial census reports tabulate teachers by sex,
one third of the total, as Figure 3 indicates, was female. The proportion continued
to increase and by the 1870s the almost equal participation of boys and girls in
schooling is reflected in a similarly balanced teaching force. That profile might

Figure 3 The teacher population, by sex, 1824–1901

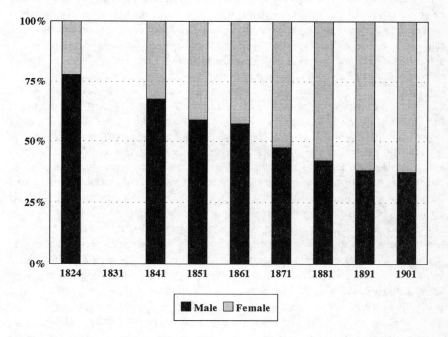

Sources *Second Report of the Commissioners of Irish Education Inquiry*, H.C. 1826–7
[12], xii appendix 22 pp. 230–1331 and *Census of Ireland, 1841–1901*
  Totals of teachers were not tabulated in the reports of the 1821 or 1831
census. Neither were they tabulated in the reports of the 1824 and 1834
enquiries, though each attempted a listing of teachers by name. These
data were not collected in a standard form nor were they complete,
though the most satisfactory, that for 1824, allow an estimate that
indicates that women teachers were then 22 per cent of the total.

33 See, for example, Lord Farnham, *A Statement of the Management of the Farnham Estates*
(Dublin, 1830).

have been maintained, but the enrolment of an increasing number of younger children and the growth of infant classes resulted in relatively fewer men being recruited as teachers.

By the end of the century 49 per cent of national schools had a single-sex profile, where men taught boys and women taught girls or infants. Such schools were almost all in the towns where an abundant child population facilitated not just separate schools for boys and girls, but separate classes for each level of ability or standard. Conversely most of the mixed schools were in the more sparsely populated parts of the countryside and in these, three quarters of the teachers were women.[34] While the consensus for segregated education had been promoted enthusiastically by the commissioners and by the clerical patrons, the low density of some rural populations saw economic considerations overrule any social or moral argument for segregation. In those instances a lone teacher would have full responsibility for all of a locality's pupils and while the regulations allowed for pupils as young as four and as old as eighteen, the bulk was clustered between eight and twelve. Just 10 per cent of schools had both a mixed pupil population and a mixed teaching force. In most cases, these were two-teacher schools, often under the care of a husband assisted by his wife. The younger classes were almost always taught by the woman while her male colleague taught the older ones. Groups would be swopped periodically so that the older girls could be taught needlework.[35]

Though central to the project of universal schooling, the female teacher was not rewarded on a basis similar to that of her male counterpart and from the beginning of national education her pay reflected the traditionally lower status of female education and the generally prevailing difference between male and female incomes. In the 1830s female salary levels were pitched at 75 per cent of those paid to males. Rates of pay were often reviewed and thereafter the scale became increasingly differentiated, but by the end of the century female rates stood at 80 per cent of those paid to male counterparts.[36] Nonetheless, for many women teaching had become an attractive occupation that provided, at the very least, a degree of financial independence. That prospect was enhanced by the possibility of promotion to a school principalship, a position that was held by two thirds of all teachers between the 1860s and the end of the century. Here however the notion that a woman was unsuitable as the superior of a male colleague prevailed: while women accounted for 55 per cent of teachers in 1900, they held but 28 per cent of the school principalships, in each case as a sole teacher.[37]

34 *Sixty-sixth Report of the Commissioners of National Education in Ireland, for the Year 1899–1900*, [Cd 285], H.C. 1900, xxii, p. 20.   **35** P.W. Joyce, *A Handbook of School Management and Methods of Teaching* (Dublin, 1872), pp. 44–70.   **36** *Seventh Report of the Commissioners of National Education in Ireland for the Year 1840*, [353], H.C. 1842, xxiii, p. 104; *Sixty-sixth Report of the Commissioners of National Education in Ireland for the Year 1899–1900*, [Cd 285], H.C. 1900, xxiii, p. 14.   **37** *Sixty-sixth Report of the Commissioners of National Education in Ireland for the Year 1899–1900*, [Cd 285], H.C. 1900, xxiii, p. 19.

Until the 1840s the most pervasive type of school was that of the teacher proprietors, who, if they became national teachers, would undergo a significant loss of independence. The national school teacher was subject to immediate and frequent surveillance by a clergyman manager and somewhat less frequently, by a government inspector. Independence in pedagogic style and school organisation had been traded for the security of a regular salary, and from 1882, the assurance of a state pension. In the poorest parishes the teacher might also be the tenant of a comfortable official residence, thereby providing a vivid example of the fruits of education and of the well-ordered domesticity that the curriculum sought to promote. In these and many other ways the role of teachers was being transformed: they were no longer the free-moving entrepreneurs of diverse background and experience who ventured to set up schools in response to popular demand. They had become, instead, paid servants in an expanding state apparatus. There is no doubt that the national school provided occupational opportunity and financial security, especially for many women, but it did so under conditions that required an unquestioning acceptance of an authoritarian and patriarchal structure.

In the space of two generations between the 1830s and the 1890s the state had ceased to view the school as a potentially subversive agency. Instead it began to promote instruction through the national school as a process that, if properly accomplished, would be essential to the formation of each citizen. Whatever the wishes of the children or of their parents, none should remain apart from the undertaking. The state was joined in that project by the churches as they came to regard schooling as a necessary part of the pastoral process. The school thus became the usual way of promoting an individual's inclusion in a national civic and religious culture. Those who looked to the national school for instruction may have imagined it to hold the key to a transformed way of life. This was certainly the case for the women who found it an increasingly accessible means of acquiring skills and knowledge and for those women who went on to become teachers. The paradox of nineteenth-century school reform is that, despite the apparent promise that it would weaken the barriers deriving from class, religion or race, it became instead an instrument that promoted a knowledge of the immutability of those forces. In the case of gender formation it provided equality of access, but to a curriculum that emphasised and reinforced gender difference.

Women and the Great Famine

DAVID FITZPATRICK

The economist Amartya Sen is justly celebrated for elaborating the thesis that famines typically result from maldistribution rather than scarcity of food.[1] Those most vulnerable to famine are the groups least well 'endowed' with property, and with the capacity to obtain employment or produce resources. The value of these endowments, termed by Sen the 'exchange entitlement', is determined by the prevailing price of commodities and labour, and by the effect of taxes and benefits. In the event of a sharp increase in the price of basic necessities, sometimes but not always the consequence of a failure in food supply, those with a substantial initial endowment may prosper while the poor starve as a result of inability to purchase the available food. 'Market forces' may therefore create famines even without eviction, expropriation, or other deprivations of endowment. Furthermore, famines may be averted by interventions designed to increase the exchange entitlement of the most vulnerable groups. By reducing taxes and providing judicious relief in cash, so stimulating demand by consumers, the state may simultaneously avert starvation and promote economic recovery at fairly low cost. Sen's initial concern was with the rôle of governments in counteracting the inequitable distribution of entitlements between social classes. Recently, however, he has proposed extension of his theory to embrace 'exchange entitlement relations' between and within families, and in particular between women and men.[2] If women were already subject to systematic discrimination, one might expect this to be manifested not only in inferior endowments, but also in relatively severe decline in the value of their exchange entitlements during a subsistence crisis. Catastrophes such as famine, in which the struggle for survival challenges established conventions of mutual obligation, should surely generate lurid evidence of the subordination of women.[3]

Ireland provides a useful case for testing and extending Sen's model, although Cormac Ó Gráda has expressed reservations about its applicability to a famine where there were few 'gainers' yet 'losers' of almost every class.[4] Sen maintains that 'the classic case of food countermovement is, of course, the Irish famine of the 1840s', noting 'that market forces would tend to encourage precisely such

1 Amartya Sen, *Poverty and Famines: An Essay on Entitlement and Deprivation* (Oxford, 1981).   2 Sen, 'Food, Economics and Entitlements', p. 41, in Jean Drèze and Sen (eds), *The Political Economy of Hunger*, i (Oxford, 1991), pp. 34–52; idem, *Hunger and Public Action* (Oxford, 1989), pp. 46–61.   3 For an inconclusive discussion of the hypothesis that women in 'male-dominated societies' are typically 'victimised' during famines, see David Arnold, *Famine: Social Crisis and Social Change* (Oxford, 1988), pp. 86–91.   4 Cormac Ó Gráda, *The Great Irish Famine* (Dublin, 1989), pp. 61–3.

food movements [as the export of corn] when failure of purchasing ability outweighs availability decline'.[5] Both James Donnelly and Ó Gráda have briefly discussed the effect of the Irish famine on 'exchange entitlement relations' within families, in accordance with Sen's suggestion. As Donnelly observes, 'by their very nature prolonged famine and epidemics of fatal disease lead to the large scale erosion or collapse of traditional moral restraints and communal sanctions'. In the Irish case, Donnelly reports 'acts of gross inhumanity ... by parents against their children, and by sons and daughters against their parents' – though not specifically by men against women.[6] Ó Gráda also detects discrimination against dependants within families, both young and old, musing that 'the Famine presumably forced many families, like the occupants of an overloaded lifeboat, to make life-and-death choices: an equal sharing of the burden of hunger might have doomed all. Were the young sacrificed so that others might live?'. Like Donnelly, he does not extend the catalogue of victims to women.[7] Translated into Sen's terminology, these depictions of famine's effect on the 'moral economy' of Irish families imply devaluation of the 'exchange entitlements' of dependants, reliant on their capacity for providing services through household production, paid or unpaid labour. This essay extends the analysis to the female experience during the Irish famine of 1845–50. How did famine affect the exchange entitlements of women as workers and producers? Were their broader entitlements as reproducers, and as providers of affection or consolation, similarly affected?[8] Does the available evidence indicate that women were more likely than men to suffer through death or disease, and less likely to obtain relief from private or public agencies (whether through food, cash or emigration)? Were women more likely than men to be thrown overboard?

Mortality is the least ambiguous index of the human cost of famine. It is scarcely surprising that no comprehensive record exists of the number of male and female deaths attributable to the Irish famine. Even if every death had been accurately recorded, the proportion caused by famine-induced deprivation or infection would remain conjectural. Nevertheless, the Irish case is documented by remarkably detailed 'tables of deaths' for each year between 1841 and 1851, recording the age and sex of those dying in each county (subdivided by deaths in rural districts, in towns and in public institutions). These tabulations were

---

5 Sen, 'Ingredients of Famine Analysis: Availability and Entitlements', p. 461, in *Quarterly Journal of Economics*, xcvi (1981), pp. 433–64. The Irish application was amplified by Sen in 'Starvation and Political Economy', an address to the International Conference on Hunger at New York University on 20 May 1995.   6 James S. Donnelly, 'A Famine in Irish Politics', p. 371, in W.E. Vaughan (ed.), *A New History of Ireland*, v (Oxford, 1989), pp. 357–71.   7 Ó Gráda, *Famine*, p. 50.   8 It is noteworthy that most analysts of famine have followed Sen's example by restricting the scope of 'endowments' to property, 'labour power' and other assets or skills directly exchangeable for money. Comparable assets such as reproductive and emotional 'power' have been ignored, despite the obvious possibility of exchanging the associated services for payments in kind such as board and lodging. This essay explores some implications of so extending the theory of entitlements.

derived from retrospective returns required from each 'Head of Family' still extant in 1851, specifying 'the Members, Visitors, and Servants of this Family, who have Died while residing with this Family, since the 6th June, 1841'. The census commissioners observed pointedly that 'the necessity for this Table is caused by the want of a General Registration of Deaths in Ireland'.[9] The census of non-institutional deaths was woefully incomplete, being restricted to those dying in households which survived until 1851. It therefore omitted vagrants and solitaries, as well as people dying in households subsequently dissolved through further mortality, emigration or simply dispersion. Only about one and a third million deaths were enumerated, less than 15 per cent more than the total for the previous decade.[10] The precise number and composition of deaths is unknowable, but ingenious calculations of 'excess' mortality have been derived from estimates of 'normal' mortality before 1846. The most systematic analysis suggests that age-specific mortality rates were roughly doubled during the years of famine, giving rise to almost a million 'excess' deaths.[11]

All of these imperfect measures of mortality suggest that women were less likely to succumb than men. Females accounted for 48.1 per cent of estimated excess mortality, being outnumbered by males in every reported age-band. The discrepancy was negligible for young children, but substantial among the elderly.[12] These contrasts are confirmed by the tables of death compiled for the census,

9 The family return (Form A) was reproduced as an appendix to the *Census of Ireland for the Year 1851: General Report*, pp. cvii–cx, in HCP, 1856 [2134], xxxi. Heads of family were instructed to return the name of each person dying, age, sex, relation to head, occupation, cause of death, and season and year of death. Similar forms were to be submitted by every public institution. Civil registration of deaths was introduced in 1864, but long remained seriously incomplete.   10 The number of recorded deaths was 441,836 between June 1831 and December 1835; 745,538 between January 1836 and June 1841; 318,066 between June 1841 and December 1845; and 1,031,589 between January 1846 and March 1851 (excluding over 11,000 deaths in workhouses for which no returns by sex were available). For analysis of the census of deaths and its defects, see S.H. Cousens, 'Regional Death Rates in Ireland during the Great Famine, from 1846 to 1851' in *Population Studies*, xiv (1960), pp. 55–74.   11 Phelim P. Boyle and Cormac Ó Gráda, 'Fertility Trends, Excess Mortality, and the Great Irish Famine' in *Demography*, xxiii, 4 (1986), pp. 543–62. 'Normal' mortality rates were estimated by comparing the age-distributions of the population in 1821 and 1841. 'Excess' mortality was calculated from the difference between the actual age-distribution for 1851 and that projected forwards from the 1841 distribution (applying the 'normal' rates of mortality and assumptions about fertility and migration).   12 Ibid., p. 555. The female components by age-group were 48.8 per cent (under five years), 49.2 per cent (5–9), 48.4 per cent (10–59) and 44.1 per cent (over 60). Since women outnumbered men at higher ages, the female advantage was even more pronounced than these proportions indicate. The female proportion of the 'average population' was 50.8 per cent, the components by age-group being 49.1 per cent (under 5), 49.1 per cent (5–9), 51.3 per cent (10–59) and 52.6 per cent (over 60). Unlike the aggregate estimate for excess mortality, the distribution of deaths by age-group and by sex is highly sensitive to the assumed volume and composition of net outward migration, for which no aggregate figures are available.

Table 1. Female percentage of deaths and population in Ireland, 1841–51

Category	Period	Age: 0	1–14	15–34	35–49	50+	Total
DEATHS	1841–45	44.1	48.3	48.6	47.6	44.3	46.4
	1846–51	46.1	49.1	47.4	45.8	43.2	46.5
INSTITUTIONS	1841–45	47.8	48.0	51.1	46.3	46.8	47.6
	1846–51	47.3	47.9	50.8	49.2	44.0	47.6
CIVIC	1841–45	43.9	48.3	46.8	44.4	46.4	46.5
	1846–51	45.6	49.7	48.0	45.6	47.0	47.9
RURAL	1841–45	43.7	48.3	48.5	48.8	43.6	46.2
	1846–51	45.8	49.9	45.6	43.8	42.2	45.5
POPULATION	1841	48.9	49.2	52.1	51.4	51.6	50.8
	1851	49.1	49.2	51.8	52.8	53.8	51.3
CIVIC	1841	49.1	49.9	56.7	55.2	57.0	54.2
	1851	49.7	49.9	56.4	55.6	58.1	54.4
RURAL	1841	48.9	49.1	51.3	50.7	50.8	50.3
	1851	49.0	49.0	50.7	52.1	52.9	50.6

Note: Statistics were derived from the reports of the Census of Ireland for 1841 and 1851 (HCP). Deaths were returned retrospectively by householders (or heads of institutions) who completed census forms. 'Civic' districts were defined as towns with a population exceeding 2,000, other districts being 'rural'. The ages of inmates in public institutions were not separately enumerated, but the female proportion was 56.8 per cent in 1851. All figures exclude those of unspecified sex; totals include persons of unspecified age.

revealing female components of 47.7 per cent in 1831–41, 46.4 per cent in 1841–45, and 46.5 per cent in 1846–51. The female advantage is further documented in Table 1, which compares famine with pre-famine mortality in various age-groups for public institutions, towns and rural districts. Male majorities were recorded in every sub-group apart from young adults dying in institutions, the surplus usually being greatest in the case of infants and older adults. As in most recorded populations, heavier infant mortality among boys rapidly counteracted the small surplus of male births. The figures strongly suggest that adult women were less at risk of death than men of the same ages, particularly beyond the age of fifty years.[13] It

13 It is, however, conceivable that the retrospective enumeration of deaths among the elderly was particularly incomplete for women, since women were more at risk of widowhood and perhaps a solitary death.

is worth noting that no such female advantage is apparent in the returns of registered deaths after 1864, which imply heavier male mortality in Leinster, heavier female mortality in Ulster, and very little difference elsewhere.[14] The particularly low female proportion of deaths in rural districts during the 1840s reflects the tendency of women to drift to the towns, as already manifested by the higher female proportion of civic as against rural residents in 1841.

The most striking lesson of Table 1 is the replication during the famine of the pattern evident between 1841 and 1845, in spite of the vast increase in the number of recorded deaths. The female component of deaths scarcely changed in the famine years, the proportion increasing slightly for children while declining still further among adults. In civic districts, the female proportion increased slightly for all age-groups, though townswomen remained markedly less at risk of death than their male peers. This minor loss of advantage was only partly accountable to the growing female surplus of population between 1841 and 1851, itself presumably in part a consequence of low female mortality. In rural Ireland, the male surplus of adult deaths actually increased, despite the declining minority of men in the population at risk. The female proportion of the middle-aged population rose from 50.7 per cent in 1841 to 52.1 per cent in 1851, yet the female proportion of middle-aged deaths fell from 48.8 per cent in 1841–45 to 43.8 per cent in 1846–51.[15] Though less marked, this contrast also applied to those aged fifty or more. In short, the official returns for Ireland as a whole confirm the supposition that women were less at risk of death than men, and that their advantage was if anything enhanced during the crisis. Even so, many hundreds of thousands died who would otherwise have survived beyond 1851.

Since the impact of famine varied sharply between regions, it is essential to document the female experience in local context. The contrasts evident for Ireland as a whole are confirmed by mortality in Fermanagh, as summarised in Table 2. With the exception of the age-group most affected by child-bearing, women were substantially under-represented in all categories by comparison with the county's population in 1841. Despite the surplus of women among surviving adults, the female advantage in rural mortality was particularly pronounced for

---

14 These comparisons refer to the probability of survival between the fifteenth and fifty-fifth birthdays, so minimising the errors attributable to unregistered deaths and misreported ages (in both cases most serious for infants and the elderly). The survivorship ratios were derived from rough estimates of annual age-specific mortality rates for the age-groups 15–19, 20–24, 25–34, 35–44, and 45–54, based on the deaths recorded in successive decades, and the corresponding mean population, in each age-group. For the cohort born in 1856, the survivorship ratios were 66.6 per cent for women and 66.2 per cent for men. Corresponding provincial ratios were 64.1 per cent and 61.1 per cent for Leinster, 64.6 per cent and 66.2 per cent for Ulster, 69.0 per cent and 68.2 per cent for Munster, and 74.0 per cent and 73.8 per cent for Connaught.   15 These figures refer to those aged 35–49 years. The cumulative effect of heavier male out-migration might conceivably account for the increasing predominance of living women at higher ages, but not for the decreasing female proportion of deaths.

Table 2. Female percentage of deaths and population in Fermanagh, 1841–51

Category	Period	Age: 0	1–14	15–34	35–49	50+	Total
DEATHS	1841–45	44.1	46.0	54.7	48.6	46.9	47.6
	1846–51	44.9	47.5	48.9	46.5	44.5	46.5
INSTITUTIONS	1841–45	*44.4	*44.4	*45.0	*40.0	*35.3	39.1
	1846–51	50.0	46.0	55.6	52.7	44.8	47.9
CIVIC	1841–45	42.6	44.1	*54.2	*19.0	*48.3	42.9
	1846–51	36.3	48.2	48.7	37.1	44.4	44.5
RURAL	1841–45	44.2	46.2	55.0	50.4	47.1	48.2
	1846–51	44.5	48.6	47.0	44.9	44.5	46.0
POPULATION	1841	48.2	48.9	52.5	52.0	51.4	50.8
	1851	50.1	49.2	51.4	53.2	52.5	51.0
CIVIC	1841	49.7	51.1	55.2	55.9	54.9	53.9
	1851	54.5	50.1	56.3	55.5	55.9	54.3
RURAL	1841	48.1	48.8	52.4	51.8	51.2	50.7
	1851	49.8	49.1	51.1	53.1	52.4	50.9

Note: For sources of statistics for total deaths and population, see note to Table 1. The only 'civic' district in Fermanagh was the town of Enniskillen. Asterisked figures represent populations of less than fifty.

those aged over thirty-five years. As in Ireland overall, the female component of mortality diminished slightly after 1845, except in the case of children. These relative gains were most notable in the case of middle-aged and younger women in rural districts. In the town of Enniskillen and in public institutions, however, there was a slight increase in the female contribution.[16] Further evidence of famine mortality is provided by the manuscript register of deaths in the workhouse and its auxiliaries in Enniskillen Union.[17] This district provides an

16 These comparisons with pre-famine mortality are somewhat spurious, since the number of deaths recorded between 1841 and 1845 was only 138 in institutions and 226 in the town of Enniskillen.   17 The registers for Enniskillen were analysed by Desmond McCabe for the National Famine Research Project. The provisional statistics given in this paper are cited with the permission of my colleagues in the Project, which is supported by the Irish government's National Famine Commemoration Committee.

instructive example of the ubiquity of suffering, which affected Catholics and Protestants in almost equal measure and culminated in the loss of about a quarter of the population between 1841 and 1851. By comparison with the proportions of women admitted to the workhouse up to July 1847, female mortality was relatively light among younger adults (Table 3). This also applied to older inmates at the height of the crisis; only in the aftermath of the famine did women account for a majority of pauper deaths.[18] In Fermanagh, as in Ireland generally, women seem to have been more likely than men to survive the ravages of famine.

Table 3. Female percentage of deaths and recipients of poor relief in
             Enniskillen Union, 1845–54

Category	Period	Age: 0	1–14	15–34	35–49	50+	Total
ENNISKILLEN WORKHOUSE:							
Deaths	1846–47	66.1	44.5	61.2	59.6	37.3	47.9
Deaths	1848–50	34.0	45.6	59.0	59.0	52.3	49.4
Deaths	1851–54	*61.1	46.9	48.3	*58.6	58.2	53.0
Admissions	1845–47	54.5	46.0	69.0	67.7	47.8	54.5
Outdoor relief	1848	None	54.4	75.1	81.4	75.8	76.3

Note: Statistics for Enniskillen Union were compiled by Desmond McCabe for
       the National Famine Research Project. The *Record of Deaths, Indoor Relief
       Register and Outdoor Relief Register* for Enniskillen Union are in the Public
       Record Office of Northern Ireland, Belfast, BG 14/KA/1, BG 14/G/1
       and BG 14/EA/1. The records of admissions to the workhouse terminate
       in early July 1847, and those for outdoor relief cover January to March
       1848. Asterisked figures represent populations of less than fifty.

A contrasting urban pattern emerges from Table 4 for the city of Dublin, one of the few populations that actually increased between 1841 and 1851. This growth of population was a by-product of in-migration, masking considerable excess mortality in 1847 and especially during the cholera epidemic of 1849. The city had a substantial female majority of 55.0 per cent in 1841. Against the national pattern for civic districts, that majority declined to 53.9 per cent in 1851. In both census years, nearly three-fifths of those who had reached fifty were women. In Dublin, as in Irish towns overall, the female minority of deaths increased slightly in each age-group after 1845. The returns of burials in Glasnevin cemetery, a major repository for northside Catholics from 1832 onwards, indicate that women

18 By 1851, according to the census, the female proportion of Enniskillen's workhouse population had risen to 60 per cent. The relative increase in female deaths therefore reflected an increasingly female intake.

Table 4. Female percentage of deaths and population in Dublin city, 1841–51

Category	Period	Age: 0	1–14	15–34	35–49	50+	Total
DEATHS	1841–45	43.8	48.2	47.7	43.7	47.6	46.8
	1846–51	45.6	49.4	48.7	45.7	48.4	48.2
POPULATION	1841	48.7	50.1	57.5	55.5	58.5	55.0
	1851	49.5	49.6	55.7	54.1	58.0	53.9

Note: For sources of statistics for total deaths and population, see note to Table 1.

were more likely than men to die poor. Table 5 indicates that the female component was almost invariably lower in the general plot than in the poor plot, where space could be secured for only 1s. 6d. Widows, always vulnerable to isolation and poverty, probably account for the over-representation of older women in the poor plot, both before and during the famine. For the destitute, however, burial was more likely to occur in an unbought and unmarked grave adjacent to the workhouse. The registers for North Dublin Union show that women accounted for just under half of the deaths recorded during the famine, whereas rather more women than men gained admission to the workhouse. Among children and older inmates, women had a slightly higher risk of death than their male counterparts.[19] These findings suggest that the general female advantage in adult mortality did not apply to Dublin's elderly poor, and that Dublin women fared relatively badly during the famine and the cholera epidemic. In regions more drastically affected, however, women proved more resilient than men.

Why were women less inclined to die? Similar findings for more recent famines have prompted perplexity, even embarrassment, on the part of analysts anticipating further evidence of female victimhood. In discussing the relatively favourable record of female mortality in recent famines, Sen suggests that this is compatible with the observation that 'adult women often bear a disproportionate share of the burden of adjustment' to such crises. 'Biological' factors insulated women from the effects of nutritional discrimination, both in famines and otherwise; and in societies where women were customarily wage-earners, as in sub-Saharan Africa, such discrimination was in any case inconsiderable.[20] Ó Gráda, while confirming that in the Irish case 'men were somewhat more likely to succumb than women', states that 'the relative advantage of women must be seen against their relative deprivation, marked in nineteenth-century Ireland, in normal

19 These comparisons are approximate, since the available analysis (by Catherine Cox, for the National Famine Research Project) refers to a sample of admissions between 1844 and 1850, which does not represent the precise population from which those dying between 1845 and 1848 were drawn.   20 Dréze and Sen, *Hunger*, pp. 81, 52–8.

Table 5. Female percentage of deaths and recipients of poor relief in north Dublin, 1841–51

Category	Period	Age: 0	1–14	15–34	35–49	50+	Total
BURIALS IN GLASNEVIN (ROMAN CATHOLIC) CEMETERY:							
Poor plot	1844	48.2	52.4	56.8	51.2	61.1	53.6
Poor plot	1847	45.7	50.7	56.4	50.9	59.2	53.4
Poor plot	1849	45.3	47.3	46.7	59.8	67.7	53.8
General plot	1844	41.2	49.2	54.7	50.4	57.2	50.5
General plot	1847	45.0	50.5	49.7	50.0	50.8	49.7
General plot	1849	35.1	46.7	46.9	57.5	53.1	48.9
NORTH DUBLIN WORKHOUSE:							
Deaths	1845–48	46.4	49.3	57.7	48.8	48.6	49.6
Admissions	1844–50	46.3	44.4	57.1	53.7	45.1	50.7

Note: The returns of burials at Glasnevin (north Co. Dublin), and statistics for the workhouse of North Dublin Union, were compiled by Catherine Cox for the National Famine Research Project. The *Indoor Relief Register* for North Dublin Union is at the National Archives, Dublin; the burial registers were kindly made available by the keepers of the Glasnevin cemetery. The age-bands for Glasnevin burials in 1847 are 0, 1–19, 20–39, 40–49, and 50+. The statistics for admissions to the workhouse, and for Glasnevin burials in 1849, are derived from a sample of one in ten.

times'.[21] Applying Sen's terminology, this juxtaposition raises the conjecture that, whereas the normal exchange value of their 'endowment' was inferior to that of men, the effect of famine was to reverse this imbalance. However, Ó Gráda (in common with many students of other famines) offers a different explanation, citing physiological rather than social factors that encouraged female survival. Superior capacity to store body-fat may have enhanced female resilience against hunger and its attendant diseases.[22] Though a significant advantage in normal

21 Ó Gráda, 'The Great Famine and Third World Famines' (unpublished draft, 1995), p. 41. 22 The alleged superiority of the female physiology in resisting famine is expounded by J.P.W. Rivers, 'The Nutritional Biology of Famine' in G.A. Harrison (ed.), *Famine* (Oxford, 1988), pp. 57–106. Rivers speculates that 'females ought to be less vulnerable to deprivation, having smaller needs for energy and most nutrients because they are smaller than men, have a lower metabolic rate and a higher body fat (*sic*). Laboratory experiments certainly often show that male animals are more vulnerable to

times and in the first months of scarcity, this capacity must rapidly have become irrelevant to both sexes as undernourishment persisted and intensified among the Irish poor.

Ó Gráda further points out that famine-induced reduction in the risk of pregnancy should have diminished maternal mortality. The frequency of births seems to have dropped quite sharply after 1845, as exemplified by the registers of the Catholic pro-cathedral in Dublin. The number of baptisms fell steadily during and indeed after the famine, sinking from an annual mean of 2,209 in 1841–45 to 1,593 in 1846–50, a decline of 28 per cent.[23] This reduction occurred in the abnormal context of Dublin's persistent increase in population after 1841. Elsewhere, the risk of motherhood may have diminished even more sharply. Returns for three Catholic parishes in Clare show reductions of up to 39 per cent in the number of baptisms registered after 1845.[24] Comparison of the age-distributions enumerated in 1841 and 1851 reveals a marked reduction in the population of children born during the famine years. Despite severe under-enumeration of infants, the number of children under five in 1841 had amounted to 96 per cent of those between five and nine years. The corresponding figure in 1851 was only 80 per cent. The later census recorded a corresponding reduction of 37 per cent in the number of infants and toddlers by comparison with 1841, whereas the reduction for those aged five to nine was only 25 per cent.[25] Even after a crude adjustment for child mortality, the estimated number of children born in 1846–50 falls 31 per cent short of the corresponding estimate for 1836–40.[26] It seems certain that fertility declined during the famine, although in the absence of more extensive analysis of parish registers the extent of that decline remains conjectural.[27]

deprivation than females' (p. 91).   **23** Returns were abstracted by Catherine Cox for the National Famine Research Project. The lowest number of baptisms between 1841 and 1850 was 1,339 (1850), compared with 1,692 in 'Black '47'.   **24** Monthly abstracts for the parishes of Quin-Clooney, Corofin and Tulla were compiled by the Clare Heritage Centre, Corofin, and kindly made available by Dr Richard Reid, Canberra. These show declines between 1841–45 and 1846–50 of 39 per cent, 36 per cent and 18 per cent respectively.   **25** The reduction for the age-group from 5 to 9 may be ascribed to higher mortality and out-migration in the 1840s, probably reinforcing a pre-famine diminution in fertility. For children under 5, the reduction since 1841 was 29 per cent in Leinster, 30 per cent in Ulster, 44 per cent in Munster, and no less than 48 per cent in Connaught. **26** These rough estimates collate the census population at each year of age with the number recorded as dying in each successive year at the most appropriate ages. Thus the estimate for births in 1848 combines the population of 2-year-old survivors in March 1851 with the number of deaths at age 2 in 1850, age 1 in 1849, and below 12 months in 1848. For each year of birth between 1846 and 1850, the estimated reduction compared with the previous decade was 25 per cent (1846), 35 per cent (1847), 34 per cent (1848), 28 per cent (1849) and 34 per cent (1850).   **27** See, however, a tantalising map indicating the percentage decline in baptisms for about 150 parishes between 1842–45 and 1847, in Cousens, 'Regional Death Rates', p. 65.

Despite the apparent reduction in child-bearing, its effect in mitigating female mortality was probably small. Child-bearing was not a major source of female mortality in pre-famine Ireland, accounting for less than one-sixth of recorded deaths even for the age-groups most at risk.[28] The number of deaths attributed to 'childbed' during the 1830s was 13,903, equivalent to 2.5 per cent of all recorded female deaths. During the famine decade 8,648 women died in childbed (1.4 per cent of recorded deaths). It is notable that the number of reported deaths in childbed actually rose for the years after 1845, though this may be a figment of improved enumeration.[29] The pre-famine importance of maternal mortality, and the rapidity of decline between the 1830s and the 1840s, was somewhat greater in Munster and Connaught than elsewhere.[30] Similar patterns emerge from comparison between the number of deaths in childbed and the principal 'population at risk', that of married women aged between seventeen and forty-five years. The ratio of childbed deaths to married women in 1841 diminished from 1.6 per cent in the 1830s to 1.0 per cent in the famine decade.[31] These findings suggest that the decline in maternal mortality antedated the famine, and that it was unimportant as a factor in mitigating female suffering. In explaining the persistence of relatively low female mortality during the famine, we are left with two hypotheses. Either the effects of relative deprivation were concealed by their superior physiological endowment, or women were not relatively deprived.

The allocation of resources between men and women was governed by many agencies, including the family, employers, landlords, ratepayers and the state. The rôle of the state was critical in determining which sub-groups of the poor should be given preferential access to relief, whether in the form of wages, food, or board and lodging. The schemes for public employment in 1846–47, administered by

---

28 For deaths between 1831 and 1841, the proportions attributed to childbed were 10.1 per cent (21–25 years), 16.6 per cent (26–30), 16.4 per cent (31–35), 10.6 per cent (36–40), and 5.9 per cent (41–45). Corresponding proportions for deaths between 1841 and 1851 (for age-groups 20–24, and so forth) were 3.5 per cent, 8.4 per cent, 10.3 per cent, 9.8 per cent, and 4.7 per cent. Deaths in childbed incorporate those attributed to puerperal fever, floodings and inflammation.   **29** The numbers of recorded deaths in childbed were 734 (1842), 812 (1843), 798 (1844), 926 (1845), 945 (1846), 995 (1847), 914 (1848), 1,010 (1849), and 1,006 (1850). The annual mean figures were 1,186 (June 1831 to December 1835), 1,557 (January 1836 to June 1841), 765 (June 1841 to December 1845), and 991 (January 1846 to March 1851). These numbers represent 2.5 per cent, 2.4 per cent, 2.3 per cent, and 1.1 per cent, respectively, of all female deaths for each period. Thus the apparent increase in maternal mortality over each decade may have resulted from more comprehensive reporting of recent deaths.   **30** In 1831–41, the proportion of female deaths attributed to childbed was 3.1 per cent in Connaught, 2.7 per cent in Munster, 2.2 per cent in Leinster, and 2.1 per cent in Ulster. By 1841–51, the corresponding proportions had fallen to 1.5 per cent, 1.2 per cent, 1.4 per cent and 1.5 per cent.   **31** The numerator gives the number of deaths of women aged 16–45 (1831–41) and 15–44 (1841–51). Division by the pre-famine number of wives tends to deflate the risk of maternal mortality in the 1840s. Upon division by the mean number of married women recorded in 1841 and 1851, the ratio for the 1840s becomes 1.1.

the Board of Works, were largely directed towards able-bodied men, who accounted for 83 per cent of recorded recipients in late January 1847. The 27,507 female wage-earners represented only 5 per cent of the workforce, a proportion subsequently reduced as a result of more rigorous exclusion of family dependants from employment.[32] In the absence of adequate alternative relief for those most vulnerable to destitution, committees in some localities had signed on far higher proportions of women, boys and elderly men: in Castlebellingham, Co. Louth, the female proportion apparently reached 35 per cent. Even there, however, wages were much higher for adult men than for women, though boys were yet worse off.[33] The manifest futility of paying cash to able-bodied men with superior 'endowment', while virtually ignoring those most in need, was a major factor in inducing the government to curtail public employment and vastly extend relief in kind through the 'soup kitchens'.[34] No record was kept of the sex of those receiving 'rations'; but the administrators directed relief towards families rather than individuals, and attempted to prevent male recipients from excluding their dependants from benefit. The relief commissioners justified their unpopular decision to provide cooked rather than raw meal by claiming that men had sold uncooked rations and become 'drunk upon the proceedings, leaving their children to starve'. The state, confronted by enraged mobs intent on wrecking soup kitchens, thus presented itself as the defender of those with inferior entitlements, against the arrogation of further benefits by persons already better endowed. The administration did not fully merit its self-image as fairy godmother to Ireland's oppressed dependants: the Temporary Relief Act of 1847 specified that male heads of family would normally collect the rations on behalf of their wives and children.[35] Had women been supplied directly with uncooked food, female and family claims might have been more effectively asserted through government of the hearth. Nevertheless, the tendency of state intervention was to undermine local hierarchies by redirecting much of the available free food to those lacking recognised entitlements.

It was through the much vilified poor law that the government most strenuously and effectively enhanced the entitlements of the weak, and to some extent of women. The rules for admission to the workhouse, and especially for provision of 'outdoor relief' once the soup kitchens had been closed down, were

32 *Correspondence … relating to the Measures adopted for the Relief of Distress in Ireland: Board of Works Series, Second Part,* pp. 48–9, in HCP, 1847 [797], lii; Thomas P. O'Neill, 'The Organisation and Administration of Relief, 1845–52', p. 232, in R. Dudley Edwards and T. Desmond Williams (eds), *The Great Famine* (Dublin, 1956), pp. 209–60. **33** Christine Kinealy, *This Great Calamity* (Dublin, 1994), p. 96. The return for Castlebellingham, in the barony of Ardee, enumerated 7,042 women and girls, 9,608 men and 3,606 boys on public works in the week ending 30 January 1847. The incomplete general return for the same week, cited in the previous note, showed only 155 women, 1,138 men and 324 boys for the entire barony, whose population in 1841 was 28,704. **34** See David Fitzpatrick, 'Famine, Entitlements and Seduction: Captain Edmond Wynne in Ireland, 1846–1851', p. 601, in *English Historical Review,* cx, 437 (1995), pp. 596–619. **35** See Kinealy, *This Great Calamity,* pp. 146, 149–50.

designed to penalise able-bodied adult men. So long as public employment or rations were available, the poor law provided only secondary relief for those otherwise disqualified. But from October 1847 onwards, almost all public assistance was managed by the Boards of Guardians or Vice-Guardians nominated by the poor law commissioners. Under the Poor Law Amendment Act of June 1847, able-bodied men could secure relief only if destitute, unemployed and virtually landless, and solely as inmates of the workhouse. Admittedly, the exclusion of able-bodied men from outdoor relief in kind was relaxed in the majority of Unions because of insufficient space in the workhouses; whereas no outdoor relief for either sex was normally permitted in twenty-five Unions.[36] Nevertheless, the allocation of poor relief was biased in favour of vulnerable classes such as widows, unhusbanded mothers and their children. The strength of this bias in assigning outdoor relief is illustrated in Table 3, which shows that during the brief period of outdoor provision in Enniskillen Union over three-quarters of the recipients were female. Women accounted for 86 per cent of unmarried and 92 per cent of widowed recipients, but only 26 per cent of married beneficiaries. The infrequency of reference to children and wives results from the evident restriction of the register to heads of family, who accepted relief on behalf of their dependants.[37]

Women were also over-represented in admissions to the Enniskillen workhouse, at least during the period up to July 1847 for which records survive. Though slightly outnumbered by men among those aged fifty or more, they constituted over two-thirds of younger adult inmates. The female proportions for unmarried, widowed and married inmates were 52 per cent, 63 per cent and 61 per cent respectively.[38] Whereas women of all categories comprised 54 per cent of workhouse admissions, their share in the population of the Union was only 50 per cent in 1841. In North Dublin Union, however, women were somewhat under-represented, constituting 51 per cent of admissions between 1844 and 1850, compared with 55 per cent of the Union's population in 1841.[39] The shortfall applied to children as well as older people, whereas women aged between fifteen and fifty had their fair share of places (Table 5). As in Enniskillen, widows were less likely than widowers to enter the workhouse.[40] The patterns of local variation

36 James S. Donnelly, 'The Administration of Relief, 1847–51', pp. 317–20, in Vaughan, *A New History of Ireland*, v, pp. 316–31.   37 The register lists 114 wives, 1,173 widows, 320 husbands, and 108 widowers. There were also 401 spinsters and 68 bachelors (including 30 girls and 21 boys under 15).   38 The female proportion of widowed inmates fell short of the corresponding figures for Fermanagh's population in 1841 (72 per cent) and 1851 (73 per cent), reflecting the under-representation of older women in admissions to the workhouse.   39 In 1851, women accounted for 51 per cent and 54 per cent of the populations of Enniskillen and North Dublin Unions, respectively. Statistics for 1841 refer to the boundaries current in 1851.   40 Women comprised 44 per cent, 59 per cent and 65 per cent of unmarried, widowed and married inmates, respectively. The female proportion of Dublin's widowed population was 79 per cent in 1841, and 77 per cent in 1851. These findings are broadly supported by Ó Gráda's tabulation of North Dublin admissions at the outset of the famine, which however implies an increase in the female component from 50.4 per cent (August 1845 to February 1846) to 56.2 per cent

in the application of poor relief remain to be fully documented and explained, and no aggregated figures for the entire country have been traced for the famine period.[41] However, returns from immediately before and after the famine indicate that the female component of Ireland's workhouse population was 53.4 per cent in 1844 and 59.5 per cent in 1851. The age-breakdown available for 1844 confirms the prominence of women among inmates between fifteen and fifty, and their relative scantiness among the young and the old.[42] Thus poor relief appears to have favoured women over men among able-bodied adults, but no female advantage is demonstrable for the more vulnerable age-groups. While offering a lifeline and often a deathline for both children and veterans, the workhouses of Ireland seem to have favoured male applicants when catering for those dependant classes.

It is not yet practicable to estimate the importance of sex in the allocation of unofficial famine relief. So long as the provision of rations or employment lay within the effective jurisdiction of local relief committees rather than the Board of Works or the Poor Law Commissioners, one would expect the order of priority to have reinforced rather than challenged normative assumptions about entitlement. Some committees further encouraged this practice by delegating the decision to the 'lower class' itself. As the secretary to a Fermanagh committee stated in seeking a matching grant from the government in February 1847: 'The inhabitants [are] but of the lower class … Instead … of asking subscriptions from them, we get them to purchase penny tickets to be given by them to those whom they know to be unable to purchase for themselves. This we know to work well.'[43] When allocation of relief remained in the hands of élites such as landlords or clergy, their choices presumably reflected both group interest and shared ideology. Landlords offering compensation for disturbance or assistance for emigration typically insisted upon the removal of entire families and the levelling of their houses, so favouring neither sex.[44] The criteria for relief administered by the Catholic church and the Society of Friends might provide interesting contrasts

(November 1846 to February 1847): Ó Gráda, *Ireland: A New Economic History, 1780–1939* (Oxford, 1994), p. 102.   **41** Ó Gráda's analysis of admissions in Antrim (January to June 1847) and Midleton, Co. Cork (August 1846 to January 1847) confirms the over-representation of female inmates among younger adults, and also their under-representation among the elderly and in the widowed population. The female proportions for Antrim and Midleton were as follows: 50.1 per cent and 46.7 per cent (age-group 0–19); 69.6 per cent and 69.8 per cent (20–49); 41.0 per cent and 42.3 per cent (over 50); 52.3 per cent and 52.0 per cent (unmarried); 58.8 per cent and 61.9 per cent (widowed); 56.8 per cent and 56.9 per cent (married): ibid., pp. 103, 100.   **42** For various age-groups, the female proportions of inmates relieved between 10 January and 9 April 1844 were 46.4 per cent (under 15); 69.2 per cent (15–34); 67.7 per cent (35–49); 46.8 per cent (over 50): *10th Annual Report of the Poor Law Commissioners*, pp. 352–4, in HCP, 1844 [560], xix. The returns for 30 March 1851 were published in the *General Report* of the 1851 census, p. xxi.   **43** James Grant, 'The Great Famine in the Province of Ulster, 1845–49: The Mechanisms of Relief', Ph.D. thesis (Queen's University, Belfast, 1986), p. 122.   **44** For discussion of assisted emigration, see David Fitzpatrick, 'Emigration, 1801–70', pp. 591–7, in Vaughan, *New History of Ireland*, v, pp. 562–622.

in the religious construction of gender. Only after comparison of social practice with state policy will it be feasible to assess the subversive potentiality and effect of state intervention.

The allocation of famine relief is at best an ambiguous indicator of the 'exchange entitlements' of women as against men. If relief were administered in strict proportion to need, then the amount of relief would be inversely related to the exchange value of each candidate's 'endowment'. In practice, local interests tended to misdirect relief towards relatively well-endowed recipients, a tendency only partially resisted or reversed by the state. We therefore cannot infer differentials in exchange entitlements from differentials in relief. For example, the surplus of men among elderly inmates of workhouses might indicate either the greater vulnerability of elderly men, or an administrative bias against women.[45] In order to evaluate the impact of famine on male and female entitlements, we must investigate the range of services offered by each sex and the extent to which their value was undermined during the crisis. The remainder of this essay is no more than a preliminary sketch.

The 'endowments' which offered pre-famine women the prospect of a livelihood ranged from paid employment to domestic enterprise, household management, reproduction and child-rearing. Women were clearly at a disadvantage in the employment market, receiving markedly lower wages than men and having inferior access to secure and long-term jobs. This probably also applied, if less emphatically, to women entering foreign employment markets through emigration. With the exception of widows, few women were endowed with the rights of a tenant occupier of land. Their importance as producers within farm households, though probably greater than in the later nineteenth century, was subsidiary to that of adult men.[46] As reproducers and household managers, however, women had unchallenged supremacy. In a society for which child-bearing provided the major source of insurance against old age and infirmity, women controlled the key decisions concerning procreation, reproduction and child-rearing. Household administration and labour, though less demanding and doubtless less highly valued in a mud cabin than in a suburban villa, entailed skills entitling women to recompense in the form of food, clothing and lodging.[47]

The contribution of adult women to the welfare of families extended further, to the provision of affection and consolation. These services were by some

45 The under-representation of women among elderly inmates in various Unions antedated 1847, as implied by Ó Gráda's tabulations in Ireland, pp. 100–3. The female component for those aged over 50 was 46.0 per cent in North Dublin (August 1845 to February 1846), 46.0 per cent in Antrim (September 1843 to June 1846), and 37.5 per cent in Midleton (August 1841 to June 1842).   46 See Mary Cullen, 'Breadwinners and Providers: Women in the Household Economy of Labouring Families, 1835–36' in Maria Luddy and Clíona Murphy (eds), *Women Surviving* (Dublin, 1989), pp. 85–116. 47 For analysis of the economic value of housework in a later period, see Joanna Bourke, *Husbandry to Housewifery: Women, Economic Change, and Housework in Ireland, 1890–1914* (Oxford, 1993).

accounts sufficiently valuable to induce penniless men and women to defy narrowly 'economic' logic by marrying without immediate prospect of land or employment.[48] Although it would be absurd to assume that affection was uniquely administered by women, it seems plausible to speculate that family services such as pampering the weary, nursing the sick, or keening the dead, were female specialities. Furthermore, cooking, washing, mending and other household services provided emotional solace as well as material betterment for the hungry, dirty, or ragged. The relative power of male and female affection is dauntingly difficult to test, although the alleged predominance of women in supplying emigrant remittances suggests greater female willingness to honour unenforceable family obligations.[49] Once the definition of 'endowments' is extended from the market-place to the household and the marriage bed, it ceases to be obvious that pre-famine women enjoyed inferior entitlements to those of men. If women were more dispensable in the paid workforce, men were perhaps less essential to the collective welfare of the affective family unit. What was the relative value attributed to material goods and emotional services? How equitably were these benefits distributed within households, and within broader networks of family or friend-ship? The unwritten history of the pre-famine Irish family should incorporate not only the allocation of material commodities between male and female members, but also the selective allocation of affection.

The famine sharply devalued most of the assets and skills with which both men and women were endowed. The drastic loss of private employment after 1845 was not confined to agriculture, and had a proportionately greater impact on men as the principal wage-earners. Specialist female occupations were also affected: for example, convictions for soliciting in Dublin diminished markedly in 1846 and 1847 before gradually recovering to pre-famine levels.[50] The value of small holdings of land, an asset predominantly in the hands of male occupiers, collapsed as a result of the potato failure. The relative ease with which tens of thousands of farmers were evicted or induced to surrender their holdings was a function of falling prices for 'tenant right', as well as the rapacity or bankruptcy

48 This argument, prevalent among pre-famine critics of Irish social organisation, underlies K.H. Connell's influential demographic analysis, *The Population of Ireland, 1750–1845* (Oxford, 1950). **49** The folklore and statistics of remittances are discussed by Arnold Schrier, *Ireland and the American Emigration, 1850–1900* (Minneapolis, 1958), pp. 108–16. Daughters were not, however, prominent among those identified in the parochial examinations for the Poor Inquiry (1835) as being dutiful in accepting their obligations towards the aged. Daughters were designated in only 3 out of 106 reports, compared with unmarried children in general (9), youngest sons (9) and eldest sons (1). The major defaulters were daughters-in-law (27) and sons-in-law (7). See *First Report from His Majesty's Commissioners for Inquiring into the Condition of the Poorer Classes in Ireland, Appendix A* in HCP, 1835 [369], xxxii part 1. **50** Maria Luddy, 'Prostitution and Rescue Work in Nineteenth-Century Ireland', pp. 52–3, in Luddy and Murphy, *Women Surviving*, pp. 51–84. Convictions peaked in 1844 (at 3,855), declining to 3,754 in 1845, 3,407 in 1846, and 3,010 in 1847. The declining trend resumed after a further peak in 1850, when there were 3,482 convictions.

of landlords. Very small plots were no longer worth buying or indeed occupying, being incapable of yielding a subsistence from less prolific substitute crops. Since poor Irishmen typically possessed.few exchangeable endowments except the capacity to labour and sometimes the possession of land, male entitlements were catastrophically devalued during the crisis. If the analysis of entitlements were confined to the monetary economy, the conclusion would be inescapable that the relative deprivation of exchange entitlements during the Irish famine was more severe for men than for women. Indeed, the Irish case appears to illustrate an unstated corollary of Sen's theory of entitlements, whereby famine should diminish rather than exacerbate inequalities within poor households.[51]

If, however, the analysis of entitlements is extended to non-monetary assets and services, the relative benefit to women is less clear. Temporarily but undeniably, the devastation of famine diminished the recognised value of children as future benefactors. The female endowment of potential motherhood was therefore devalued, a process reinforced by the reduction in fecundity resulting from malnutrition and consequent amenorrhoea during famines.[52] The decline in fertility (discussed above) was compounded by a sharp drop in the number of marriages reported in 1847.[53] The reductions in nuptiality and fertility, though relatively unimportant in improving the survival chances of adult women, signified rapid deterioration in the most important of female exchange entitlements. The diminished appeal of child-bearing and marriage was parodied in the reports of 'outrages' for 1847, which revealed an increase in infanticide but reductions in rape, attempted rape and abduction.[54] The devaluation of female services within families was compounded by the razing of cottages, the dissolution of households,

---

51 Whereas famines tend to exaggerate class inequalities by their selective devaluation of the entitlements of poor labourers and farmers, they should reduce intra-family inequalities by depriving male bread-winners or potato-winners of their comparative advantage. The greater the male advantage in normal conditions, the greater the levelling effect of famine.   52 Michael W. Flinn, *The European Demographic System, 1500–1820* (Brighton, 1981), p. 31.   53 The *General Report* of the 1851 census, pp. 658–61, reveals that the number of marriages reported by surviving family heads declined from 34,433 in 1846 to 25,906 in 1847, thereafter somewhat recovering. The number in 1847 fell 25 per cent short of the mean annual figure for 1841–46. Corresponding provincial reductions were 36 per cent in Munster, 31 per cent in Connaught, 18 per cent in Ulster, and 17 per cent in Leinster. A similar change is evident in the Registrar-General's returns, restricted to non-Catholic marriages, showing a decline of 26 per cent between 1846 (9,344 marriages) and 1847 (6,943), followed by 9,048 in 1848 and 9,493 in 1849: *Thom's Official Directory* (Dublin, 1850 edn.), p. 191.   54 The pattern is somewhat spoiled by the reduced incidence of concealment of birth and desertion of children, crimes which (like infanticide) were more prevalent in 1844 than during the famine. The number of reported infanticides was 135 in 1844, 107 in 1845, 100 in 1846 and 131 in 1847. Corresponding figures for other crimes were as follows: rape, 114, 102, 105 and 35; attempted rape, 43, 50, 49 and 23; abduction, 28, 17, 18 and 10; concealment of birth, 64, 63, 66 and 55; desertion of children, 191, 125, 147 and 116. See National Archives, Irish Crime Records, i, *Returns of Outrages reported to the Constabulary Office.*

and therefore the redundancy of managerial skills. On the roadside or in the workhouse, the power of the domestic administrator was negated.

Even without a physical territory, however, women continued to offer the unquantifiable services of affection and consolation. According to one version of the 'lifeboat' model of response to famine, female providers of mere affection would be thrown overboard by men with potentially greater earning power. This argument relies on two dubious assumptions: that the distribution of power within the family group is determined by the relative earning capacity of its members, and that the resultant inequalities acquire a normative force outlasting the economic rationale that engendered them. According to a more credible hypothesis, the effect of the sudden devaluation of normal male entitlements would be to enhance men's demand for 'psychic' services such as protection and cosseting. Faced with the certainty of hunger and the consequent risk of illness and death, the potential victim might rationally seek comfort and succour at the cost of sharing food with his protector, so trading current consumption for future security.[55] For both sexes, indeed, the probability of survival was determined not merely by nutrition, but by access to helpers and nurses in periods of incapacity. To the extent that women (particularly able-bodied women with families) were the primary suppliers of care and affection, the rising value of that endowment favoured the female.[56] Alone among the major sources of either male or female entitlement, the price of love may have been inflated by famine.

If mortality provides the best index of victimhood, emigration is the surest evidence of transcendence over the crippling assaults of famine. Admittedly, the decision to emigrate was often unwelcome and largely involuntary, being therefore identified in many studies as a variety of victimhood. Nevertheless, emigration was widely regarded, even by those who deplored its genesis, as the most effective means of securing a livelihood for most survivors of the famine. Despite the restoration of land values and increase in wages, over a third of most cohorts in

55 This hypothesis is superficially at odds with Becker's model of 'altruism' within the family, in which the (male) altruist transfers part of his money income to the (female) beneficiary, in exchange for 'psychic income'. When a 'disaster' cuts the altruist's income by a larger amount than that of the beneficiary, he reduces the transfer and therefore her consumption. Becker does not discuss disasters such as famine, in which such a decision might cause starvation for the beneficiary by pushing her (initially lower) consumption below subsistence level. The optimal strategy for maximising the family's welfare might be to keep the beneficiary alive by actually raising the transfer, in the expectation that the altruist's further loss of money income would be compensated by life-preserving psychic services. By keeping a nurse in the lifeboat, the altruist's chance of survival might be increased despite his own consequent loss of consumption. Cf. Gary S. Becker, *A Treatise on the Family* (Cambridge, Mass., 1981), esp. pp. 176–7, 194–5.   56 This hypothesis is consistent with the reduction in the female proportion of middle-aged deaths between 1841–45 and 1846–51, discussed above. The association between survival and succour was mainly confined to family groups, and cannot account for mortality among the growing proportion of isolated men without potential female protectors, and women without potential male food-suppliers.

the later nineteenth century found it appropriate to seek employment and establish households outside Ireland. During the famine, departure had the further attraction of sharply raising one's probability of immediate survival, provided that the journey was not to Québec or the Maritimes in 1847. Access to emigration provides a crucial test for the prevalence of discrimination against women: the vital choice concerned those who would be helped aboard the lifeboat, not those who would be thrown overboard. Unfortunately, no aggregate record of Irish emigration was compiled before May 1851, so precluding definitive analysis. Between 1851 and 1855, however, there was a slight female surplus of recorded emigrants, an Irish aberration not replicated until the turn of the century.[57] For the famine years, official returns by sex were compiled for each country of departure but not nationality, so leaving unknown the sex ratio of Irish passengers from Liverpool and other British ports. There was a small male surplus among the minority of Irish emigrants using Irish ports, a surplus which peaked at the height of the crisis in 1847.[58] A study of over 6,000 Irish passengers reaching New York in 1847 and 1848 also indicates a male majority, amounting to 55.6 per cent by comparison with 53.8 per cent for a sample of sailings between 1840 and 1846.[59] It therefore seems likely that men gained preferential access in the earlier years of famine, progressively losing their advantage to women by 1851. Yet these fluctuations cannot mask the most striking characteristic of Irish emigration in European context: the enduring absence of a substantial male majority. Before, during and after the famine, women and men enjoyed roughly equal opportunities to seek sustenance beyond Ireland's shores.

The intention of this essay is to provoke discussion of the evidence for discrimination against women in Irish history, by comparing male and female suffering and survival during an unexampled economic, social and familial crisis. To the extent that the incidence of mortality indicates relative victimhood, women had a marked initial advantage which was extended during the famine. The allocation of official relief, at least through the workhouse, favoured women among younger adults but males among children and the elderly. The state thus protected and enhanced the entitlements of dependants in general, and of non-dependant women. These relief measures affected a society in which the superiority of male endowments was less obvious than is usually assumed. If household and family services are analysed along with assets and skills with a

57 See David Fitzpatrick, 'The Unimportance of Gender in explaining Post-Famine Irish Emigration' in Eric Richards (ed.), *Visible Women: Female Immigrants in Colonial Australia* (Canberra, 1995), pp. 145–67.   58 The reports of the Colonial Land and Emigration Commissioners, in HCP, indicate that the female proportion of non-cabin passengers from Irish ports was 48.3 per cent in 1843, 50.0 per cent in 1844, 50.0 per cent in 1845, 49.3 per cent in 1846, 46.1 per cent in 1847, 46.3 per cent in 1848, 47.7 per cent in 1849, 50.5 per cent in 1850, and 50.6 per cent in 1851.   59 Cormac Ó Gráda, 'Across the Briny Ocean: Some Thoughts on Irish Emigration to America, 1800–1850', p. 126, in T. M. Devine and David Dickson (eds), *Ireland and Scotland, 1600–1850* (Edinburgh, 1983), pp. 118–30.

monetary exchange value, the apparent differential in pre-famine entitlements is greatly diminished. The effect of famine was to reduce the value of most of these endowments, while increasing the demand for the provision of affection and solace, perhaps a female speciality. The roughly equal access of the sexes to emigration suggests that women were not effectively excluded from the most efficient path to survival and revival. If women were indeed the victims of systematic discrimination during the Irish famine, the evidence in support of that hypothesis has yet to be assembled.[60]

60 I am grateful to Cormac Ó Gráda, Timothy Guinnane and Joanna Bourke for their searching critiques of my argument and suggestions for its development.

'Ireland's trained and marshalled manhood': the Fenians in the mid-1860s

TOBY JOYCE

'War', at least in the sense of combat, 'has the supremely important limitation that it is an entirely masculine activity', according to the military historian John Keegan.[1] It could be truly said that a large part of the so-called 'art of war' lies in persuading or coercing men, particularly young men, to bear arms in pursuit of a cause. An armed rebellion is no exception to this, a point to be kept in mind when examining the organisation known as the Fenians in Ireland during the period 1861 to 1865.

Manhood

Strictly speaking, only the American branch of the organisation should be called the 'Fenians', but the name is generally used for both branches. The Irish branch was known as the IRB, or Irish Revolutionary Brotherhood, and later still as the Irish Republican Brotherhood; in this paper the 'IRB' refers to the Irish move-ment. Throughout its history, the IRB was a tightly-knit secret society, but in its mid-1860s manifestation, it constituted a mass movement with probably over 50,000 in membership,[2] and possibly as many as 100,000. Given the circumstances, the figure compares favourably with the public recruitment of 150,000 men by the Irish Volunteers during the 1914 Home Rule crisis.[3] Except for the 1918–22 period, this was the only time that radical separatism commanded such support, and it represented a remarkable achievement for its chief organiser, James Stephens.

The picture of the 'average Fenian' is well known from arrest records in the 1865–7 period. The vast majority were townsmen of the lower middle class: clerks, tradesmen, shopkeepers or shopkeepers' assistants, while less than 20 per cent were labourers or farmers.[4] Lord Straithnairn, Commander of the British forces in Ireland, described the Fenians accurately as having come from the 'class above the masses'.[5] Members of this class were excluded from the franchise, but were

1 John Keegan, *A History of Warfare* (London, 1994), p. 76.   2 R.V. Comerford, *The Fenians in Context: Irish Politics and Society 1848–82*, (Dublin, 1985), p. 124.   3 David Fitzpatrick, 'Militarism in Ireland, 1900–1922' in Thomas Bartlett and Keith Jeffrey (eds), *A Military History of Ireland* (Cambridge, 1996), p. 386.   4 K. Theodore Hoppen, *Elections and Popular Politics in Ireland 1832–1885* (Oxford, 1994), pp. 359–61.   5 Ibid. p. 359.

important because of the moral pressure they could bring in public meetings and demonstrations. The Fenians exploited this potential to the full. Excluding the north-east, the movement was strongest in the most 'modernised' regions of the country: a broad swathe running eastward and south from Longford-Westmeath, and around to West Cork.[6] It was weakest along the west coast, generally.

In his paper, 'Patriotism as Pastime',[7] R.V. Comerford has discussed the background to the success of Fenianism in the 1860s. He points to the increased leisure time of young men in urban and town environments, to the association of Fenian recruiting with public houses, and to the communal nature of nocturnal drilling. This leads to his conclusion that the Fenianism of the 1860s had its base in the need of young men for socialisation and self-actualisation, and that it was mainly a public and social movement, rather than a secret and military one. Yet, on another level, a 'social' organisation may be turned to military purposes. One example, highlighted by Kevin Whelan, is that of the United Irishmen, some of whose most effective units were formed from hurling teams and local factions in the Carlow-Wexford area.[8] The United Irishmen found public houses, with their charged atmosphere of local male solidarity, political discussion and patriotic singing, to be excellent recruiting grounds.[9] The Fenians adopted the same recruiting techniques seventy years later, but Comerford is surely incorrect in deducing that Fenianism was therefore confined to the alehouse and football pitch. History reveals many examples of young men joining military organisations for social reasons: the weekend soldiers of the FCA, the National Guard or the Territorial Army. Their effectiveness as soldiers depends less on initial motivation than on the methods of the organisation in training what often seems like unlikely material, and often with reasonable success.

It is the argument of this essay that while the 'Patriotism as Pastime' thesis goes some way to explaining the phenomenon of Fenianism in the 1860s, it cannot fully account for the influx of so many men into the IRB at that time. While it is true that the men who joined the Irish Fenians were searching for self-actualisation, they deliberately chose to do so in the manner suggested by the masculine ethos of nineteenth-century nationalism – through the pursuit of soldiering. This effect was achieved by the IRB chiefly through use of the contemporary example of the American Civil War, in which many Irishmen were serving in the Union army.

The IRB set out consciously to politicise and militarise a large section of the Irish people, in particular the urban and town-dwelling males. To do this, they drew on the nineteenth-century popular cult of 'manhood' that accompanied the growth of nationalism and the militarisation of society across Europe at that

6 Comerford, *The Fenians in Context*, p. 208.   7 R.V. Comerford, 'Patriotism as Pastime: the Appeal of Fenianism in the mid-1860s' in *Irish Historical Studies*, xxii, 87 (1981), pp. 239–50.   8 Kevin Whelan, 'The United Irishmen, the Enlightenment and Popular Culture' in David Dickson, Daire Keogh and Kevin Whelan (eds), *The United Irishmen: Republicanism, Radicalism and Rebellion* (Dublin, 1993), pp. 288–9.   9 Ibid., p. 292.

time. In general, the Victorian ideal of 'manhood' or 'manliness' incorporated 'qualities of physical courage, chivalric ideals, virtuous fortitude with additional connotations of military and patriotic virtue'.[10] Gerald Lindemann, studying the letters of Civil War soldiers, has found copious evidence of the cult of manhood, expressed by one young private as the expected bearing of the soldier: 'If he shows the least cowardice, he is undone. His courage must never fail. He must be manly and independent.'[11] This mobilisation of manhood extended even into the non-military societies of Great Britain and the United States.

In Britain, during 1857, rumours of an invasion from Imperial France gave rise to the formation of 'Independent Rifle Companies' across England, Wales and Scotland. These units drilled and practised under elected officers in contrast to the gentry-led local defence volunteers of the Napoleonic Wars.[12] In the United States, during the excitement that accompanied Abraham Lincoln's presidential campaign of 1860, thousands of young men, calling themselves Wideawakes, drilled and publicly marched in torchlight processions at Republican rallies.[13] The first volunteers for the Union army must have included many of these Wideawakes in their number. Similarly, in the American south, companies of young men drilled with old muskets and broom handles in anticipation of secession. The outbreak of the Civil War was greeted north and south by rejoicing similar to that which greeted the outbreak of World War One in Europe. Many of the regiments, on both sides, were composed of men from a single community who elected their own officers and took their sense of identity with them into the war. 'The average Civil War [military] company began with all the discipline of a lodge of Elks,' comments one social historian in reference to soldiers and their communities; details are available of regiments setting up Bible classes, buying regimental libraries, organising Christian associations and holding Sunday prayer meetings.[14]

Ireland was not immune from such military enthusiasm, as was shown in 1860 when a thousand-man brigade was raised to assist the Pope, whose territory had been invaded by the new Italian state.[15] Many of the men who joined the brigade went on to join the Union army in the Civil War. Others remained in Ireland and later joined the Fenians.

10 Norman Vance, *Sinews of the Spirit: the Ideal of Manliness in Victorian Literature and Religious Thought*, quoted in J.A. Mangan and James Walvin, *Manliness and Morality: Middle Class Masculinity in Britain and America, 1800–1940* (Manchester, 1987), p. 1.   11 Gerald Lindemann, *Embattled Courage*, (New York, 1989), p. 7.   12 Comerford, *The Fenians in Context*, p. 44.   13 There is a fascinating photograph of a group of New York Wideawakes in Philip B. Kundhardt et al, *Lincoln: an Illustrated Biography* (New York, 1992), p. 132. Their uniforms and torches hefted like rifles give them a distinctly martial air. 14 Reid Marshall, 'The Northern Soldier and his Community' in Maris Vinovskis (ed.), *Towards a Social History of the American Civil War* (Cambridge, 1990), pp. 78–92.   15 E.R. Norman, *The Catholic Church and Ireland in the Age of Rebellion 1859–1873* (London, 1965), pp. 45–51.

Fenian History

The Fenian organisation emerged from the disunity of Irish nationalism in the late 1850s. It was founded by a group of exiles in New York, chief among them the veterans of 1848, Michael Doheny and John O'Mahony.[16] Contact was opened with James Stephens who had just returned to Ireland following exile in France. Stephens set about organising the Irish Revolutionary Brotherhood, a secret oath-bound organisation, and, despite resistance from established nationalist leaders, began gradually to put together the movement.

Michael Doheny was arguably the most important influence on Fenian militarism, though it was O'Mahony who became head centre in the United States. Doheny had long been at the forefront of Irish-American radical separatism. In the early 1850s, he had encouraged Irish emigrants to join the New York militia, and founded the Irish New York regiments, including the famous 'Fighting Irish' 69th which so distinguished itself in the Civil War.[17] In a public letter, written in December 1860 and published in *Phoenix*, the Fenians' New York newspaper, Doheny wrote to the Mullinahone contingent of the papal brigade:

> [After coming to the United States,] our first care was to create, incite and extend military organisations among Irishmen ... The result is that there are, at least, 25,000 Irishmen in these States – some of them fully drilled and disciplined – all of them more or less so ... A similar organisation in Ireland is just what is needed. Every man has a natural right to be a man in the highest acceptation of the term; and no one is such unless he knows the use of arms.[18]

Fenianism in the United States received a major boost during the Civil War. Anti-British attitudes pervaded the US army and government because of what seemed an ambiguous British policy towards the Confederacy. Irish regiments such as those created by Doheny were fertile recruiting grounds. Army life gave plenty of scope for discussion and persuasion while the men were in camp.

In Ireland, James Stephens used the growing power of the Fenians in America as leverage to generate further recruits. Even before 1861, however, the movement had begun to attract support. In West Cork, a nucleus for further expansion was provided by the Phoenix Society, founded in Skibbereen by Jeremiah O'Donovan Rossa. The West Cork movement quickly developed, as Rossa recalled in his memoirs: 'In the cellars, in the woods, and on the hillsides, we had men drilling in the night-time, and war and rumours of wars were on the wings of the wind.'[19] The particular recruiting technique of the Fenians was begun here: 'We set our eyes on the young men who could carry their district, in case of a rising.'[20]

---

16 Comerford, *The Fenians in Context*, pp. 43–66.   **17** Patrick O'Flaherty, 'Michael Doheny, Young Irelander and Fenian' in the *Irish Sword*, xvii, 67 (1988), pp. 81–9. **18** *Phoenix* [New York], 10 December 1860.   **19** Jeremiah O'Donovan Rossa, *Rossa's Recollections 1838–1898* (New York, 1898), p. 199.   **20** Ibid.

Stephens was to repeat this early success on a far larger scale in the 1863–1865 period. However, the Skibbereen overture ended in disaster: an informer within the movement, and the local parish priest, tipped off the authorities, and the episode ended in a gaol term for O'Donovan Rossa and exile for others. But this setback was offset by the first public success of the movement, gained by playing a dominant role in the Terence Bellew McManus funeral procession (November 1861), the first in a series of great nationalist funerals. Here was indeed a symbol that Fenianism marked a new departure. Instead of the loose gatherings of the O'Connell era,[21] with their Catholic-style ritual, the focus was on a quasi-military procession of marching men, with the McManus remains more a symbolic excuse for a large public demonstration.

The main vehicle for the success of the IRB was the publication between 1863 and 1865 of the newspaper, the *Irish People*. With John O'Leary as editor, and with Charles Kickham and Thomas Clarke Luby on the staff, the *Irish People* proved as effective as the *Nation* of the 1840s in stimulating a new generation of nationalists. As journalist Richard Pigott later wrote in his recollections,

> The aim of the *Irish People* was to impress upon the people that freedom could only be won 'by the sword'; that it was possible so to win it; that the American war showed that as Irishmen had, by their genius and courage, helped America to win battles, so had they the same ability to conquer the independence of their own country.[22]

The drive for many thousands of young men to join the Fenians came from the success of Irishmen in the American Civil War, and the belief spread by Stephens and his lieutenants that Irish-American soldiers would be available to spearhead a rebellion in Ireland after the war. The war also helped the *Irish People* to stress the military prowess of Irishmen:

> [The American Civil War] has revived the somewhat tarnished military prestige of our race. It has restored the Irish people's weakened confidence in the courage of their hearts and the might of their arms ... this American war has given us back our military reputation in its pristine lustre ... every Irishman, worthy of the name, believes once more that he has a soldier's heart and arm.[23]

The newspaper also revelled in the democratic nature of the Federal army:

> It has shown to us the Irish people, in our own days, a living example of what a people's army can do – an army officered exclusively by men sprung from

21 Gary Owens, 'Constructing the Repeal Spectacle: Monster Meetings and People Power in Pre-Famine Ireland' in M.R. O'Connell (ed.), *People Power* (Dublin, 1993), pp. 80–93.   **22** Richard Pigott, *Recollections of an Irish Nationalist Journalist* (Dublin, 1883), p. 131.   **23** 'Fruits of the American War' in *Irish People*, 26 December 1863.

the ranks of the people, and (what touches us more nearly) a large proportion of whom are Irish-born.[24]

There are signs that before the publication of the *Irish People*, the movement had been faltering. Thomas Clarke Luby, one of Stephens' chief lieutenants, baldly stated in his recollections that the IRB in early 1863 was losing ground,[25] and reflected on how little had been achieved between 1858 and 1863. If that is so, then the publication of the newspaper created, in Luby's words, a Fenian 'boom'. Later, referring to this phase of Fenian history, O'Donovan Rossa recalled: '[The] movement generated a spirit of manhood in the land ... [The] Fenian organisation ... in a great measure broke up the faction fights and the faction-parties.'[26] Here O'Donovan Rossa makes an important claim to having suppressed faction-fighting, something the United Irishmen also attempted.[27] A similar claim was made by Charles J. Kickham in 1865:

> Drunkenness and faction-fighting are disappearing. Our young men are becoming more intelligent and manly, and, consequently, more moral every day. And this change is most apparent precisely where the *Irish People* is most read, and 'Fenianism' is said most to abound.[28]

The message of the *Irish People* resonated with the literate middle and lower-middle class. 'The American Civil War was the principal topic of public interest in Ireland from 1861 to 1865', writes Joseph Hernon.[29] Ireland was linked to the USA by ties of history and emigration. The state of mind produced by the war can be seen vividly from the speeches given at an outing of young men (and their female companions) in July 1863.[30] One long toast included reference to 'John O'Mahony ... [who] will be, perhaps, the liberator of his country ... [and] the patriot soldier, Thomas Francis Meagher. Methinks I see him at the head of 100,00 exiles, standing on his native sod'. This could be dismissed as bibulous rhetoric on a summer afternoon, but it shows that 'raw material' existed for revolutionary purposes. Indeed, many of the young men attending were probably already in the IRB. A toast to 'the Association' was possibly a coded reference to the movement,[31] whose members used such ellipses in referring to the organisation,

24 Ibid.   **25** '[H]ow little the "Fenian" work done from 1858 to 1863 (inclusive) seems as compared to the expenditure of labour and the monetary expense', Ms 331 (Thomas Clarke Luby Papers), National Library of Ireland.   **26** O'Donovan Rossa, *Recollections*, p. 205.   **27** Whelan, 'The United Irishmen, the Enlightenment, and Popular Culture' in *The United Irishmen*, pp. 293–4.   **28** 'Fenianism Metamorphosed' in *Irish People*, 17 June 1865. This unsigned leading article is attributed to Kickham by R.V. Comerford in *Charles J. Kickham* (Dublin, 1979) p. 245.   **29** Joseph Hernon, *Celts, Catholics and Copperheads: Ireland views the American Civil War* (Ohio, 1967), p. 7.   **30** *United Irishman and Galway American*, 15 August 1863.   **31** *The United Irishman and Galway American* was the journal of a public body, the National Brotherhood of St Patrick, which shared goals and members with the clandestine IRB. The reference would have been clear to all readers in either movement.

rather than the 'Association of Grocers' Assistants', its official title.[32] Young men in this particular trade constituted very typical IRB recruits.

The 'spirit of manhood' is linked to 'respectability' which carried connotations of virtue and nobility. Leaders aimed to recruit outstanding young men in each town, the ones who would 'carry the district' in Rossa's words. Recruiting in Dublin, Thomas Luby described some draper's assistants he was recruiting as 'respectable young men', adding: 'recognising their smartness, I made them all B's [officers] on the spot'.[33] When Michael Davitt joined the Fenians in 1864 in Haslingden, Lancashire, it was said 'every smart, respectable young fellow' was a member.[34] Furthermore, the Fenians eschewed another popular social pastime of the period: electoral violence. According to K.T. Hoppen, conditions in Ireland between 1850 and 1870 were such that 'it was the absence rather than the presence of violence [at elections] which seems to have been thought worthy of comment and explanation'.[35] The riotous groups of these occasions were composed mainly of the poor labourers who lived in the cottages surrounding most Irish towns. One Irish election mob, at Cavan in 1855, is described as follows: 'A body of stout, active young fellows, numbering some five or six thousand and each brandishing an enormous cudgel, came down the street and advanced to the court house, roaring vociferously.'[36] Women often formed part of these election crowds. At Cashel, in 1865, 'well-looking, well-dressed girls, one a perfect Amazon, bared their arms, wound their shawls tightly around them, and rushed with the melee.'[37] The Fenians did not mobilise women or the lower classes, or, their spokesmen emphasised, participate in these electoral brawls. In replying to the charge of 'rowdyism', Charles Kickham pointed out, in the article quoted above: 'If denouncing rowdyism affords them any pleasure, they have a rich treat before them. They will find one "nomination day" worth fifty years of "Fenianism".'[38] This aim to develop discipline among their supporters, and help make respectable the country, bolstered a general Victorian trend.

While a Fenian Sisterhood was founded in the United States, and Fenian wives worked diligently for their men when imprisoned, there is a marked absence of female participation in Fenian activities in Ireland in the period under question. Women are conspicuously missing from Fenian gatherings. Like the 'Grocers' Assistants' meeting mentioned above, they appear mainly as dancing partners![39] Women were not allocated any auxiliary role such as intelligence-gathering, message-carrying, medical or commissary duties – roles traditionally filled by women in revolutionary movements. Fenianism in the 1861–1865 period appears to have been totally in the male sphere. Unlike the *Nation*, only one female poet

---

32 See Luby papers, National Library of Ireland, where Luby refers to the use of such coded names as 'our body', 'our movement' and 'our organisation'.   33 Luby papers. 34 Letter of Frank Haran to Mrs Mary Davitt, 7 November 1907, quoted in T.W. Moody, *Davitt and Irish Revolution* (Dublin, 1984), p. 44.   35 Hoppen, *Elections, Politics and Society*, p. 390.   36 Ibid., p. 403.   37 Ibid., p. 407.   38 'Fenianism Metamorphosed' in *Irish People*, 17 June 1865.   39 See also Comerford, 'Patriotism as Pastime', p. 248.

was published regularly by the *Irish People*: Eva O'Leary, sister of the editor John O'Leary.

It was to landlords and police that the Fenians refused the deference that had hitherto been the norm in Irish society. James Roche, an American Fenian who returned to edit a newspaper in Galway, posed the question in an editorial: 'Instead of the whining gait and tone of the mendicant, should we not adopt the manly bearing and tone of the freeman?'[40] The 'manly bearing and tone', thus defined, closely resemble the demeanour of a soldier. In the mid-nineteenth century, the soldier had become the 'epitome of manhood', and even the middle class aspired to the aristocratic values which had once been the monopoly of the knight: chivalry, honour and courage.

Military drilling, performed in secret, was the major pursuit of the Irish Fenians. Its significance extended far beyond the social dimension identified by some historians – alternative to the faction fight, and forerunner of the later inter-parish football match. Drill is still important to armies in standardising the movements of large masses of soldiers; it was even more important in the mid-nineteenth century when armies still did battle in massed formations. It also had important functions in instilling a military ethos, as a morale-builder and as a preparatory ritual for battle.[41]

Irishmen were certainly familiar with the image of the soldier, since the country was heavily garrisoned by a large army presence and a paramilitary police force, the Royal Irish Constabulary. It was the heady mixture of soldiering and nationalism which attracted so many of the younger members of the middle classes. They aspired to emulate the manly deeds of their cousins who were fighting in the battles of the American Civil War. They heeded the call of 'manhood' as the masculine defenders of a national community. The Fenian 'boom' of 1861–1865 was an Irish version of the military enthusiasm that had fuelled the Independent Rifle Companies in Britain and the large-scale volunteering on both sides in the early years of the American Civil War. The contemporary social gatherings, at public houses or football matches, provided the raw material, just as a later generation of IRB men would be recruited from the ranks of the Gaelic Athletic Association. The primary appeal for these recruits lay, not in group socialising, for which they had many options, but in the prospect of war as a test of manhood in which patriotism was focused into a simple challenge of courage and character. In this, they were heeding Michael Doheny's words, when he proclaimed that the Irish regiments were influenced by two leading motives:

> First, they ardently desire some opportunity to prove their fidelity to the nation that entrusts its honor and its flag to their keeping. And secondly, they desire,

40 *Galway American*, 30 May 1863. **41** Richard Holmes, *Firing Line* (Penguin, 1987), pp. 42–3.

and more fervently if possible, to meet the old enemy on some fair field, and leave the result to the God of battles.[42]

One can easily imagine versions of Doheny's words repeated by IRB recruiters. That such ideas were commonly accepted is demonstrated by the outing of the 'Grocers' Assistants' mentioned above. Within a long toast to 'love of country' which, according to the speaker, among Irishmen 'prevails with them in a higher degree than people of other countries', a list of military heroes from Brian Boru to Robert Emmet is included.[43] Other examples of such rhetoric abound in contemporary nationalist newspapers, including reports of meetings of the National Brotherhood of St Patrick, the IRB's public 'twin' organisation.[44] It is easy to dismiss this with the jaded scepticism of the twentieth century but at the time such sentiments could be taken very seriously. The 1863–5 period could plausibly be argued to present a 'time of opportunity' for Ireland, with an Anglo-American war looming, and with the growing influence of Fenians in the United States.

The rhetoric of James Stephens, with its anticipation of Pearse, further exemplifies this:

> We witness the 'periodical slaughter' of our people; we see the grass growing upon their hearths; we watch the stalworth manhood and virtuous womanhood of our race flying away to distant lands – and seeing all this we must be men and no thanks to us ... Youth of Ireland! all depends on you ... You are our vanguard. Be prepared to meet the foe in an ordered phalanx, and your measured tramp shall hush the voice of denunciation ... UNITED Ireland leaping to her feet, shall, with one sweep of her unfettered arm, hurl the invader into the sea.[45]

In a letter to John O'Mahony of December 1861, Stephens argued that the Irish alone must win Irish freedom, though American assistance would be welcome. He wrote: 'Ireland's trained and marshalled manhood alone can ever make could ever have made Ireland's opportunity.'[46] The striking phrase captures the vision of the IRB that prevailed among its leadership. The IRB's ultimate failure was to prove less to do with the nature of its recruits than with the lack of arms, planning and proper military organisation. Thomas Kelly, former US army captain, writing from Ireland to John O'Mahony in 1865, expressed no concerns about the demeanour or morale of the men he encountered in Ireland: 'Personally, I am well satisfied, judging from all I have seen and heard, of the numbers and discipline, and the ability of the men here to achieve success, if properly equipped and led.'[47] Yet it was arguably to Ireland's benefit that it avoided a bloody rising, as improvements in the country's political position from 1870 onwards suggest.

---

42 *New York Phoenix*, 10 December 1860.   **43** *United Irishman and Galway American*, 15 August 1863.   **44** See *United Irishman and Galway American*, July 1863 to April 1864. **45** 'Liberty or Destruction' in *Irish People*, 23 January 1864.   **46** Letter from James Stephens to John O'Mahony, 16 December 1861, O'Donovan Rossa Papers, National Library of Ireland.   **47** Thomas Kelly to John O'Mahony, 21 June 1865, Fenian Brotherhood

Conclusion

In a number of ways, the Irish Fenians of the 1860s were typical mid-century Victorians. The young males who joined the IRB at this time were spurred on by the same motives that impelled their contemporaries in Europe and America to participate in military and quasi-military activities. Also clear is the value placed on 'respectability'; in this regard Fenianism had some role in the creation of the more disciplined nationalist electorate that underpinned the party of Parnell and Redmond. Paradoxically, an organisation dedicated to violent overthrow of the government assisted in the dominance of constitutional politics for a half-century.

The 'Patriotism as Pastime' thesis, while possessing some validity, does not fully explain the extraordinary success of Fenianism in the mid 1860s in creating a mass movement. It is true that the increased leisure time of young men employed in towns did provide a ready raw material for recruitment but a view of Fenianism as purely a social phenomenon is an insufficient one. When placed in the contemporary political, ideological and military context, as well as the social one, the IRB of 1863–5 becomes credible as a quasi-military movement with revolutionary potential. The appeal to 'manhood' shaped by the IRB leaders found a ready response among the males of the middle and lower middle classes. While peer pressure, the desire to jump on an apparent bandwagon, may have provided the motive for some, there was undoubtedly a core of men intent on the Fenian objectives: men like Michael Davitt and Mark Ryan, who joined the Lancashire Militia to acquire military training and returned to Tuam in 1865 to join the expected rebellion.[48] These men were fulfilling the gender role assigned to men by the new nationalism: to become soldiers and die, if necessary, for the country as a whole.

As an attempt to create a rebellion by politicising and militarising Irish men, the IRB ultimately failed, though not because of any lack of seriousness on the part of its members. On the contrary, the IRB leadership did arouse a pitch of enthusiasm and support for their cause in a sizeable number of men. It failed because it did not underpin the movement with a realistic strategy, adequate logistics and consistent co-ordination with the US branch of the movement. Stephens himself ultimately realised the futility of a rising once the promise of American aid receded and the police penetrated the Irish organisation. His refusal to order a rising in 1865 signalled the end of his reign as 'Fenian Chief', and the end of any realistic prospect of a rebellion.

The Fenian Rebellion of 1867 was a dismal, and in many ways farcical, failure but it took place two years after the optimum time for rebellion – 1865, when the movement was at its peak. Comparisons of 1865 with 1916 are very illuminating: a similar core of literary nationalists constituted the separatist leadership; the

Records, collection no. 14, Catholic University of America Archives, Washington, D.C., by kind permission from the Department of Archives and Manuscripts, CUA.   **48** Mark Ryan, *Fenian Memories* (Dublin, 1945), p. 17.

wordy rhetoric of 'the sword' and 'striking a blow' are echoed, as are the hopeful, though futile, signals of an overseas ally. The differences are just as illuminating: the 1860s failed to produce a great crisis of the empire as 1914–1918 did, and James Stephens, unlike Patrick Pearse, failed to live up to his own rhetoric. While Thomas Bartlett and Keith Jeffery have recently stated that the 1916 Rising lay outside the 'recognised Irish military tradition',[49] it could be argued that the 1916 leaders drew on an alternative Irish 'paramilitary' tradition, one conceived by the Young Irelanders but given its essential characteristic by the Fenians that of the courageous, manly and noble Irish rebel.

49 Thomas Bartlett and Keith Jeffery, 'An Irish military tradition?' in Bartlett and Jeffery (eds), *A Military History of Ireland*, p. 22.

II

Unstable Unions: Early Nineteenth-Century Fiction

Sex and Sensation in the Nineteenth-Century Novel

SIOBHÁN KILFEATHER

To dream of a hearse with white plumes is a wedding; but to dream of a wedding is grief, and death will follow.
To dream of a woman kissing you is deceit; but of a man, friendship; and to dream of a horse is exceedingly lucky.[1]

The fact is, though it is difficult for an outsider to believe it, that the whole subject of love, of passion of any kind, especially from a girl and with regard to her own marriage, is such an utterly unheard-of one amongst Grania's class that the mere fact of giving utterance to a complaint on the subject gave her a sense not merely of having committed a hideous breach of common decency, but of having actually crossed the line that separates sanity from madness.[2]

Emily Lawless, in *Grania* (1892), tackles a problem that haunts much nineteenth-century Irish fiction: how to represent the (presumably) inarticulate masses, without merely re-presenting stereotypes associated with stage-Irishry and the brogue. Lawless gestures towards a recognition of this problem in her dedication: 'the possibility of an Irish story without any Irish brogue in it – that brogue which is a tiresome necessity always'. In her heroine, Grania O'Malley, named for an almost mythical figure from Irish history, Lawless creates a subjectivity whose complexities are indicated by sense, feeling and intuition rather than articulation, a woman isolated from her community by a superior sensibility which she has no words to explain, even to herself. The grandeur of Grania's nature is mapped directly onto the bleak grandeur of the landscape – the novel's subtitle is 'the story of an island', and the frontispiece is a map of the Aran Islands. None of Lawless's characters is liberated – except in death – from the confines of what the novelist presents as a narrow and rigid world-view. Grania never succeeds in articulating her discontents to her lover or to herself. The drama of their conflict requires a richness of language in the interplay between free indirect discourse and omniscient narrative to suggest to the reader the meaning of Grania's social, sexual and spiritual frustrations.

---

1 Jane (Lady) Wilde, *Ancient Legends, Mystic Charms, and Superstitions of Ireland. With Sketches of the Past* (1888; republished Galway, 1971), p. 208.   2 Emily Lawless, *Grania: The Story of an Island*, (London, 1892), p. 249.

Terry Eagleton writes that in nineteenth-century Ireland 'the sexual culture of the nation belonged to a complex economy of land and inheritance, property and procreation. As far as sexuality goes, we are speaking less of the erotic or psychological than of dowries and matchmakers'.[3] At one level, Lawless's novel would seem to concur with the view that Irish sexuality is so materially located as to exclude expressions of desire and sensuality, to make such expressions seem absurd or insane. At another level, the very posing of the problem of how to articulate desire within the novel suggests that the sociological or anthropological model for recording Irish sexualities is inadequate to the lived experience of those sexualities. Eagleton argues that it is with the modernism of Moore, Wilde and Joyce that 'sexuality becomes a metaphor for political revolt'. Eagleton's description of the sociological model is true to one dominant discursive mode of constructing Irish sexualities, the sketches of Irish life that run through those texts of political economy, travel writing, fiction, memoirs, journalism and apologies that seem to look to a British as well as Irish audience. Many of these incorporate an homage to the possibility of self-representation of the masses, in so far as they include documentation such as interviews or testimonies presented in court, to journalists, or to officials such as census takers or Poor Law Commissioners. In general these texts offer a contrast between the obfuscation of Irish speech – its deviousness, its foreignness, its intrinsic absurdities – and the apparent transparency of hunger and poverty as written on the body of the peasant. I began this essay with a quotation from Jane Wilde to indicate that there was some recognition in nineteenth-century literature that popular superstitions, folklore and ballads might be some of the languages in which ordinary people articulated the complexities of desire, and that the inverted logic of dreams has a pronounced role in such articulations. I want to argue that the novel is a significant source of information about sexuality because of its special ability to incorporate conflicting discourses, without necessarily reconciling them, and that in nineteenth-century Irish fiction there are recurring dramatisations of a great silence around sex.

Terry Eagleton, *à propos* his argument that the major nineteenth-century Irish novelists are 'engaged in a kind of performative contradiction', producing texts 'colonial in their very letter', cites William Carleton as an example.

> [T]he speech of Carleton's characters can also veer from one linguistic form to the other within one sentence ... Young Dalton, one of the labouring poor of *The Black Prophet* (1847), manages to produce this earthy, monosyllabic praise of the woman he loves: 'Upon my honour, Donnel, that girl surpasses anything I have seen yet. Why, she's perfection – her figure is – is – I havn't [*sic*] words for it – and her face – good heavens! what brilliancy and animation!' Young Dalton's problem is that he has all too many words for it ...[4]

3 Terry Eagleton, *Heathcliff and the Great Hunger: Studies in Irish Culture* (London, 1995), p. 227.   **4** Ibid., p. 209; William Carleton, *The Black Prophet: A Tale of Irish Famine* (Belfast, 1847), p. 118. Eagleton slightly mis-remembers here: the speaker is young Dick but the elaborate performance of speechlessness is the relevant point.

Eagleton makes this point in a context where he argues that what the Irish *novelists* have no words for is a history so 'crisis-racked, excessive, hyperbolic, unlikely,' where 'life itself is sometimes a great deal more improbable than the most sensationalist of tales'. I make no apology for returning to the question of realism in the nineteenth-century novel, since criticism has so readily agreed that this is *the* issue.[5] Although the narrative of nineteenth-century fiction is often traced from Edgeworth to Somerville and Ross, I would argue that in this debate there is an exclusion of a certain kind of women's writing and a demotion of the melodramatic and sensationalist aspects of nineteenth-century fiction that in Britain were associated with an appeal to women readers.[6] It is when he tries to describe the body of Sally M'Gowan that words fail young Dick. Nineteenth-century Irish novels have as much trouble representing bodies and sexuality as in representing famine, dispossession and emigration. This is not because sex is simply an unspeakable subject in nineteenth-century Ireland, but because Irish writers reject the domestication of sexuality in ways that disrupt and depose the conventions of realist fiction.

The use of the word 'sensation' to describe excited or violent feelings dates from the late eighteenth century and by the beginning of the nineteenth century 'sensational', like the recently coined term 'melodramatic', was being associated strongly both with popular theatre and with newspaper reporting of crime. In literary criticism 'sensation fiction' is a term very specifically applied to a group of novels published in England in the 1860s, many published by Bentley and by Maxwell, some serialised in periodicals edited by women: the best-known of the sensation novelists are Wilkie Collins, Mary E. Braddon, Mrs Henry Wood, Sheridan Le Fanu, Charlotte Riddell and Rhoda Broughton. Jenny Bourne Taylor suggests that Wilkie Collins transposes 'the disruptive and disturbing elements of Gothic fiction into the homely setting of the family and the everyday, recognisable world, thus generating suspense and exploiting undercurrents of anxiety that lie behind the doors of the solid, recognisable, middle-class home.'[7] While many critics have followed W.J. McCormack's analysis of Le Fanu into recognition of

---

5 See Thomas Flanagan, *The Irish Novelists, 1800–1850* (New York, 1959); John Cronin, *The Anglo-Irish Novel, Volume One: The Nineteenth Century* (Belfast, 1980); Seamus Deane, *A Short History of Irish Literature* (London, 1986); Barry Sloan, *The Pioneers of Anglo-Irish Fiction: 1800–1850* (Gerrard's Cross, 1986); Seamus Deane (ed.) *The Field Day Anthology of Irish Writing* (3 vols; Derry, 1991).   6 'The sensationalists made crime and violence domestic, modern, and suburban; but their secrets were not simply solutions to mysteries and crimes; they were the secrets of women's dislike of their roles as daughters, wives, and mothers. These women made a powerful appeal to the female audience by subverting the traditions of feminine fiction to suit their own imaginative impulses, by expressing a wide range of suppressed female emotion, and by tapping and satisfying fantasies of protest and escape'; see Elaine Showalter, *A Literature of Their Own: British Women Novelists from Brontë to Lessing* (1977; revised edition, London, 1984), pp. 158–9.   7 Jenny Bourne Taylor, *In the secret theatre of home: Wilkie Collins, sensation narrative and nineteenth-century psychology* (London, 1988), p. 1.

the symbolic and allegorical valences of the so-called Protestant Gothic, with its narratives of aristocratic decay, there has been a concomitant denigration of, or apology for, 'Catholic' bourgeois fiction (McCormack is an exception).[8] Eagleton, for example, recognises Protestant Gothic as 'the political unconscious of Irish society';[9] but in discussing *The Black Prophet* he identifies a striking 'hiatus' between 'story and society': 'Carleton can find no way of anchoring his narrative in the social conditions he depicts; instead the latter threaten at times to become a mere context for the former, which irrelevantly revolves on a twenty-year old murder.'[10] Other critics have depicted the Irish novel as undermined by these dislocations. According to Thomas Flanagan,

> The history of the Irish novel is one of continuous attempts to represent the Irish experience within conventions that were not congenial to it ... The best of them, which seek to move beyond these forms, make their strongest points and exist most vividly through indirection, symbol, allusion, and subtle shifts of points of view.[11]

John Cronin precedes Terry Eagleton in finding the plot of *The Black Prophet* inadequate to its anthropological and political concerns:

> Ideally the terrible realities of the truths in his novel cried out for a sturdy plot-structure to match them and symbols grand enough to do justice to his fearsome theme. Sadly, what he offers instead is an unconvincing story of rural murder and mystery which is intended to generate, in relation to the contemporary events of the novel, an atmosphere of tension and horror.[12]

It might be profitable to move from the presumption that these are failed realist texts to think of their sensational and melodramatic elements as the vehicles for certain kinds of critique. It is not simply that Irish life had its sensational and melodramatic aspects, for which novelists such as Carleton strove to achieve what Margaret Oliphant ascribed to the sensation novelists – 'a kindred depth of effect and shock of incident'.[13] *The Black Prophet* is, of course, exemplary of a narrative and imaginative problem foregrounded in the debate between Edmund Burke and Thomas Paine on the French Revolution, the problem of representing the suffering of the masses as dramatically or affectively as the story of an individual, particularly of a literate, self-reflective individual. Sensational fiction offered writers the opportunity to interrogate the mechanisms by which grand historical narratives invade and evacuate individual subjectivities in what are conventionally presented as the private spaces of home, family and sexuality.

8 See W.J. McCormack, *Sheridan Le Fanu and Victorian Ireland* (Oxford, 1980) and McCormack's introduction to 'Language, Class and Genre' in *The Field Day Anthology of Irish Writing* i, pp. 1070–82.   **9** Eagleton, *Heathcliff and the Great Hunger*, p. 187.   **10** Ibid., p. 212.   **11** Flanagan, *The Irish Novelists*, p. 334.   **12** Cronin, *The Anglo-Irish Novel*, p. 92. **13** Margaret Oliphant, article in *Blackwood's Edinburgh Magazine* 1862, quoted by Taylor, *In the secret theatre of home*, p. 3.

I am aware of the dangers of adapting the very specific use of 'sensation fiction' to include a much larger group of generically mixed texts over a much longer period in Ireland. I have argued elsewhere that there existed amongst eighteenth-century Irish and Scottish writers a sufficient alienation from English literature to foster the development of gothic fiction as a critique of 'progress' from the margins.[14] I want to argue here that in the nineteenth century Irish writers responded to the demands of new discursive formations about Irish reality, and to the tensions of negotiating between the slightly different demands made upon them, by a variety of British readerships and Irish readerships, to discover the uses of sensationalism. As a specifically literary, historical argument I would identify Gerald Griffin's *The Collegians* (1829) as the foundational fictional text in this transformation. It would be mistaken, on several counts, to insist too schematically either on a rigid distinction between English and Irish novelists – after all, Charlotte Riddell and Sheridan Le Fanu can be incorporated into the narrative of English sensation fiction – or between sensational and realist texts. One might question the usefulness of categorising *Clarissa* or *Emma* as realist novels, in so far as such categorisation necessarily belies interesting elements of those texts. More importantly, perhaps, Jenny Bourne Taylor warns of the dangers of privileging sensational novels as the site of madness and 'otherness', 'making them the bearers of a more authentic truth'.[15] It is possible to look at the sensational aspects of writers such as Griffin, Carleton, Le Fanu, Frances Browne, Sarah Grand and George Moore without denying that they have other striking generic affiliations, not all of which are necessarily best read in an Irish context.

Jenny Bourne Taylor describes the middle-class English home of sensation fiction as a 'secret theatre', operating behind closed doors. Irish novels place much more emphasis on open doors, from cabin to big house, but the house open to hospitality and community is also open to surveillance. In the most famous depiction of the middle-class home in nineteenth-century fiction – breakfast at the Dalys' in *The Collegians* – the room is an over-determined text, the apparently transparent domesticity riven with incongruity and contradiction. One of the novel's motifs, in fact, is spatial contrast. In terms of landscape this involves a reiterated mystique of the west, where landscapes are more dramatic and life lived at a greater pitch of intensity.[16] The nobility of Myles and the unruliness of Poll both have their true homes in the west, and it is appropriate that at the novel's conclusion Hardress is seeking his death on a westward voyage, just as Mihil is being carried to a grave in the west.

The allegorisation of space is just as striking in the representation of interiors, particularly in the repeated use of adjacent rooms to house irreconcilable narratives. The chasm between the classes is represented, for example, when

14 Siobhán Kilfeather, 'Origins of the Irish Female Gothic' in *Bullán*, i, 2 (Autumn 1994), pp. 35–45. 15 Taylor, *In the secret theatre of home*, p. 17. 16 For a discussion of the western landscape, and particularly Killarney, in Victorian melodrama, see Luke Gibbons, 'Landscape and character in Irish romantic melodrama' in Kevin Rockett, Luke Gibbons and John Hill, *Cinema and Ireland* (London, 1987), pp. 210–21.

Hardress cripples Danny Mann by pushing him downstairs; while Hardress's muted alienation from his own class is most strikingly presented when he stands at the deathbed of Dalton, the huntsman, who is being teased by drunken revellers in the adjoining room. The organisation of domestic space is also a mode for conveying several undercurrents of passion that cannot erupt into social space. In the chapters at the Dairy Cottage, for example, while Kyrle is advocating the necessity of certain social hypocrisies, he is opening his heart to Hardress, while Hardress, the advocate of frankness, refuses to acknowledge the anguish of Eily, pacing the floors of another room. At Poll Naughten's cottage, Eily is repeatedly represented as moving in and out of her own room, and this movement provides Danny Mann's testimony with one opportunity for evasion:

> Questioned, If he were not present in said Naughten's house, when said Eily (deceased) said Looby being then in Naughten's kitchen, did give a letter to Poll Naughten, sister to prisoner, addressed to Dunant O'Leary, hair-cutter, Garryowen, and containing matter in the handwriting of said Eily; answereth, How should he (prisoner) see through stone walls.[17]

The anti-naturalistic presentation of space also opens up possibilities for representations of the fantastic. At her first appearance Anne Chute is passing around a drawing of Castle Chute the house in which the party is gathered and yet Hyland Creagh does not recognise the scene. Castle Chute is the place of two 'supernatural' visions; Dan Dawley's comic encounter with the Chute family ghosts at the start of the novel is echoed by a moment towards the end when Danny Mann's guards mistake Hardress for a ghost.

Luke Gibbons, in an essay on Killarney and the politics of the sublime, argues that the recurrence of supernatural motifs in eighteenth-century Irish literature provides one of the few means by which the legitimacy of the colonial settlement can be contested, and quotes Tzvetan Todorov: 'The function of the supernatural is to exempt the text from the action of the law, and thereby to transgress that law'.[18]

Griffin presents the Irish peasantry as a people 'at war with the laws by which they are governed ... There is scarcely a cottage in the south of Ireland, where the very circumstance of legal denunciation would not afford, even to a murderer, a certain passport to concealment and protection'.[19] There is a more textually interesting association with the law in Griffin. What chiefly justifies describing *The Collegians* as sensational is the novel's relationship to crime reporting. Showalter and Taylor point out that sensation fiction in England is concurrent with a huge public interest in murder trials, particularly trials of young women

17 Gerald Griffin, *The Collegians: A Tale of Garryowen* (1829; London, [1842]), p. 242. **18** Luke Gibbons, 'Topographies of Terror: Killarney and the Politics of the Sublime' in *SAQ*, 95,1 (Winter 1996), pp. 23–44, p. 38; Tzvetan Todorov, *The Fantastic: A Structural Approach to a Literary Genre* (Ithaca, 1975), p. 33.   **19** Griffin, *The Collegians*, p. 243.

such as Madeleine Smith and Constance Kent. Jonah Barrington's recollections are one testimony to Irish public interest in crime. It has been observed that Griffin's historical setting for *The Collegians* is complicated by public memory of the much more recent murder of Ellen Hanlon. Later editions of the novel reiterate that memory by printing Curran's narrative of the murder from the *New Monthly Magazine* as an appendix. The juxtaposition of novel and narrative has the effect of demonstrating how inadequate explanation and motivation are to the crime. The discrepancies within and between the two texts draw attention to the ways in which various discourses – law, reportage, imaginative fiction – stand in for and gesture towards sexual passion and domestic violence but can never sufficiently account for that excess. The seduction of Eily, as much as her murder, happens off-stage.

It has been persuasively argued that newspaper reporting of sex crimes tends to produce conservative and normative versions of appropriate female behaviour, blaming the victim.[20] It is tempting but unproductive to suggest that what has been silenced in *The Collegians* is Eily's voice. Eily's voice is, in fact, foregrounded in a bizarre call to realism within the text, namely the dream of Hardress Cregan, where he introduces Eily to his rich and fashionable acquaintances, and is shamed by 'the bashfulness, the awkwardness, and the homeliness of speech and accent, with which the ropemaker's daughter received their compliments' and at the sight of her peeling a potato with her fingers. 'He dreamed, moreover, that when he reasoned with her on this subject, she answered him with a degree of pert vulgarity and impatience which was in "discordant harmony" with her shyness before strangers'.[21] The dream, like the scene at the Dairy Cottage, suggests that Hardress is not at all free from social concerns, as he pretends, but it is tonally a very different kind of revelation from that found in dreams in other novels, where the dreamer is overwhelmed by memory or unacknowledged, even unfocused, desires. In *The Black Prophet*, Donnel Dhu dreams that Condy Dalton is hammering a nail into his coffin. Sarah Grand's *The Heavenly Twins* and George Moore's *Evelyn Innes* are just two examples of novels featuring young women who live 'in a state of exquisite feeling', sexually aroused by powerful dreams.[22] Dreams perform many different functions in texts; in these novels they permit an indulgence of sensuousness without reflection or judgement. In *The Heavenly Twins*, of course, the end consequence of Edith's dream is her syphilitic baby and her own descent into insanity.

20 For accounts of this phenomenon in different periods see Anna Clark, *Women's silence, men's violence: sexual assault in England 1770–1845* (London, 1987); Keith Soothill and Sylvia Walby, *Sex Crime in the News* (London, 1991); Judith Walkowitz, *City of Dreadful Delight* (London, 1992); James Kelly, '"A Most Inhuman and Barbarous Piece of Villainy": An Exploration of the Crime of Rape in Eighteenth-Century Ireland' in *Eighteenth-Century Ireland/ Iris an dá chultúr*, 10 (1995), pp. 78–107.   **21** Griffin, *The Collegians*, p. 126. **22** Sarah Grand, *The Heavenly Twins* (London, 1893; reprinted Ann Arbor, 1992), pp. 157; 'The face rose up to hers. She looked into the subtle eyes, and the thrill of the lips, just touching hers, awakened a sense of sin, and her eyes when they opened were frightened and weary', George Moore, *Evelyn Innes* (London, 1898) p. 33.

Elizabeth Bowen, in an introduction to a reprint of Sheridan Le Fanu's *Uncle Silas*, suggests that

> *Uncle Silas* is, as a novel, Irish in two other ways: it is sexless and it shows a sublimated infantilism. It may, for all I know, bristle with symbolism; but I speak of the story, not of its implications – in the *story*, no force from any one of the main characters runs into the channel of sexual feeling.[23]

Bowen, in her own fiction a mistress of indirection, knows quite well, of course, how the novel bristles with sexuality, but in distinguishing between the story and implications she executes a divorce which everything in the text militates against. Maud's dream of her father's face 'sometimes white and sharp as ivory, sometimes all hanging in cadaverous folds, always with the same unnatural expression of diabolical fury' connects the sexuality and infantilism.[24] Only in her dreams can Maud accuse her father of terrorising her, and only in fiction is there an acknowledgement that illicit intergenerational passions can fracture the home.

I began by suggesting that novelists have as much problem representing bodies and sexuality as famine and dispossession. One reason for this may be that the two had become intimately associated in discursive constructions of nineteenth-century Ireland. Feminists in Britain, many of whom offered powerful critiques of the family as a British institution, identified it as a site of resistance in Ireland.[25] In particular, they drew on the work of the Poor Law Commission to suggest that Irish chastity and domesticity were undermined by poverty and misgovernment. 'The admirable tales of Banim and Carleton have, I trust, paved the way for the success of the TRUE STORIES of the Irish Peasantry told to the Poor-Law Commissioners,' announces Christian Johnstone. Johnstone and successive apologists for the Irish peasantry contributed to the production of a moral climate in which unruly, illegitimate sexuality became unrepresentable. Frances Power Cobbe offers a powerful image of this unspeakability: 'There is a peculiarly ferocious scream, really worthy of wild beasts, practised among these wretched girls whenever a mutiny takes place. It is called the poorhouse scream'.[26] In

---

23 Sheridan Le Fanu, *Uncle Silas: A Tale of Bartram-Haugh* (1864; reprinted with an introduction by Elizabeth Bowen, London, 1947). Introduction reprinted in *Collected Impressions* (London, 1950) and in *The Mulberry Tree*, edited by Hermione Lee (London, 1986) pp. 100–13; 101–2.   **24** Le Fanu, *Uncle Silas*, ch. 29.   **25** Christian Johnstone, *True Tales of the Irish Peasantry, As Related by Themselves, Selected from the Report of the Poor Law Commissioners* (Edinburgh, 2nd edition, 1836), preface; Frances Power Cobbe, *Essays on the Pursuits of Women Reprinted from Fraser's and Macmillan's Magazines* (London, 1862); Annie Besant, *Coercion in Ireland and Its Results* (London, 1882); Josephine E. Butler, *Our Christianity Tested by the Irish Question* (London, 1887).   **26** Cobbe, *Essays on the Pursuits of Women*, p. 192. I must emphasise that I am interested here primarily in modes of representation. For a discussion of women's historical experience, see Maria Luddy and Clíona Murphy (eds), *Women Surviving: Studies in Irish Women's History in the Nineteenth and Twentieth Centuries* (Dublin, 1989), particularly chapters by Luddy on prostitution and by Dympna McLoughlin on workhouses.

contrast to this scream novelists increasingly present a chasm of silence on the subject of sexuality.

The turn to melodrama or sensation allows the juxtaposition, as opposed to reconciliation, of violently disparate material. If the black prophet's murder is insufficiently motivated or explained then so is the behaviour of Sally's 'unnatural' mother, and so is the famine, but these things are not made to stand for one another. Sensational plots also require an interrogation of the borders of sanity and insanity, sometimes the terrain of dreams. At the height of sensation fiction's popularity, which was also the period when feminists were campaigning for repeal of the Contagious Diseases Acts, Frances Browne's novel, *The Hidden Sin* (which starts, like *The Black Prophet*, with an old Irish murder for money) situates insanity precisely as a colonial legacy:

> 'Yermiska was a Tartar Moslema, accustomed to think of revenge, but never of revolt or disobedience; and the night before her marriage she deliberately drank a potion ... How, or of what that draught was compounded, the Powers of Darkness best know; but the Princess declared, and time has proved her statement true, that it would transmit hereditary and irremediable madness to the utmost generation of her descendants.
>
> 'You look incredulous, my friend. There are secrets in nature for which the boasted science of Europe has neither name nor place ... That knowledge, like all the deeper and higher sorts, has no written records. It cannot be found in books; they contain but the husks and rinds of learning, being meant for the common eye and mind. It exists, nevertheless, among primitive and unlettered races; the African slave and the Hindoo pariah have visited the sins of the fathers upon the Anglo-Saxon families by means similar to those which the unwilling bride employed against mine.'[27]

D.A. Miller, in his study of Wilkie Collins and other Victorian English novelists, suggests that the point of the nineteenth-century novel 'is to confirm the novel-reader in his identity as "liberal subject", a term with which I allude not just to the subject ... but also to, broadly speaking, the political regime that sets store by this subject'.[28] In his chapter on Collins, Miller suggests that what is sensational about the sensation novel is the somatic experience of sensation in reading it, and that these sensations the ones felt on the pulses of the reader's body, help to disavow the text's apparent interpretations of its own sensationalism. 'Reader, if you have shuddered at the excesses into which he plunged, examine your own heart ...' begins the final paragraph of *The Collegians*, confident that the reader has been physically, sensibly and sensationally, as well as morally and mentally moved by the events.[29] One might argue that in asking the reader to identify, however provisionally, with Eily's seducer and murderer Griffin acknowledges a

27 Frances Browne, *The Hidden Sin* (3 vols; London, 1866), iii, pp. 101–2.   **28** D.A. Miller, *The Novel and the Police* (California, 1988), p. x.   **29** Griffin, *The Collegians*, p. 282.

failure to identify with Eily and her class. On the other hand, a recognition of the power of sexual passions casts a melancholy and sinister hue on the rational domesticity of the Dalys, whose expression is as much the childbed death as the family breakfast feast.

At the close of the century Horace Plunkett was to express his concern that excessive sexual surveillance was driving people to emigration: 'In some parishes the Sunday cyclist will observe that strange phenomenon of a normally light-hearted peasantry marshalled in male and female groups along the road, eyeing one another in dull wonderment across the forbidden space'.[30] If some novels sought to represent this bleakness, other chose to intervene and breach the space by concentrating on fantasy rather than realities.

30 Horace Plunkett, *Ireland in the New Century* (London, 1904; revised edition, London, 1905), p. 116.

History, Gender and the Colonial Moment:
Castle Rackrent

COLIN GRAHAM

By-the-by, interrogatories artfully put may lead a suspicious reasoner, you know, always to your own conclusion.[1]

In *Castle Rackrent* (1800) the legislative merging of Ireland and Britain is figured in terms of gender, power and subversion. Edgeworth's novel, shifting uneasily on the pressured historical moment of Union, places the authoritative, textual, legal point of the colonial process in a complex intersection of cultural and gender identity, and its most extraordinary achievement is to produce a text in which it is textual and linguistic strategies, rather than commonly shared oppressions, which link gender and Ireland. Through 'sly civility', silences and feigned innocence, *Castle Rackrent* charts the nature of the Union in political terms and union in gender terms, its 'artful interrogations' pushing the reader unknowingly towards naively stated disturbances of established, complacent ideological discourses.

Edgeworth's text expresses its scepticism about the phenomenon of Union through an analogy which centres on a gendered notion of union. Union becomes both a marital and political act in *Castle Rackrent* and each union is viewed as a relationship of power in which dominance and counter-dominance co-exist, so that *Castle Rackrent* can eventually be read as a text which supports the notion that dominant discursive formations can be undercut without their knowledge. In order to substantiate this line of argument it will first be necessary to describe a critique of colonial textuality derived from the post-colonial critic Homi Bhabha. Bhabha's notion of 'sly civility' as a counter to colonial discourse can be traced in specific gendered terms onto Edgeworth's 'Essay on Self-Justification'. It can also lead to a view of Edgeworth's texts as potentially undermining gendered unions and to a reading of *Castle Rackrent* in which the examination of union/ Union uncovers resistances to a teleological notion of union/Union as a monologically healing process.

I

Using post-colonial criticism may be contentious enough in a Irish cultural setting. As Gerry Smyth has recently commented, its status is 'uncertain and its

1 Maria Edgeworth, 'An Essay on the Noble Science of Self-Justification' in *Letters for Literary Ladies*, edited by Claire Connolly (London, 1994), p. 72.

93

relationship with indigenous initiatives troubled'.[2] It certainly needs to be adapted and exploited in the specific context of Ireland. Post-colonial criticism and the theoretical relationship between gender and post-colonialism constitute an infinitely wider issue than can be dealt with in this essay. A degree of applicability will be assumed in the following discussion of how the ideas of Homi Bhabha can be used to untangle some of the possibilities inherent in Edgeworth's text. Bhabha's essay 'Sly Civility'[3] will be used to discuss his notions of the doubleness of colonial/official discourses, how alternative, ironising forms can be inserted into the official. The aim here will be to turn these ideas onto the ways in which *Castle Rackrent* addresses gender and history at the same moment.

Bhabha's 'Sly Civility' has two main purposes. Firstly, it attempts to establish what he calls the 'ambivalence at the very origins of colonial authority'.[4] In the broadest terms this can be seen as the gap between dominance and liberality in Western thought: the dichotomy between notions of the civilising mission of empire and all the ideologies and narratives of domination which go with it, on the one hand, and the trappings of freedom, individuality and humanism which are basic to Western thought and exist in tandem with dominance in an imperial context, on the other. Bhabha explores this 'space' in the predominant discourse in many ways, but perhaps his best example comes in his use of that arch utterer of imperial truths, Thomas Babington Macaulay. Bhabha quotes Macaulay's essay on Warren Hastings in which Macaulay says that Hastings' 'instructions, being interpreted, mean simply, "Be the father and the oppressor of the people; be just and unjust, moderate and rapacious."'[5] Of this piece of colonial advice, Bhabha says:

> What is articulated in the doubleness of colonial discourse is not simply the violence of one powerful nation writing out the history of another. 'Be the father and the oppressor ... just and unjust' is a mode of contradictory utterance that ambivalently reinscribes, across differential power relations, both coloniser and colonised. For it reveals an agnostic uncertainty contained in the incompatibility of empire and nation; it puts on trial the very discourse of civility within which representative government claims its liberty and empire its ethics.[6]

The 'agnostic uncertainty' Bhabha describes in colonial discourse, where its self-contradictions cannot close on each other, constitutes the space into which a counter-discourse can press its resistance. Having initially established the existence of this space, Bhabha moves on to his second major aim, to identify the means by which 'interpretation and misappropriation'[7] can enter the space. Here Bhabha envisages the counter-discourse in the terms described by the title of his essay, 'Sly Civility'. He takes this phrase from an Archdeacon Potts writing in 1818 about Indian natives:

2 Gerry Smyth, 'The Past, the Post and the Utterly changed: Intellectual Responsibility and Irish Cultural Criticism' in *Irish Studies Review*, 10 (1995), p. 27.   3 Homi K. Bhabha, 'Sly Civility' in *The Location of Culture* (London, 1994), pp. 93–101.   4 Ibid., p. 95. 5 Ibid.   6 Ibid., pp. 95–6.   7 Ibid., p. 95.

> If you urge them with their gross and unworthy misconceptions of the nature and the will of God, or the monstrous follies of their theology, they will turn it off with a sly civility perhaps, or with a popular and careless proverb. You may be told that 'heaven is wide place, and has a thousand gates'; and that their religion in one by which they hope to enter.[8]

Bhabha suggests that this sly civility, a resistance which can never quite be entirely construed as resistance or acquiescence, deepens a crisis of paranoia in colonial discourse and widens the space in its doubleness. The importance of Bhabha's description of this psycho-political split is that it breaks the configuration of colonial interaction originally set up by Edward Said's notion of orientalism in which the west is, in effect, entirely dominant as a discourse. Textuality in the colonial context changes from being monolithic and complacent to being complex and unsettled, if still reflecting dominance.

The notion of sly civility can be used then in various ways. It has obvious political implications in that it suggests that colonial dominance does not necessarily imply a complete paucity of modes of resistance, though any modes of resistance included in the notion of sly civility will be restricted to oral and textual irony and slippages. For present purposes the idea of sly civility can be used to build a notion of textuality in which texts can be inscribed with both dominant *and* counter-discourses; in which colonial textuality can be self-parodying of its own dominance through the unwitting inclusion of sly civilities. Ireland was in a liminal position in the colonial encounter. It was on the threshold of what might be called entire colonisation, but its position was complicated by geography and blurred race issues. Such factors were central to the production of texts in Ireland which are not fixed in their cultural and discursive positions.

The notion of sly civility describes with some degree of accuracy the textual tactics at play in *Castle Rackrent.* These tactics, moreover, effect a paralleled linkage between the coloniser-colonised relationship and the gender relationships of marriage. The crucial factor in aligning colonial and gender relations in Edgeworth is the very notion of Union – as political event and as social marriage. Marriages are central to the narratives of *Castle Rackrent*, a text placed precariously on the moment of Union, and the novel's marriages are the points at which Edgeworth most obviously aligns cultural and sexual politics. But for the beginnings of Edgeworth's contemplation of sly civility in union/Union we can look back to her 'Essay on Self-Justification' (1785). In this deeply ironic and shifting text she describes the means by which women can subvert, counter, even control dominant male discourses without men's knowledge:

> Nothing provokes an irascible man, interested in debate, and possessed of an opinion of his own eloquence, so much as to see the attention of his hearers

---

8 Ibid., p. 99.

> go from him: you will then, when he flatters himself that he has just fixed your
> eye with his *very best* argument, suddenly grow absent.[9]

The tactics described here are those of the provoking frustration over which
Bhabha sees colonists in India worrying. The authority of a discourse is undermined by the deliberate exploitation of the apparent incapacities of those
subjected to it; for example, the 'feminine' inability to concentrate or the native's
inability to discourse 'rationally' on religion. Yet these are also the very incapacities
which justify the initial dominance. On either side of this paradox is the doubleness Bhabha describes. Edgeworth's 'Essay' alerts its readers to a gendered, subaltern
consciousness which exists in the same social context as its dominant counterpart
and which may even exist beside but without the knowledge of that which it
undermines. It is a textual version of this sly civility of self-justification which is
embedded in *Castle Rackrent*, and which makes it such a complex text in historical,
cultural and gender terms.

The possibilities of this type of reading of *Castle Rackrent* are immense. What
follows are examples of how the text can benefit from a Bhabha-derived analysis
of its positioning of history and gender. These illustrate the possibilities for reading
which Bhabha's ideas offer, yet none allows the theory to fit exactly or compla-
cently as a epistemological framework for the text. This in turn confirms the
notion implicit in Bhabha's essays that colonial discourse and its countering
discourses co-exist in unpredictable and continually ironic ways.

Figuring the Act of Union as a marriage aligns gender questionably but
temptingly alongside politico-cultural relations and allows the text to clash its
component discourses in variant ways. The readings below imply that gender can
exist on either the 'official' or 'unofficial' side of colonial discourse. Taken together,
they suggest, in Edgeworth, a sceptical and radical examination of the potential
of the political and gender Unions which circulate in *Castle Rackrent*.

II

As Marilyn Butler points out,[10] the 'Preface' to *Castle Rackrent* is, most likely, a
work of collaboration between Maria Edgeworth and Richard Lovell Edgeworth.
Given this knowledge it is tempting to view the work as the kind of dialogue of
gendered sly civility which Bhabha transcribes in colonial terms in his essay. Such
an analysis need not necessarily involve dissecting the language or authorship of
the text in gender terms. As the 'Preface' puts it, 'there is much uncertainty even
in the best authenticated ancient and modern histories'[11] and the 'Preface' itself
replicates this textual ambiguity about authenticity, authority and written history.

---

9 Maria Edgeworth, 'An Essay on the Noble Science of Self-Justification', p. 70.
10 Maria Edgeworth, *Castle Rackrent and Ennui* (Harmondsworth, 1992), p. 347.   **11** Ibid.,
p. 61.

It thus ends with the apparent hope and potential of the Act of Union: 'When Ireland loses her identity by an union with Great Britain, she will look back with a smile of good-humoured complacency on the Sir Kits and Sir Condys of her former existence.'[12] The teleology of assimilation and loss of identity here are already undermined by the 'Essay on Self-Justification', which has contorted the notion of the possibility of a post-union 'good-humoured smile'. At the very least the 'Essay' implies that the husband can never be certain of the intention of what appears as complacency and compliance. According to this view, the loss of identity is credible in only the most superficial of understandings of union/Union.

This leads to a consideration of the ways in which the 'Preface' deals with unofficial discourse, especially that of space Thady's voice. In a text which assumes an *'ignorant* English reader',[13] it is important to know if the 'Irishness' of the text is understood as a counterpart or a counter to 'Englishness'. The 'editor' of the 'Preface' says that s/he

> had it once in contemplation to translate the language of Thady into plain English; but Thady's idiom is incapable of translation, and *besides*, the authenticity of his story would have been more exposed to doubt if it were not told in his own characteristic manner.[14]

The grammatical construction used here, especially the use of 'besides', suggests an elision of the knowledge of sly civility. By not translating Thady's idiom, its existence as something which may cast doubt on the 'complacent' loss of 'Irish' identity after Union is never, as the 'Preface' says, 'exposed to doubt'. Indeed it may be this which makes Thady untranslatable: not because he is insurgent – as an ideological or representative character he is certainly not – but because his otherness to 'plain English' is a reminder of the difficulty of union; and because this notion of misunderstood idiom in Union is tied, in gender and political terms, to the polite insurgency described in Edgeworth's 'Essay on Self-Justification'.

The 'Preface', which is at least in part a doubly-authored text, may then already signal the role of gender in simultaneously covering and exploiting the spaces opened by sly civility. The Union is presented in idealised terms in the 'Preface', though this presentation is at least potentially ironic. It is undercut by the notion of Thady's language as untranslatable. As for the process of the loss of Irish/'her' identity, it remains unexplained in a text that merely reinforces the difficulty associated with identity.

Given these enclosing presumptions about the text, understood through Bhabha's writings, Edgeworth's 'Essay' and the Edgeworths' 'Preface', the text can effectively be opened and examined in many ways. The sly civility exhibited in *Castle Rackrent* could be said to constitute the basis of the novel's ambiguities, ironies and humour; similarly, Tom Dunne identifies 'other aspects of the Irish stereotype – deviousness, flattery and dishonesty'[15] in *Castle Rackrent*, which in

12 Ibid., p. 63.   **13** Ibid.   **14** Ibid. My emphasis.   **15** Tom Dunne, *Maria Edgeworth and the Colonial Mind* (Cork, 1984), p. 7.

themselves almost act as an anatomy of sly civility. And yet sly civility is more than a stage Irish stereotype in *Castle Rackrent*, it is the mobilisation of language and of silence, sometimes both, as a way of speaking back. Like Edgeworth's advice to 'suddenly grow absent', sly civility relies on a curious and paradoxical ability to make less more. The moment of sly civility fills a gap in colonial discourse, but fills it with an unfathomable hollowness. In Bhabha's Archdeacon Potts' example of this disturbing linguistic reduction in the native's use of 'a popular and careless proverb', it is the correctness of the answer which is suspicious (the natives' linguistic competence is in itself worrying for Potts here). Richard Pococke, on his tour of Ireland in 1752, finds himself having to explain away a similarly replete linguistic void: 'Asking here about the road, if it was hilly ? they told me it was, but that the hills were all level, by which I suppose they meant that they were not high.'[16] The exquisite moment of ambiguity here is quickly rationalised, but the indeterminacy it employs (whether deliberate or not on the part of the 'colonised') again reveals language and textuality to be central to sly civility's existence. The voice of 'here' (which is as specific as Pococke gets about who he asked) is dissolved as far as possible into the discourse of the traveller's prose but still a glimpse of the space it invokes remains.

Sly civility in *Castle Rackrent* is most readily identifiable in Thady, of course, and in his case it is deliberative silence masquerading as acquiescence which marks his relations with his masters. Most commonly this is expressed through the repeated phrase 'but I said nothing'. This first appears, appropriately enough, when the text's first 'union' is being discussed (the marriage of Sir Murtagh): 'it was a strange match for Sir Murtagh; the people in the country thought he demeaned himself greatly, but I said nothing'.[17] The immediate irony here is that Thady does not 'say nothing': the text itself is Thady saying everything, so that textually at least his sly civility parallels his longevity. Thady's 'but I said nothing' also takes us back, both grammatically and linguistically, to the 'Preface' and its 'Thady's idiom is incapable of translation, and besides'. Thady's 'but' and Edgeworth's 'besides' have equally unstable grammatical functions, perhaps because they both hinge on an uncertain assertion made either in or about Thady's 'idion'. Edgeworth, discussing Thady's voice, finds her own prose pre-echoing Thady's (and to an extent thus already aligning this tactic of sly civility with the writing of *Castle Rackrent*).

Thady's silence then is a tactic of sly civility and is employed at moments crucial to the narrative, and to union. Sir Condy's 'toss-up' to decide on his marriage partner is accompanied by Thady's usual apparent shrinking quietude: 'my heart was all as one as in my mouth when I say the halfpenny up in the air, but I said nothing at all; and when it came down, I was glad I had kept myself to myself'.[18] But this moment, like most others when Thady says 'nothing', is preceded by a more active subversion:

16 John McVeagh (ed.), *Richard Pococke's Irish Tours* (Dublin, 1995), p. 31.   17 Maria Edgeworth, *Castle Rackrent and Ennui*, p. 68.   18 Ibid., p. 89.

'to prove it to you, Thady' says he, 'it's a toss up with me which I should marry this minute, her [Judy McQuirk] or Mr Moneygawl of Mount Juliet's town's daughter so it is.' 'Oh, boo! boo!' says I, making light of it, *to see what he would go on to next*; 'your honour's joking, to be sure; there's no compare between our poor Judy and Miss Isabella, who has a great fortune, they say.'[19]

Again, and as with the first use of 'but I said nothing', the moment of sly civility accompanies a decisive moment *before* union. Thady's role here is to push the narrative, moving the linear progression of novelistic history towards the marital act which should underpin the novelistic plot. And yet Thady turns this central narrative, social and ultimately political decision into an act of purest chance – one which (having acted as catalyst) he observes in silence. Thady has here taken Edgeworth's advice to her 'fair readers' on dealing in their 'adversaries', men: 'Remember, all such speeches as these will lose above half their effect, if you cannot accompany them with the vacant stare, the insipid smile, the passive aspect of the humbly perverse.'[20]

Gender and sly civility can be linked in more than tactical ways, though, in *Castle Rackrent.* One of the most obvious is through the metaphor and narrative device of marriage, which closes the 'Preface', as a projected mode of hope. Yet the text itself delineates a succession of failing marriages and unions. While not necessarily insisting on a continual parallel between Ireland and femininity in Union, a gender perspective on the text can focus on the difficulties, perhaps impossibilities of union. Sir Condy and Mrs Jane, for example, come to represent a marriage which the woman would never have entered into with a fuller knowledge:

my lady couldn't abide the smell of the whiskey punch. 'My dear,' says [Condy], 'you liked it well enough before we were married, and why not now?' 'My dear,' said she, 'I never smelt it, or I assure you I should never have prevailed upon myself to marry you.' 'My dear, I am sorry you did not smell it, but we can't help that now,' returned my master, without putting himself in a passion, or going out of his way, but just fair and easy helped himself to another glass, and drank it off to her health.[21]

If it can be argued that this is merely narrativity, a 'novelistic' marriage without resonances through gender into politics, the footnote which accompanies the incarceration of Sir Kit's Jewish wife undeniably and explicitly pushes the political into the gender sphere. The 'editor' tells the story of a Colonel McGuire's wife who was imprisoned by her husband for over twenty years. The footnote ends:

19 Ibid. My emphasis.   **20** Maria Edgeworth, 'An Essay on the Noble Science of Self-Justification', p. 77.   **21** Maria Edgeworth, *Castle Rackrent and Ennui,* pp. 91–2.

These circumstances may appear strange to the English reader; but there is no danger in the present times, that any individual should exercise such tyranny as Colonel McGuire's with impunity, the power now being all in the hands of government, and there being no possibility of obtaining from parliament an act of indemnity for any cruelties.[22]

Such a reassurance, which, like much of the text, is addressed with some irony to the English reader, rests of course on the authority of an act of parliament. Apart from a potentially deliberate and joking ambiguity about which parliament is referred to in 1800, the authority which the editorial voice invests in this legislation echoes that hopeful note in the 'Preface' about the effects of the Act of Union. The same undermining process, an ironic interjection into a discourse of safety in legislation, must be seen at work here, and it begs the obvious question as to whether Sit Kit's behaviour would have been different after political Union and parliamentary legislation. Indeed it would be possible to argue that Sir Kit's treatment of his wife is not a pre-Union but a post-union/Union phenomenon, which comes about as much through the frictions of cultural as gender unions. His wife's Jewishness is continually emphasised by Thady's account, functioning mainly as a definition of her non-Irishness; as when she calls a turf stack 'a pile of black bricks' or describes a bog as 'a very ugly prospect' or laughs 'like one out of their right mind' when she hears the place name 'Allyballycarricko'shaughlin', as Sir Kit '[stands] by whistling all the while'. As Thady says, 'I verily believe she laid the corner stone of all her future misfortunes at that very instant; but I said no more, only looked at Sir Kit.'[23] Gender, cultural nationality and parliamentary act meet at this moment in the text, pressuring the notion of Union as benign change, implying dissent beyond the beginning of assimilation and allowing a space for the insertion of what remains outside the teleology and remit of the dominant.

Castle Rackrent not only plays with marriage as the act of union – it also looks forward to the end of union. (The Rackrents' marriages tend to dissolve simultaneously with their deaths.) Sir Murtagh's marriage (about which Thady has ominously 'said nothing') closes in a confusion over narrative time appropriate to the hiatus of Union in which *Castle Rackrent* is placed. (The hiatus at this point in the text is emphasised by surrounding footnotes, one of which suggests that, whereas in 'the last century' banshees visited Irish families, these visits have 'latterly' 'discontinued'; the next footnote, on the word '*childer*' notes that this is how the word children was '*formerly* pronounced'.[24]) If this is (or could at least be seen as) celebratory subversion, it is certainly not 'civil' and Thady recognises it as such: 'But in a dispute about an abatement, my lady would have the last word, and Sir Murtagh grew mad; I was within hearing of the door, and now I wish I had made bold to step in.'[25] The 'abatement' is, of course, legalistically, a 'quashing' and allows, indeed insists on, a 'last word'. It is an act of foreclosure on marriage and union and prefigures Sir Murtagh's death; the Glossary, usually helpfully garrulous but

22 Ibid., p. 79.   **23** Ibid., pp. 77–8.   **24** Ibid., pp. 71, 72.   **25** Ibid., pp. 71–2.

here ironically tautologous, says only of 'Sir Murtage grew mad': 'Sir Murtagh grew angry'[26]. Thady's silence is awkwardly complicit here with this disruption of civility, and is made inactive both by his listening and the very notion of a 'last word'.

While Sir Murtagh's death and marriage end almost before they are over, other Rackrent unions have equally ludicrous and confused beginnings and terminations: Sir Condy's begins with the toss of a coin and ends with a freak accident (he believes), while his life ends with a staged wake. Sir Kit's 'second' marriage is on the verge of being decided by duel when one of his opponents gets his wooden leg 'stuck fast' in a 'ploughed field',[27] as if the text wishes to veer away from direct confrontation and towards the pleasure of farcical civility (the two parties 'shook hands cordially, and went home to dinner together'[28]). Sir Kit himself is killed and his wife lives. Having from her 'confinement' been much obliged to Sir Kit and drunk, in absentia, 'the company's health', Lady Rackrent, as Thady notes, 'got surprisingly well after my master's decease'.[29] Thady's 'surprise' is inherent in his sly civility: it is dutifully and superficially innocent but contains an understanding complicity with 'the Jew Lady Rackrent', who survives her imprisonment through her ability to fill the fake politeness of her husband's address with a countering weighty politeness of her own. Thady cuts off any sympathy he has for Lady Rackrent with civility at her expense in the staffering naiveté of saying: 'she had taken an unaccountable prejudice against the country'.[30]

Thady's narrative style is thus attuned to contain the quiet carnivalesque it sees in acts of union, including civility and growing absences, with pleasurable ease; but against this it sets the disjunction caused by direct incivility. For Thady himself, Jason is disturbing, most obviously because he usurps the social order; equally Jason's disturbing tendencies arise from his increasing confidence in moving outside the power relations which necessitate sly civility:

> Now I could not bear to hear Jason giving out after this manner against the family, and twenty people standing by in the street ... I could scarcely believe my own old eyes, or the spectacles with which I read it, when I was shown my son Jason's name joined in the costodiam ... so I said nothing, but just looked on to see how it would all end.[31]

Jason's 'giving out' in this public way is ironically juxtaposed to the novel itself but what it lacks is irony and civility. Jason's name is 'joined in the custodiam', another affront, and another perversion of 'union'. Thady's response is now almost stock, and, since the unspoken nature of his sly civility has been broken by Jason's directness, Thady's response of saying nothing seems increasingly hollow.

This episode precedes the ending of Sir Condy's marriage to Bella, and in the latter's conclusion there is a breaking of the strategies of 'self-justification' of gendered relations recommended by Edgeworth. Bella, having told Condy to

26 Ibid., p. 131.   **27** Ibid., p. 89.   **28** Ibid., p. 81.   **29** Ibid., p. 82.   **30** Ibid., p. 83.
31 Ibid., p. 100.

shave, sees him do so: 'But she took no notice, but went on reading.'[32] In a way this mimics Thady's 'but I said nothing'; however this follows *direct* instruction and acquiescence by the husband. The double 'but' serves as an over-emphasis and differentiates it from the subtlety of Thady's civility; this is followed by Bella questioning the very basis of her marriage to Condy.

So for Thady and *Castle Rackrent's* sly civility, and the tactic of growing absent, there is an alternative figuration of gender and union/Union which builds in the text: once the power relations which produce sly civility are challenged or changed (as with Jason) or made explicit (as with Bella), the possibilities of sly civility are altered too. And yet Thady's narrative itself is intent on collapsing these challenges into its own sly civility – Jason's triumph is achieved through the tactics and strategies he has learnt from his father. And Jason himself is ultimately caught up in the narrative innocence which 'fools' the 'Editor' of *Castle Rackrent* who at the end of the text says:

> The Editor could have readily made the catastrophe of Sir Condy's history more dramatic and more pathetic, if he thought it allowable to varnish the plain round tale of faithful Thady. He lays it before the English reader as a specimen of manners and character, which are, perhaps, unknown in England. Indeed the domestic habits of no nation in Europe were less known to the English than those of her sister country, till within these few years.[33]

Thady is given his ultimate audience and the tag he needs to play it: 'honest Thady' is now 'faithful Thady'. At this crucial moment of Union the 'domestic' is rendered through a series of gendered unions which are 'allowed' to the sly civility of Thady; Ireland is rendered to 'the English reader' by a narrator capable, as the 'Editor' goes on to say, of combining 'simplicity, cunning ... shrewdness and blunder'.[34] Where the text toys with the possibility that sly civility is redundant (since Jason ceases to need to 'grow absent' into silence), it finally leaves the reader at the mercy of a narrator who has made slyly civil his own power relations, and has delineated union/Union in terms of tragedy, farce, mistimed narratives and death.

III

In *Castle Rackrent* the cultural politics of metaphoric marriages becomes laden with the possibility of sly civility. The text pushes towards the notion of marriage as the appropriate construction for understanding the union/Union, yet ironises its own expressed belief in the ability of union to facilitate a loss of identity tantamount to a discursive monologism. Its notion of the untranslatable idiom, necessary for a treasured 'authenticity', can be used to place its delineation of the cracks in colonial, dominant discourses in the context of Bhabha's idea of the double articulation of colonialism and the nature of sly civility.

32 Ibid., p. 102.   **33** Ibid., p. 121.   **34** Ibid.

Edgeworth's text expresses something implied but unexplored in Bhabha's essay:[35] the double-facedness of the coloniser may be seen from outside the coloniser's discourse, but if seen it cannot be fully, dialogically articulated by the colonised. It can only be mimicked, parodied in sly civility. A knowledge of the space between the double-face of colonialism can only be voiced where the coloniser is deaf to it. And yet however small this space may be, any insertion into this space begins the process of undermining and exploding the authority of colonialism. To borrow the metaphor Edgeworth uses in her 'Essay on Self-Justification', when advising a woman on how to gain the sympathy of bystanders when confronted by her irascible husband, 'the simple scratching of a pick-axe, properly applied to certain veins in a mine, will cause the most dreadful explosions'.[36] Reading *Castle Rackrent* in this way reorientates it as an ironic, multi-voiced text. It certainly serves to contradict one historian's literal reading of the novel as one in which Edgeworth was 'careful to assure her [English] readers that the events she unfolded bore no resemblance to the Ireland of her own time'.[37] *Castle Rackrent* pressurises the notion and the moment of Union through a gendered understanding of cultural interaction; against the colonial discourse which implies a loss of identity, it pits an awareness of dissent which is dangerous for its untranslatable, slyly civil qualities.

35 Bhabha expands on aspects of the theories central to 'Sly Civility' in 'Signs Taken for Wonders: Questions of Ambivalence and Authority Under a Tree Outside Delhi, May 1817' also in *The Location of Culture*, pp. 102–22.   **36** Edgeworth, 'An Essay on the Noble Science of Self-Justification', p. 70.   **37** D. George Boyce, *Nineteenth-Century Ireland: The Search for Stability* (Dublin, 1990), p. 22.

'The whole fabric must be perfect':
Maria Edgeworth's *Literary Ladies* and
the Representation of Ireland

CLÍONA Ó GALLCHOIR

This essay combines a stylistic analysis of the first part of Maria Edgeworth's *Letters for Literary Ladies*, entitled 'Letter from a Gentleman to his Friend, upon the Birth of a Daughter, with a reply', with a closer examination than has so far been offered of the literary-historical context of this work. Recent criticism on Edgeworth has begun to dismantle the traditional divisions between her four 'Irish Tales', *Castle Rackrent* (1800), *Ennui* (1805), *The Absentee* (1812) and *Ormond* (1817), and her other writing;[1] this essay extends this re-examination of Edgeworth's representation of Ireland in the context of her work as a whole, by deriving a theory of representation from the 'Letter from a Gentleman' which can be applied to her fiction. More specifically, I argue that the strategies by which Edgeworth sought to represent Ireland (an ambitious undertaking in the development of the novel which she virtually pioneered) must be acknowledged to be historically grounded in her position as a woman writer in post-revolutionary culture. The 'Letter from a Gentleman', based on an incident in 1782, was eventually published in 1795, thus spanning the chasm which the French Revolution created in European history, and providing a perspective on Edgeworth's engagement with history which has not yet been examined.

I

Letters for Literary Ladies was Maria Edgeworth's first published work.[2] This is highly ironic, given that 'Letter from a Gentleman' is based on an exchange of letters between Edgeworth's father, Richard Lovell Edgeworth, and his friend,

---

1 W. J. McCormack rejects as 'self-obscuring' the 'relentless, if unconscious classification of Edgeworth's fiction into mutually exclusive categories'; see W. J. McCormack, 'The Tedium of History: An Approach to Maria Edgeworth's *Patronage*' in Ciarán Brady (ed.), *Ideology and the Historians* (Dublin, 1991), pp. 77–98, p. 84. See also Siobhán Kilfeather, '"Strangers at Home": Political Fictions by Women in Eighteenth-Century Ireland' (PhD thesis, University of Princeton, 1989); Kilfeather advances important political readings of Edgeworth and earlier fictions by women, notably Frances Sheridan.   2 Marilyn Butler notes that the 1795 edition of *Letters for Literary Ladies* carries an advertisement stating that *The Parent's Assistant*, a collection of stories for children by Maria Edgeworth, had already been published, but no copies of a 1795 *Parent's Assistant* have been located – the earliest date from 1796: Butler, *Maria Edgeworth: A Literary Biography*, (Oxford, 1972), p. 159n.

Thomas Day, in which Day expresses his opposition to R.L. Edgeworth's plans to encourage his daughter's literary career. This debate took place in 1782, when plans were made to publish Maria Edgeworth's translation of Mme de Genlis's *Adèle et Théodore*. In this same year, the Edgeworth family returned to Ireland and legislative independence was granted to the Irish Parliament.

The subject of 'Letter from a Gentleman' is a defence of women's right to education and to literary activity. In the initial letter, the 'Gentleman' in question congratulates a friend on the birth of a daughter, but warns him of the undesirable consequences of his plan to educate his daughter to the same high standards as men, with the possibility that she may prove an intellectual, a 'literary lady', with the ability to write and publish. This is followed by a reply from the progressive father which rebuts his friend's criticism, maintaining that the education of women does not necessarily result in the collapse of the social order, and may indeed help to sustain it. Most criticism and commentary on the composite *Letters for Literary Ladies* has come from feminist criticism and from feminist literary history, rather than from Irish critics and literary historians, and most of it has damned with faint praise. It is commonly included somewhere in the roll-call of eighteenth-century works by women which advocated high standards in the education of girls and women, but it appears to be a text incapable of generating enthusiasm in readers. Marilyn Butler describes it as 'earnest and stiff', while Jane Rendall calls it a 'modest argument', and, in fact, most feminist critics and literary historians of women's writing prefer to focus on more easily categorised figures such as Mary Wollstonecraft and Hannah More.[3] Claire Connolly, a recent editor of the text, has gone beyond this polite but ultimately unhelpful commentary to declare that 'the argument has no real impact' due to the fact that the text 'addresses its readers in the plain style revered by Enlightenment thinkers. It does not deign to offer anecdote or example'.[4] Connolly's analysis of the text's lack of persuasiveness focuses on the inadequacy of Enlightenment itself, which she says is characterised by a 'fear and distrust of women', of which Edgeworth was at some level aware.[5] I would however like to focus on the text itself, which, contrary to Connolly's assertion, offers a large number of anecdotes and examples. It is worth asking why they have somehow faded into oblivion. These take the form of literary anecdotes and learned or scientific references, as well as phrases and attitudes which exemplify national manners and modes of behaviour. On the whole these illustrative references are characterised by disparity and a certain eclecticism, ranging from the accounts of the volcano watcher Sir William Hamilton to observations on exotic plants and animals. It is therefore necessary

3 See Butler, *Jane Austen and the War of Ideas* (1975; reissued with a new introduction, Oxford, 1987), p. 127; Jane Rendall, *The Origins of Modern Feminism: Women in Britain, France and the United States, 1780–1860* (Basingstoke, 1985), p. 110; for a comparison of Wollstonecraft and More see Mitzi Myers, 'Reform or Ruin: "A Revolution in Female Manners"' in *Studies in Eighteenth-Century Culture*, 11 (1982), pp. 199–216. 4 Maria Edgeworth, *Letters for Literary Ladies*, edited by Claire Connolly (London, 1993), p. xxiii, p. xxii. 5 Ibid., p. xvi.

to analyse these strangely inarticulate anecdotes in order to understand why, in spite of what is in fact a wealth of illustration, the argument of 'Letter from a Gentleman' has 'no real impact'.

In a letter to Charlotte Sneyd written in 1799, while Edgeworth was passing through Dublin on her way to England, she describes as a curiosity a 'political print' which she has seen, depicting 'a woman meant for Hibernia dressed in *Orange & Green* & holding a pistol in her hand to oppose the Union'.[6] The insertion of the explanatory phrase 'meant for Hibernia' indicates either an incomprehension or a desire on Edgeworth's part to distance herself from the meaning of this image, or, perhaps, from the image as conveyer of meaning. Before we can speculate on how Edgeworth might have responded to such a figure, we must decide how to name the patriotically-draped woman. An immediately appropriate term would be allegory, a system of representation in which there is a relatively simple and one-to-one correspondence between signifier and signified; in this case a female figure represents the Irish nation, united in patriotic resistance to Britain and the threat of legislative union with Westminster. The allegorical representation of Ireland as a woman was by the late eighteenth century an established trope in Gaelic poetry. In *Aisling* poetry, as it is called, the young and beautiful woman who appears to the poet in a dream or vision (*aisling*) functions according to a system of absolute identification, in which her sorrows are those of Ireland, and the lover whose faithlessness she laments refers to the descendants of the Stuarts.

Twentieth-century feminism's search for foremothers has focused on women who adopted the kinds of identifications which puzzled Edgeworth in 1799. For women to make common cause with other groups excluded from power and political representation was to reject the idea that women's lives were 'naturally' conducted in a sphere which had no connection with the public and the political. Much feminist criticism, however, is guilty of constructing a continuous narrative in which women's growing consciousness of their rights is signalled by an increasing willingness to identify themselves with others whom they perceive as similarly oppressed. '[A]ll victims of prejudice and oppression found champions among women writers, but no race of mankind was so widely and commonly assigned to angry women as the slave', writes Ellen Moers in *Literary Women* (1978).[7] In a typical and still highly compelling example of early feminist literary criticism, Moers here excludes those women who did not adopt this self-representation, which helps us to understand why Edgeworth has received no more than dutiful acknowledgement from most twentieth-century critics. Among eighteenth-century writers, feminist critics have located Mary Wollstonecraft as a 'first feminist' precisely because her work is shaped by a series of identifications of this kind. The highly skilful and rhetorically powerful use of metaphor is

6 ME to Charlotte Sneyd, 2 April 1799, National Library of Ireland, Ms 10,166.   7 Ellen Moers, *Literary Women* (London, 1978), p. 15.

perhaps the single most important feature of Wollstonecraft's enduringly popular *Vindication of the Rights of Woman* (1792). Women in the *Vindication* are by turns, slaves, tyrants, even brutes, utterly devoid of the power of reason:

> Women it is true, obtaining power by unjust means, by practising or fostering vice, evidently lose the rank which reason would assign them, and they become either abject slaves or capricious tyrants. [8]

Metaphor operates on an underlying assumption of likeness or analogy. Throughout the *Vindication* women, or 'woman', becomes identified with a series of other groupings: the very wealthy, standing armies, Turkish bashaws, animals, corrupt ministers, and with recurring frequency, slaves and tyrants. It is this array of possible and reiterated identifications which gives Wollstonecraft's polemic much of its force and vitality. The metaphors are extended and built upon – women 'grovel' and 'patiently bite the bridle', they are 'depraved by lawless power'.

The images in 'Letter from a Gentleman', by contrast, although frequently arresting when considered individually, do not when taken together acquire rhetorical force. Ignorant women are compared to Italian nuns who haven't the wit to flee an erupting volcano, but warm themselves instead in the glow of the lava, and to frogs who swallow burning charcoal – 'deceived by resemblances, they mistake poison for food'.[9] In spite of (or perhaps because of) the odd aptness of these illustrative examples, they do not lend the argument additional force and persuasiveness. Each is independent of the other, serving its purpose of illustrating and underlining the author's particular point (the necessity of cultivating the reasoning faculty; the transient nature of custom and customary belief and so on): they certainly do not act in concert to create a sense of women's group identity. The reasons for which women writers like Edgeworth avoided the type of identification found in Wollstonecraft and endorsed as feminist by Moers are of course not ideologically innocent. The politics of identification are very clear: an identification of the kind found in Wollstonecraft's *Vindication* tears down the wall which divides the public from the private sphere, and the rational man who defends women's right to education in 'Letter from a Gentleman' makes very clear that this is wholly undesirable. The role proposed for educated and rational women is strictly defined: 'their influence must be private'.[10] The sense of delimitation is reflected in the manner in which Edgeworth isolates the text's examples and anecdotes within their immediate context, as if to prove that the education of women does not imply the transformation, destruction or revolutionising of the social order.

In place of revolutionary metaphor Edgeworth offers a metonymic system of representation. Rewriting Mandeville on the relationship between private and public she asserts:

8 Mary Wollstonecraft, *A Vindication of the Rights of Woman* (1792; Harmondsworth, 1992), p. 133.   9 Edgeworth, *Letters for Literary Ladies*, p. 23.   10 Ibid., p. 31.

> Private *virtues* are public benefits: if each bee were content in his cell, there
> could be no grumbling hive; and if each cell were complete, the whole fabric
> must be perfect.[11]

In spite of Edgeworth's unwillingness to place women in the public sphere, and
her support for the idea that 'their influence must be private', she here seems to
suggest that there is no public sphere independent of the numerous private spaces
which make it up. The 'whole fabric' of society cannot be understood without
reference to its constituent parts. Edgeworth, therefore, although often portrayed
as a cautious adherent to the status quo, in fact challenges the whole notion of
separate spheres. Her rejection of metaphorical representations, while clearly
indicating her refusal to claim for her writing a direct political role, does however
allow her a potentially authoritative voice without breaking with decorum.
Metonymy is not a hierarchical relationship: the part may stand for the whole
and *vice versa*. This lack of an original term captures perfectly the elusive nature
of Edgeworth's representation of the relationship between public and private, as
illustrated in the image of the hive, above: the public is no more than the sum of
its domestic parts, yet the domestic is in its turn a perfect microcosm of the larger
fabric. Having asserted that women's influence must be private, it is added that
'human affairs are chained together': 'female influence is a necessary and important
link, which you cannot break without destroying the whole'.[12]

Aside from the flexibility offered by representation based on the image of the
interconnected hive or chain, the very lack of identification which might seem
to render Edgeworth's work utterly incapable of political engagement can function
to facilitate the investigation of difference. Umberto Eco suggests that metonymy
is best understood as representation in the form of an encyclopaedia, which
indicates a system midway between the classical linear tree structure and the total
interconnectedness of the rhizome.[13] Referring to D'Alembert's prefatory remarks
to the *Encyclopaedia*, Eco elaborates:

> D'Alembert says with great clarity that what an encyclopaedia represents has
> no centre. The encyclopaedia is a pseudotree, which assumes the aspect of a
> local map, in order to represent, always transitorily and locally, what in fact is
> not representable because it is a rhizome – an inconceivable globality.[14]

Eco's 'inconceivable globality' can be sensed in the resolute localness of Edgeworth's
text and the refusal to assimilate difference. From the evidence of 'Letter to a
Gentleman' it is clear that Edgeworth is unable or unwilling to identify women

---

11 Ibid., p. 37.   **12** Ibid., p. 31.   **13** Eco derives the image of the rhizome (a 'tangle
of bulbs and tubers') from Deleuze and Guattari. In their work, the rhizome represents
a structure in which 'every point can and must be connected with every other point'.
See Umberto Eco, *Semiotics and the Philosophy of Language* (Bloomington, 1986), p. 81.
14 Ibid., p. 83.

with other groups she is even unwilling to identify modern European women with women of other cultures, because of her acute perception of difference:

> The changes that are made in the opinion of our [the male] sex as to female beauty, according to the different situations in which women are placed, and the different qualities on which we fix their ideas of excellence, are curious and striking. Ask a northern Indian, says a traveller who has lately visited them, ask a northern Indian, what is beauty, and he will answer, a broad flat face, small eyes, high cheek bones, three or four broad black lines across each cheek, a low forehead, a clumsy hook nose &c. These beauties are greatly heightened, or at least rendered more valuable, when the possessor is capable of dressing all kinds of skins, converting them into the different parts of their clothing, and able to carry eight or ten stone in summer, or haul a much greater weight in winter.[15]

Marilyn Butler's account of Edgeworth's method of composition bears out the theory that the technique of representation evident in 'Letter from a Gentleman' anticipates the manner in which she wrote her later and more successful fictions. Butler describes the way in which Edgeworth collected striking character sketches and solicited anecdotes, examples and facts from friends and family, and made notes of anything she came across in her reading, to use as sources for her writing. Maria's father encouraged her to regard her writing as compendious and miscellaneous, predicting for instance that *Professional Education* (1811) would 'be an admirable vehicle for anything we can say on any subject'.[16] Butler remarks that although 'an objective interest in human nature and the way it manifests itself in social custom no doubt lies behind Maria Edgeworth's liking for facts', Edgeworth 'never makes a general declaration of this kind'.[17] However, the plain style of 'Letter from a Gentleman', in which carefully collected facts and anecdotes are not transformed into a fictional narrative, but retain their sometimes awkward difference, can, I suggest, be read as a 'general declaration'. Edgeworth's ability to represent Ireland in the genre which came to be known as the national tale relies fundamentally on the principle that the claim to representation at the national level, through metonymy, did not represent a challenge to the public sphere as then established. Her success as a novelist of local circumstances and manners is plainly based on the belief in the reality of difference which is also a feature of this, her earliest published text.

II

The insistence on the interconnectedness of distinct spheres which is most clearly and, indeed, plainly expressed in 'Letter from a Gentleman' can therefore be argued

15 Edgeworth, *Letters for Literary Ladies*, p. 37. This passage is close to the entry on 'Beauty' in Voltaire's *Philosophical Dictionary*; see *Philosophical Dictionary*, trans. Theodore Besterman (Harmondsworth, 1971), pp. 63–4.   16 Marilyn Butler, *Maria Edgeworth: A Literary Biography* (Oxford, 1972), p. 245.   17 Ibid., pp. 239–240.

to be a characteristic feature of Edgeworth's technique of representation. It was a belief that she shared with the most notorious admirer of her novels, Jeremy Bentham.[18] Here is Bentham's own unequivocal statement of the distinctions to be made between the private matter of education and the public activity of government:

> Human creatures, considered with respect to the maturity of their faculties, are either in an adult, or in a non-adult state. The art of government, in so far as it concerns the direction of persons in a non-adult state, may be termed education.[19]

Bentham's method rests, like Edgeworth's, in the first instance on a theory of individual psychology: this accounts for his beginning his *Introduction to the Principles of Morals and Legislation* with a list of thirty-two 'circumstances influencing sensibility'. Bentham's determination to fix the contours of difference is married with a boundless faith in the translatability of method: Bentham's reforming zeal extended itself in many directions – he wrote on penal reform, civil and criminal law reform, education, and for Arthur Young's *Annals of Agriculture*. Bentham's most enduring legacy, the Panopticon, acts as an image of this translatability. The full text of the title runs as follows: *Panopticon*, 'or, The Inspection House; containing the idea of a new principle of construction applicable to any sort of establishment in which persons of any description are to be kept under inspection; and in particular to penitentiary-houses; prisons, houses of industry, work-houses, mad-houses, lazarettos, hospitals and schools'.[20] A belief in 'translatability' is equally evident in the curious examples of 'Letter from a Gentleman': nowhere is likeness between the subject and its illustration suggested, but the assumption that *method* is translatable is undeniable.

Bentham's most consistent interest was the formulation of legislative systems, which he hoped to form according to a rational plan that would be validated by their geographical translatability. The successful transplantation of laws cannot however be achieved without the provision of a mass of documentation, as follows:

> a general table of the circumstances influencing sensibility; tables or short accounts of the moral, religious, sympathetic and antipathetic biases of the

---

18 Edgeworth came into contact with Benthamite ideas through her translator, Etienne Dumont, who edited and translated several of Bentham's works. For specific comments by Bentham on Edgeworth, see J. R. Dinwiddy, 'Jeremy Bentham as a Pupil of Miss Edgeworth's' in *Notes and Queries*, 29 (1982), pp. 208–11.   19 *Introduction to the Principles of Morals and Legislation* in *Works of Jeremy Bentham*, edited by Sir John Bowring (11 vols; Edinburgh, 1843), i, p. 143. An edition of Bentham's works to replace that edited by Bowring is in progress, but as it is not yet complete I have for the sake of consistency referred here to the earlier edition of the works.   20 Bentham, *Panopticon; or, The Inspection House* in *Works*, iv.

people for whose use the alterations [in legislation] are to be made; a set of maps as particular as possible; a table of the productions of the country.[21]

It will be clear that Bentham's programme for rational legislation is crucially dependent on new forms of knowledge and knowledge-gathering, which at the time he was writing were still being developed. The rational and translatable legislation he proposes is therefore contingent on historical progress. In Bentham's view, the crucial shift in cultural description took place with Montesquieu:

> Before Montesquieu, a man who had a distant country given him to make laws for, would have made short work of it. 'Name to me the people', he would have said; 'reach me down my Bible, and the business is done at once.' ... Since Montesquieu, the number of documents which a legislator would require is considerably enlarged. 'Send the people,' he will say, 'to me, or me to the people; lay open to me the whole tenor of their life and conversation; paint to me the face and geography of the country; give me as close and minute a view as possible of their present laws, their manners, and their religion.'[22]

Bentham's method may at first sight seem completely concerned with the present, specifically with the documenting and control of present circumstances. As his last remark makes clear however, it is a method firmly rooted in a historical mentality. Given that Edgeworth and Bentham shared certain beliefs and principles, it is of particular interest to consider this assertion of confident historical progression in relation to Edgeworth's representations of Ireland, most strikingly in *Castle Rackrent*. The time 'before Montesquieu' to which Bentham refers was in the case of Ireland not a hypothetical case, but a historical reality, and one of which Edgeworth, for instance, was fully aware. In his *True Causes why Ireland was never entirely subdued* (1612), a work which Edgeworth read at least twice, John Davies states that 'to give Lawes to a conquered people is the principalle marke and effect of a perfect Conquest'.[23] Davies' notion of 'giving laws' has the same uncompromising ring as Bentham's 'reach me down my Bible'. What remains in doubt is whether, in the case of Ireland, it is possible to assert, with the same degree of certainty displayed by Bentham, that the time 'before Montesquieu' is in fact past. Edgeworth acknowledges that Ireland has experienced the pre-Montesquieuvian type of administration in the first note to *Castle Rackrent*, in which she quotes Spenser's *A View of the Present State of Ireland* (1596), a view notable for its marked lack of interest in the present laws, manners and religion of the Gaelic Irish who were to be governed. This citation is clearly ironic, and is therefore of a piece with the editorial insistence that Thady's narrative is to be understood as historical. The embattled intention of the editorial voice centres on the reiterated use of the word 'formerly' in the preface, notes and glossary to *Castle Rackrent*. The

21 Bentham, *Of the Influence of Time and Place in Matters of Legislation* in *Works*, i, p. 173.
22 Ibid., p. 173n.   **23** John Davies, *The True Causes why Ireland was never entirely subdued* (1612; facsimile reprint, Shannon, 1969), p. 100.

enduring fascination of *Castle Rackrent*, however, lies in its failure to maintain the separation of these two times, the barbaric past and the enlightened present. The title suggests that the past is defined by the date of 1782, which as remarked above was the year in which the return of the Edgeworth family to Longford coincided with the removal of the more obvious obstacles to Irish legislative independence; the 'Introduction', however, is dated 1800 and proposes the imminent union between Great Britain and Ireland as the moment from which Ireland's progress can be dated. Whereas the title suggests that barbarism lies before 1782, the 'Introduction' nervously suggests that Ireland's entry into a history of progress did not in fact take place as anticipated in the optimistic 1780s, thus throwing into doubt all such assertions of new beginnings, including the 'Editor's' own.

III

At the outset, I noted that 'Letter from a Gentleman' spans the historical chasm of the French Revolution, and that the text is marked by the need to uphold the principle of historical progression. As in *Castle Rackrent*, the problem of persuasive chronology lies at the heart of this short text. As noted earlier, the incident on which 'Letter from a Gentleman' is based took place in 1782, while Edgeworth was translating *Adèle et Théodore*. The specifics of the period of composition are unknown, but it was published in 1795, by which time Revolution in France had turned to Terror, followed by war with England, and the optimism of the drive for constitutional reform in Ireland via the Volunteer movement had been replaced by a polarisation of society as the United Irishmen prepared, with French help, for armed rebellion.

The post-revolutionary context of 'Letter from a Gentleman' is trumpeted in the opening pages, in which the Rousseau-worshipping Thomas Day has been transformed into an unmistakably Burkean figure, who remarks that the days of chivalry are past and warns of the dreadful consequences of abandoning custom and precedent. We might wonder why a progressive such as Day is fictionalised by Edgeworth along the lines of Burke, who was in the vanguard of reaction, but we need look no further than Day's ideas on the proper place of women for an answer. Day's objections to female authorship were based on a view of female nature and character whose debt to Rousseau is clear. He believed that women's 'weakness of body, and imbecility of mind, can only entitle them to our compassion and indulgence'.[24] In fact, he was such an admirer of Rousseau's theories on women that he pursued the plan of raising two foundling girls in seclusion in order to produce a creature as much like Rousseau's Sophie as possible, and from the two to choose a wife. When this plan failed to produce a suitable spouse he proposed to Honora Sneyd, who later became R.L. Edgeworth's second wife,

24 Letter to RLE, quoted in Richard Lovell Edgeworth and Maria Edgeworth, *Memoirs of Richard Lovell Edgeworth* (2 vols, 1820; Shannon, 1969), i, p. 224.

but she refused him on the grounds that she 'would not admit of the unqualified control of a husband over all her actions'.[25] Edgeworth subsequently fictionalised Day's extraordinary behaviour in *Belinda*. Day's admiration for Rousseau's ideas implied a similar view of the corrupting effeminacy of French society: he was, he wrote to R.L. Edgeworth, disgusted to see that, in France, women 'regulat[ed] the customs, the manners, the lives and the opinions of the other sex, by their own caprices, weaknesses and ignorance'.[26]

In the aftermath of the upheavals which struck Europe between 1782 and 1795, conservative reaction tended to claim that Rousseau's critique of the corrupting feminisation of society had been effectively proven by the course of the French Revolution. Just as Mary Wollstonecraft's *Vindication of the Rights of Woman* is only half-understood without reference to its revolutionary origin, Edgeworth's 'Letter from a Gentleman' is in part a contribution to the Revolution controversy, with a distinct gender inflection. The damage done to progressive ideas after the events of 1792 in France had, as Edgeworth suggests here, particular consequences for women, who were threatened with the withdrawal of the opportunity which Enlightenment philosophy had held out to them. This is made explicit in the references to the corrupting effects of female leadership, specifically in relation to France:

> Trace the history of female nature, from the court of Augustus to the court of Louis XVI, and tell me whether you can hesitate to acknowledge that the influence, the liberty and the *power* of women have been the constant concomitants of the moral and political decline of empires; – I say the concomitants: where the events are thus invariably connected I might be justified in saying they were *causes* – you would call them *effects*; but we need not dispute about the momentary precedence of evils, which are found to be inseparable companions: – they may be alternately cause and effect, – the reality of the connexion is established.[27]

Edgeworth answers the post-revolutionary conservatism of the first letter with the restrained rationality of the reply. In her own life and in the immediate past the reverse was true: optimistic rationalism had been replaced by a reaction which eschewed reason in favour of custom and the maintenance of the status quo. Historical chronology is thus reversed in Edgeworth's rewriting of the 1782–1795 period in 'Letter from a Gentleman', and therein, I suggest, lies its lack of persuasiveness. Looking, for instance, at some of the most obvious sources for the two pieces, Edgeworth responds to Burke with reference to Voltaire. Recent criticism, in its polite acknowledgement of Edgeworth's only explicit contribution to the debate on women's roles, has judged her particular brand of rationality inadequate to counter the power of post-revolutionary conservative rhetoric. 'Letter from a

25 Ibid., i, p. 250.   26 Ibid., i, p. 224.   27 Maria Edgeworth, *Letters for Literary Ladies*, p. 4.

Gentleman' has a value outside this context, however. It sheds light on Edgeworth's response to a post-revolutionary crisis that affected women who wished to challenge custom, in her own case by the adoption of a writing self. It also indicates that Edgeworth favoured a system of representation based on metonymy in order to facilitate her position as a woman writing in a post-revolutionary world, in which women were threatened with the withdrawal of freedoms and opportunities, based on the claim that feminine power was intimately bound up with the corruption which preceded Revolution.

IV

Metonymic schemes and problematic chronologies are a feature of Edgeworth's other work from this period, *Practical Education*, published jointly with her father in 1798. In a chapter entitled 'On Rewards and Punishments', although the theme is the education of young children, the Edgeworths characteristically draw their examples from the writings of Voltaire, Blackstone and Beccaria on law and penal systems. Chronology becomes an issue of importance when deciding whether or not punishment is effective. Punishment as revenge on the past is, the Edgeworths appear to say, of absolutely no utility: 'The past is irrevocable; all that remains is to provide for the future'.[28] Characteristically post-revolutionary caution becomes apparent however when the Edgeworths qualify this radical statement:

> It would be vain to plead the necessitarian's doctrine of an unavoidable connexion between the past and the future in all human actions; the same necessity compels the punishment, that compelled the crime; nor could, nor ought, the most eloquent advocate, in a court of justice, obtain a criminal's acquittal by entering into a minute history of the errors of his education … It is the business of education to prevent crimes.[29]

In both *Castle Rackrent* and 'Letter from a Gentleman' Maria Edgeworth proposes that humanity is both largely the product of environment and susceptible of change and improvement. These positions were central to her commitment to the continued improvement in women's lives, and her belief in the necessity of governing Ireland rationally and justly. This optimistic idealism is exemplified by the reforming zeal of Bentham. However, Bentham's writings indicate that the implementation of rational systems depends crucially on the definition of irrational, or more precisely non-utilitarian belief and practice, as conclusively 'past', whereas 'Letter from a Gentleman', in its rhetorical inadequacy, acknowledges implicitly that rationality itself has been superseded by reaction. Bentham's confident assurance that irrationality has become past is thrown into doubt both by the

28 Richard Lovell Edgeworth and Maria Edgeworth, *Practical Education* (2 vols; London, 1798), i, 228.   **29** Ibid.

post-revolutionary, anti-feminist reaction, and by the continued political upheaval in Ireland; the contradictory claims of *Practical Education* indicate that the past continues to exercise influence on the present through the search for cause and the felt need to apportion blame and punish accordingly.

Castle Rackrent's narrator, Thady Quirk, has been described the embodiment of 'colonial man',[30] but for Edgeworth, he is incomplete without reference to the society which produced him, the 'whole fabric' of which he is a part. The editorial apparatus which so many readers find irritating, patronising or intrusive, is, in addition to its function as apologist for the leadership of the ruling class, an attempt to supply what Edgeworth saw as a necessary referent in representation, and a deliberate obstacle to symbolic interpretation. Marilyn Butler has suggested that, in the tension between the 'Englishness' of the editorial voice and the 'Irishness' of the narrative voice, it is possible to locate the 'split cultural personality of the coloniser';[31] one could also suggest that the 'split' evinces a profound ambiguity on Edgeworth's part as to the more fundamental question of the location of 'personality' in any circumstance, in particular as a response to the historical crisis of the 1790s. In Edgeworth, the categories of gender and race or ethnicity can thus be said to overlap, though not in any metaphorical sense. Woman cannot *be* the nation, since the source of being lies always in some supra-individual force that is not susceptible to representation. The best Edgeworth can do is to indicate that her representation is partial; hence the extra-narrative voice of *Castle Rackrent's* 'Editor'. Ultimately this serves not to generate an impression of totality, though this controlling motive has been ascribed to Edgeworth, but to underline the partiality of the narrative voice and to fragment the representation. Based on a reading of Edgeworth's early work from the 1790s it is possible to characterise Edgeworth's narrative technique as sharing the qualities of the learned examples from 'Letter from a Gentleman', in that her plots and scenarios tend towards translatability and internationalism, but function through delimitation and contraction. The use of this method of representation is conditioned partly by Edgeworth's experience of the obstacles to women writers in post-revolutionary Britain and Ireland, an experience which undermines the apparent confidence in progress which her works propose.

---

30 P. F. Sheeran, 'Some Aspects of Anglo-Irish Literature from Swift to Joyce' in *Yearbook of English Studies*, 13 (1983), p. 102.   31 *Castle Rackrent* and *Ennui*, edited and with an introduction by Marilyn Butler (Harmondsworth, 1993), p. 16.

Imperfect Concord: Spectres of History in the Irish Novels of Maria Edgeworth and Lady Morgan

ANNE FOGARTY

The dual modes of realism and romance are frequently used as a convenient means of charting opposing tendencies in the history of the novel. At first glance, the work of Maria Edgeworth and of Lady Morgan would appear to illustrate these polarities. Where Edgeworth spearheads the use of naturalism and of social realism in her rational fictions about Ireland, Lady Morgan by contrast initiates and promotes a romantic and mythical view of the country and its history in her novels.[1] Edgeworth's highlighting of the intricacies of social interaction cede to a rival emphasis in the work of Lady Morgan on the alluring but threatening sublimity of the Irish landscape and of its inhabitants. On closer inspection, however, this neat dichotomy breaks down.

This essay aims to trace the continuities and differences between two novels by these interrelated writers which were published in the aftermath of the Act of Union in 1801. The texts which I shall examine are Maria Edgeworth's *The Absentee* (1812) and Lady Morgan's *The Wild Irish Girl* (1806).[2] I shall argue that the initial counterpoint between the enlightened utopianism of Edgeworth and the Gothic romanticism of Lady Morgan masks the shared political and aesthetic concerns of their work. In thus cross-comparing and picking out points of connection between their novels, my purpose is to consider the difficulties which both writers encounter in simultaneously depicting the vicissitudes and conflicts of Irish history whilst yet outlining a resolution of the political problems of the country.

I shall make the case that the attempt by Maria Edgeworth and Lady Morgan to write totalising fictions which use a moment of social concord to achieve a form of closure is countermanded by the contradictions and conflicts in Irish society which their work exposes. My argument will be not so much that their imaginations and political sympathies are at odds, as critics frequently contend, but that their very means of envisioning and emplotting Irish colonial history and its fateful consequences are themselves divided and riven.[3] Both writers, it

1 For an account of the philosophical underpinnings of the work of these writers, see Marilyn Butler, *Maria Edgeworth: A Literary Biography* (Oxford, 1972) and J. T. Leerssen, 'How *The Wild Irish Girl* Made Ireland Romantic' in *Dutch Quarterly Review*, 18 (1988), pp. 209–27. 2 *The Absentee*, edited by W.J. McCormack and Kim Walker (Oxford, 1988); *The Wild Irish Girl* (London, 1986). 3 Terry Eagleton, in his account of the formation of the Anglo-Irish novel, contends that there is a tension between the ideological beliefs and the imaginative insights of Edgeworth and Lady Morgan. See *Heathcliff and the Great Hunger: Studies in Irish Culture* (London, 1995), pp. 145–225.

will be seen, produce hybrid fictions which are seamed with doublings, hauntings and ambiguities which remain obdurately at odds with the harmonious endings which round out their texts.[4] Their composite creations combine aspects of the courtship novel and of the romance with panoramic surveys of Irish history, culture and society.

Both writers too use the viewpoint of the dispossessed outsider in order to constitute a vantage point from which to make sense of the entangled affairs of the country. The difference of Ireland is apparently lessened and made more amenable in their novels because it is looked at from the perspective of an other, a sympathetic visitor who is finally revealed to have a claim on the place because he is the disaffected son of an absentee landlord. Edgeworth and Lady Morgan ultimately endeavour to domesticate the wildness and intractability of Irish history by turning their sprawling accounts of the political conflicts which impede the cause of progress and of national cohesion into forms of family romance.[5] The hero reconfirms his stake in the country by embarking on a marriage which represents a strategic and problematic fusion of the interests of native and colonist. The prior education of the hero is made, however, contingent on this putatively happy outcome. Hence, Lord Colambre in *The Absentee* and Horatio Mortimer in *The Wild Irish Girl* are both exposed to conflicting aspects of their environment which permit them to reflect on and revise their attitudes.

However, the marriage of the hero hinges not just on the expansion of his sensibility and understanding but also on the re-establishment of his claims as a landowner and the renegotiation of the identity of the woman who becomes his wife. In each case the construing of the 'Irishness' of the heroine complicates and in part undermines what the protagonist has come to know about the country. As a consequence, the marriages which act as tentative signs of political resolution at the endings of these two novels prove simultaneously to be highly ambiguous renderings of the union between Ireland and England which they in part mirror. Unlike English domestic fictions of the same period in which, as Nancy Armstrong argues, the private sphere slowly begins to eclipse the public world, the sexual contract which is symbolically realised through the marriage of the revitalised landlord and his Irish bride with her refurbished national identity never succeeds in displacing the problems attached to the problematic social contract on which a colonial society is based.[6] Romance proves an uneasy solution to the political difficulties of Ireland.

4 For a discussion of the pervasive use of gothic conventions in eighteenth- and nineteenth-century fiction, see Terry Castle, *The Female Thermometer: Eighteenth-Century Culture and the Invention of the Uncanny* (Oxford, 1995) and Siobhán Kilfeather, 'Origins of the Irish Female Gothic' in *Bullán*, 1 (1994), pp. 35–45.   **5** Christine van Boheemen analyses the way in which the plotting of the identity and the establishment of the family origins of an orphaned outsider is a recurrent theme of the novel in different eras. See *The Novel as Family Romance: Language, Gender and Authority From Fielding to Joyce* (Ithaca, 1987). **6** Nancy Armstrong, *Desire and Domestic Fiction: A Political History of the Novel* (Oxford, 1987).

Both Edgeworth and Lady Morgan set out to combat false representations of Ireland by providing accounts of the country which are authentic and accurate. Prejudiced misrepresentations are thus to be countered by a new political vision which attempts to avoid the distortions and errors of the past. The sins of the fathers, their novels suggest, can be cancelled out by the actions of sons who know and experience Ireland in an altogether different fashion. Empirical reportage and the establishment of authentic local colour are as a result signal aspects of their work. The oedipal rivalry between generations becomes part of this process whereby the present cancels out and makes good former atrocities. The past has to be known and acknowledged before it can be overcome. However, although their work presents a corrective portrait of the Irish and of Irish history and points to the injustices perpetrated during the several centuries of English government and mismanagement, it also betrays a fear that Anglo-Irish relations will always be punctuated by crises and conflicts. A sense of irresolution lies at the heart of the fictional solutions proffered by these two narratives.

In what follows, I shall argue that different and contradictory representations of Ireland vie for attention in *The Absentee* and *The Wild Irish Girl*. Although both authors have the purpose of readjusting our views of Ireland by producing didactic fictions which enable us to distinguish between veracious and distorted descriptions of the country and its people, both find that their subject escapes them or that they cannot fully marry the lessons of history with the utopian solutions of fiction. Both texts uncover and insist upon the connections between politics and aesthetics and demonstrate that the manner in which we view a people and a society materially affects the judgements which we make about them.

However, it is this very premise, the impossibility of dissevering seeing from judging, which leads to the many moments of contradiction in these narratives. Borrowing a set of terms from Jacques Derrida's suggestive re-interpretation of Marx, I propose that *The Absentee* and *The Wild Irish Girl* represent the fictional Irelands conjured up by their authors as rooted in a type of 'spectropolitics'.[7] Although neither of these texts would seem at first glance to be a Gothic fiction, they both contain uncanny effects which take the form of displacements, ghostly doublings, and coincidences. As a result, these novels indicate that Ireland is not just a space onto which people project various competing political visions which can be assessed according to their ethical or moral worth, but that the many conflicting representations of the country uncannily repeat and duplicate each other and hence elude the magisterial scrutiny of the author's political vision.

Both Edgeworth and Lady Morgan use the device of the travel narrative in order to review Irish history and politics. Lord Colambre and Horatio Mortimer undertake a kind of sentimental journey which allows them to experience at first hand the plight of the Irish and to make them painfully aware of the inadequacies and abuses of the landlord system in the country. As outsiders who have a secret

---

7 Jacques Derrida, *Specters of Marx: The State of Debt, The Work of Mourning and The New International*, trans. Peggy Kamuf (London, 1994).

connection with this strange land through which they travel, they waver between a subjective and objective view of Irish society. They react to a world which is at once an alien space and their future abode or home. As Derrida explains, the strange familiarity associated with the spectre depends upon its visibility. However, paradoxically, the visibility of a ghost is a visibility of the invisible:

> The spectre appears to present itself during a visitation. One represents it to oneself, but it is not present itself, in flesh and blood. The non-presence of the spectre demands that one take its time and its history into consideration, the singularity of its temporality or of its historicity.[8]

In the interpretations that follow I shall suggest that Edgeworth and Lady Morgan focus on the spectral presence of Ireland in their narratives in order to illustrate its singularity and the materiality of its political and social conflicts. However, at the same time, the country that they describe seems like Derrida's spectre to be caught in a temporal dimension of its own, forever trapped in a past that refuses to be either fully present or to accord with a utopian vision of the future. In addition, while the spectropolitical vision of Ireland in *The Absentee* and *The Wild Irish Girl* problematises and extends our view of the place, it also has aspects of a negative conjuration or haunting. As Derrida points out, the *revenant* or ghost can be either a welcome or a dreaded apparition. It can alternatively be a *Geist* in the positive sense of spirit or essence, or a *Gespenst* in the negative sense of a spook or phantom. The spectral Irelands portrayed by Edgeworth and Lady Morgan hover precariously between these two spheres; their novels both conjure up an amenable and forward-looking vision of the country and depict it as a space of uncanny repetitions, visitations and hauntings.

The rambling journeys of the heroes of *The Absentee* and of *The Wild Irish Girl* through Irish history and society are given contour by contrasting notions of the aesthetic. While the key term in Edgeworth's novel is that of taste, the crucial concept in Lady Morgan's novel is that of the sublime. By tracing in turn the manner in which these concepts inform the political re-education of their respective protagonists, it is possible also to examine the moments of ambivalence which threaten to undermine the apparently demonstrable political theses of these texts.

The moral worth of Lord Colambre in *The Absentee* and the gradual emergence of his desire to get to know Ireland are initially signalled by his repugnance for London taste. The effete values of the metropolis are exposed in the descriptions of his mother's inept attempts to be accepted by English society. The soirées which she holds in order to ingratiate herself with the snobbish custodians of London fashion are characterised by their empty pageantry and cultural eclecticism. By decorating her rooms in various Oriental and African styles, she merely mirrors the parasitical and decentred nature of English upper class society. The decadence of this community seems to be less the result of its cannibalisation and appropriation

---

8 Derrida, *Specters of Marx*, p. 101.

of other cultures than of its incapacity to realise the connection between aesthetic and moral interests. The dependence of Colambre's father on a Jewish money-lender provides a further illustration of the moral errancy of this Anglo-Irish family which is dangerously adrift in English society. By transforming Irish colonial capital into the empty signs of English class distinction, Colambre's mother moreover highlights her own moral blindness and failure to live up to her political responsibilities. Colambre, by contrast, seeks to close the gap between objects and values. Eschewing the world of fashion and declaring at one point that he has no taste at all, he heads off for Ireland in order to discover for himself the true nature of the place. Initially, thus, the narrative seems to suggest that Ireland is the inverse of England: a counterfoil to English decadence and moral dissolution, it is intimated to be a place of innocence, purity, and originary natural virtue. Colambre, it would appear, moves from the greed and rapacity of England to the unpolluted domain of Ireland where society is not held hostage to base materialism.

However, his experience of Ireland from his very first approach to Dublin is also mediated by an interleaving of framing visions and competing ideologies. Colambre's identity is no less dubious and unstable in this other world. Alienated from London, he enters his country of origin as an alien. Ireland too, the text shows, is created by conflicting and potentially corrupting tastes and fashions. Colambre's initial experiences of his lost homeland are as disorientating as any of his mother's inept social pastiches. In swift succession, he learns of the superiority of Dublin life, sees the vulgar display of the Raffarty estate in Wicklow, is brow-beaten by the jaundiced, English fortune-hunter, Lady Dashfort, and is charmed by the benign but befuddled antiquarianism of Count O' Halloran.[9]

Following this bewildering patchwork of impressions, the text attempts to channel our perceptions and the moral choices of its protagonist by cross-comparing in what would seem a schematic way the behaviour of the two agents employed by Colambre's father, Mr Burke and Nick Garraghty. The opposing worlds of these two men are presented in polar terms: the domain of the good agent is redolent of order and progress while that of the corrupt agent epitomises disorder and anarchy. However, this alluringly simple object lesson which nestles inside all of the other warring frameworks on Ireland which have hitherto been proffered to Colambre leads to further complexities. The very doubling that occurs through the stark opposition of good and evil estate management suggests that the society which Colambre visits is inherently unstable and divided. This instability is made all the more evident through the disguise which Colambre is forced to adopt for most of the course of the novel. He visits his father's estates, *incognito*, as a *revenant* wrapped in a self-effacing cloak. On one level, this image of the masked landlord with his occluded identity acts as a reification of the moral obfuscation which has resulted from the mismanagement of the family property.

9 For an illuminating discussion of these assorted scenes and figures, see W.J. McCormack, *Ascendancy and Tradition in Anglo-Irish Literary History From 1789 to 1939* (Oxford, 1985), pp. 123–168.

However, on another level, it would seem that Colambre himself has been forced into the role of spectre. His alias ironically casts him as the ghost in the machine and shows him to be as much the cause of, as the solution, to the problems from which his father's tenants are suffering.

Despite the anomaly of his position, Colambre draws the correct conclusions from these vivid illustrations of how landlords should and should not comport themselves. He finally acts in accordance with that enlightened and paternalist landlordism favoured by Edgeworth and her father.[10] However, his justification of his actions and retrospective account of what he has seen from the postillon window and learnt from the narrative of Larry Brady, the loyal family retainer who roundly denounces Garraghty, are curious:

> The higgling for the price of the gold; the time lost in disputing about the goodness of the notes, among some poor tenants, who could not read or write, and who were at the mercy of the man with the bag in his hand; the vexation, the useless harrassing of all who were obliged to submit ultimately – Lord Colambre saw: and all this time he endured the smell of tobacco and whiskey, and the sound of various brogues, the din of men wrangling, brawling, threatening, whining, drawling, cajoling, cursing, and every variety of wretchedness.
>
> And is this my father's town of Clonbrony? thought Lord Colambre. Is this Ireland? No, it is not Ireland. Let me not like most of those who forsake their native country, traduce it. Let me not, even to my own mind, commit the injustice of taking a speck for the whole. What I have just seen is the picture only of that to which an Irish estate and Irish tenantry may be degraded in the absence of those whose duty and interest it is to reside in Ireland, to uphold justice by example and authority; but who neglecting this duty, commit power to bad hands and bad hearts – abandon their tenantry to oppression, and their property to ruin.[11]

It is striking that Colambre refuses here to see the squalid, debased Ireland which he has visited as anything other than a 'picture'. Although he has come face to face with the harsh realities of landlordism and particularly of the absentee system, he cannot accept his unvarnished vision of the country except in mediated and symbolic terms. He spectralises what he has seen and places it inside a picture frame in order to keep it distant from himself. Despite his rejection of taste and of the false perspectives offered by fashionable culture, he still insists on viewing Ireland within aesthetic and epistemological frameworks which involve a denial

---

10 For an analysis of the complex and contradictory political position of Edgeworth and her family, see Tom Dunne, *Maria Edgeworth and the Colonial Mind* (Cork, 1984); idem, "'A Gentleman's Estate Should be a Moral School": Edgeworthstown in Fact and Fiction, 1760–1840' in Raymond Gillespie and Gerard Moran (eds), *Longford: Essays in County History* (Dublin, 1991), pp. 95–121; and Michael Hurst, *Maria Edgeworth and the Public Scene: Intellect, Fine Feeling and Landlordism in the Age of Reform* (London, 1969).   11 Edgeworth, *The Absentee*, p. 162.

as well as an acceptance of what he has witnessed. By delimiting his experience of Ireland in this manner, he enables himself to perform the righteous actions which are required of him. However, he simultaneously places himself at a remove from the injustices exposed. Colambre establishes his presence as a landlord by keeping himself outside of this framed perspective which threatens to reveal too much about the inequities of the colonial system in Ireland. It is as if the text has perforce to bury some of the political insights which it brings to light because they have implications which do not coincide with the morality which it propounds. In keeping with the Kantian adage, Colambre has the courage to use his own understanding in coming to terms with the chaotic and disturbing nature of Irish social reality.[12] Yet, equally, he has to acknowledge the limitations on his freedom before putting into effect the meliorating social philosophy which Edgeworth and her father saw as the fitting basis of enlightened landlordism. In considering the proper uses of unfettered thought, Kant came to the conclusion that 'the public use of man's reason must always be free and it alone can bring about Enlightenment among men; the private use of reason may be quite seriously restricted'.[13]

At this juncture in the narrative, Edgeworth's hero seems to limit the radicalism of his own insights by restricting the ambit of his private powers of reason. While his public self is ready to denounce Garraghty for his corruption and inhumanity, his private self dissociates itself from the knowledge of such evil. Of course, Edgeworth uses this scene in part to convey to us the refinement of Colambre's sensibilities which make him back off in distress from the brute reality of Ireland. The text, however, begs the question as to whether the right-minded son of an erstwhile absentee landlord will ever be in a position to see the 'real' Ireland which he desires. The framed and spectral scene from which he turns away seems to have as its counterpart another more ghostly scene which the text is incapable of depicting. The advent of Colambre's beneficent regime lies beyond the horizon of our field of vision in a vague future which the ending of the novel firmly and ironically holds in abeyance.

An earlier episode in the tale illustrates why Colambre ultimately finds it necessary to excise from his memory certain aspects of Irish life in order to hold things within bounds. In a scene in which the discomfiting otherness of the country threatened to engulf him, he is evicted along with Widow O'Neill from her cottage. In a curious overlaying of dispossessions, the eviction of a native Irish tenant from her land dovetails with the expulsion of the absentee landlord from his estate. The incident of course forms part of Colambre's empirical education; he experiences at first hand the grievances of his tenants by partaking in the

12 Immanuel Kant, 'An Answer to the Question: What Is Enlightenment?' in *Kant's Political Writings*, edited by Hans Reiss and translated by H.B. Nisbet (Cambridge, 1971), pp. 54–60. At the beginning of this essay, Kant declares that 'sapere aude!' or 'have the courage to use your own understanding' is the motto of the Enlightenment.   13 *Kant's Political Writings*, p. 55. For a summary of the contradictions of Enlightenment philosophy, see Dorinda Outram, *The Enlightenment* (Cambridge, 1995), pp. 1–13.

eviction. The English audience for which the text was intended would presumably have taken greater umbrage at this injustice because it is so patently absurd.

However, the ambiguity of the scene belies these simple didactic objectives. The double eviction of landlord and tenant indicates a moment of irresolution and almost of political deadlock. Both coloniser and colonised seem equal victims of this system of misrule. The dual injustices which Colambre and Widow O'Neill jointly experience shade into each other and the plight of the absentee English landlord seems almost to eclipse that of the native Irish. The text appears to have to disavow as well as acknowledge the corruption of the landlord system. It makes it visible as an invisibility. In addition the scene enacts, in an oblique fashion, a general fear of native Irish retaliation which the novel represses. The threat of a peasant rebellion against an unjust system is converted here into a phantom but ultimately harmless eviction of the landlord by his own conniving agent.

Similarly, the text leavens and somehow short-circuits the injustices caused by absenteeism through the constant interjection of the comic commentary of Larry Brady, the loyal retainer of the Colambre family. His language and witticisms act as a shield that buffers the protagonist against too close an encounter with the hardship which is a direct result of his family's pursuit of taste and fashion. Moreover, Brady is a ghostly double of an earlier pivotal figure in Edgeworth's work, Thady Quirk in *Castle Rackrent*. Unlike his predecessor, this revised version of the family retainer is marked by his unswerving loyalty and innocent devotion. However, his garrulousness and disingenuous chatter whilst recalling Thady's self-serving deviousness serve the further function of keeping the spectre of disloyalty at bay.[14]

The shift of perceptions which enables the rehabilitation of the identity of Colambre's cousin, Grace Nugent, depends upon a similar pattern of acceptance and denial, seeing and not seeing. As with his experience of Ireland, Colambre seems initially to have to deny the evidence of his senses which persuade him of her fundamental virtue before he can succeed in vindicating her and saving her reputation. By the end of the novel, his penniless Irish cousin has transmogrified into an English heiress. All of the numerous associations with Irishness, illegitimacy and scandal which have tainted her reputation have been removed. She swaps her original surname, which, as W.J. McCormack has pointed out, potentially connects her with dissident Irish nationalism, for an English name, Reynolds.[15] Only after this transformation is the marriage between Colambre and herself possible. The heroine has, thus, to be rewritten and to become her own ghostly double before she can take up her predestined role as the wife of an Anglo-Irish landlord. The re-naming of Grace Nugent reminds us of the precarious nature of identity in a colonial society. Her symbolic marriage with Colambre comes about only when her virtue is translated into English terms and she is absolved of any connection with Catholic Ireland.

14 Marilyn Butler analyses the political objectives underlying the depiction of Thady. See *Castle Rackrent and Ennui*, edited by Marilyn Butler (London, 1995), pp. 1–54.
15 McCormack argues that the Nugent family would have had particular associations with recusancy and Jacobite politics. See 'Introduction', *The Absentee*, pp. xxii–xxv.

The ending of the novel, however, demonstrates that such convenient exorcisms of social tensions do not hold good. Instead of a final view of Colambre, we are treated instead to a re-play of events in a letter of Larry Brady to his brother in England which describes the recent reinstatement of Lord and Lady Clonbrony on their demesne. Brady concludes his missive with a request to his absentee brother, a tenant farmer who had been driven from his holdings by the evil Garraghty, also to return home. This recursive letter thus suggests that the consolidation of benevolent English rule of Irish society will be borne out by the desire of the native population to accept this new and enlightened regime.

The question of ghostliness, however, still hovers over the text. As Derrida comments, it is one of the aspects of the spectre that it sees you before you see it.[16] Brady, by having the final say, spectralises the revenant landlords for us. In superimposing his vision on theirs, he dislocates the presence which they seem to have established in the country. Further, he diverts our attention to the abiding problem of the political role which will be played by the native Irish in this regime which is not of their making. His witty but portentous dislocation of the term 'absentee' to describe his brother's enforced exile implicitly raises the question as to whether the mutual presence of the Anglo-Irish landlord and Irish tenant will not still involve future banishments, exiles and conflicts of interest. The healing salve of Brady's comic and genial rewriting of the plot uneasily masks the political rivalries which remain a constant aspect of colonial society. The conflicts which Edgeworth's novel attempts to circumvent and defuse seem to be always already inscribed in the spectropolitical discourses which haunt her fiction.

Horatio Mortimer (H.M.), the hero of Lady Morgan's *The Wild Irish Girl*, similarly discovers Ireland to be a site of ambivalence. Like Colambre, he travels to Ireland in order to restore himself, to banish the ill-effects of English dissipation, and to become acquainted with his neglected patrimony, the decaying estates of his absentee father. H.M. oscillates between approbation of the romantic aspects of Irish culture and dismay at its uncouthness. In particular, he seems to be torn between two countervailing attitudes towards the sublimity of the Irish landscape. At the beginning of his trip, he revels in its untamed qualities and uses the pleasurable feelings of terror which it inspires to secure his identity. The following passage describes his reaction to the scenery in an unspecified part of the west of Ireland:

> Mountain rising over mountain, swelled like an amphitheatre to those clouds which, faintly tinged with the sun's prelusive beams, and rising from the earthly summits where they had reposed, incorporated with the kindling aether of a purer atmosphere. All was silent and solitary – a tranquillity tinged with terror, a sort of 'delightful horror', breathed on every side. I was alone, and felt like the presiding genius of desolation![17]

16 Derrida, *Specters of Marx*, p. 101.   **17** Morgan, *The Wild Irish Girl*, p. 7.

Here, it is clear that H.M. gives in to the painful transports of the sublime in order ultimately to reassert control over himself. The overwhelming spectacle of the mountains allows him to secure and anchor himself in his solitary identity.[18] He is transformed through this aesthetic experience from an anonymous spectator into 'the presiding genius of desolation'. In such moments, he is exposed to what David Morris describes as the eighteenth-century sublime which occurs primarily 'in a world of stable meanings, where interpretation is not openly at issue'.[19] By contrast the feelings of terror and mystery which are sparked off by H.M.'s contemplation of the castle of Inismore and its inhabitants, as he ventures further into the vortex of Irish wildness, plunge him into that state of dislocation and disempowerment linked with the Gothic sublime. The contradictory emotions of fear and fascination conjured up by this negative encounter with the sublime ultimately centre on the figure of Glorvina, the wild Irish girl herself.

Glorvina is described as an impossible amalgam of nature and culture, innocence and mystery, desire and terror. As the final member of a moribund Gaelic tribe, she is at once *Geist*, the distillation of this lost Irish civilisation, and *Gespenst*, a ghost from an irredeemably remote past. A nightmare which H.M. experiences during his sojourn in this final ruined outpost of Gaelic supremacy makes evident the lurking horror which he paradoxically links with her beguiling seductiveness:

> What had I to expect from the unpolished manners, the confined ideas of this Wild Irish Girl? Deprived of all those touching allurements which society only gives; reared in wilds and solitudes, with no other associates than her nurse, her confessor, and her father; endowed indeed by nature with some personal gifts, set off by the advantage of a singular and characteristic dress, for which she is indebted to whim and natural prejudice, rather than native taste: I who had fled in disgust from even those whose natural attraction the bewitching blandishments of education, the brilliant polish of fashion, and the dazzling splendour of real rank, contributed their potent spells ...
>
> While given up to such reflections as these – while the sound of the Irish harp arose from the hall below, and the nurse muttered her prayers in Irish over her beads by my side, I fell into a gentle slumber, in which I dreamed that the Princess of Inismore approached my bed, drew aside the curtains, and raising her veil, discovered a face I had hitherto rather guessed at, than seen. Imagine my horror – it was the face, the head, of a *Gorgon*![20]

---

18 For an examination of the role of the sublime in literature of this period, see Marjorie Hope Nicolson, *Mountain Gloom and Mountain Glory: The Development of the Aesthetics of the Infinite* (New York, 1959), Neil Hertz, 'The Notion of Blockage in the Literature of the Sublime' in Geoffrey H. Hartman *Psychoanalysis and the Question of the Text* (Baltimore, 1978), and Thomas Weiskel, *The Romantic Sublime: Studies in the Structure and Psychology of Transcendence* (Baltimore, 1976). **19** David Morris, 'Gothic Sublimity' in *New Literary History*, 16 (1985), pp. 299–319 (p. 299). **20** Morgan, *The Wild Irish Girl*, p. 51.

In construing the unspeakable dread with which he associates Glorvina, Lady Morgan's hero invokes a confused array of gothic images. The wild Irish girl in his feverish imaginings is a composite of oriental dancer, classical monster and succubus. Ultimately, the narrative shows that the spectral ambiguities of Glorvina are an emanation not just of her ethnic otherness but of the rapacity of his own family. The gothic sublimity of the Castle of Inismore has as its absent cause the depredations of colonialism. H.M. finds that the double with which he has to grapple is, in fact, his father who has planned to marry the wild Irish girl and thus ensure his sovereignty over her lands.

By ousting his father and himself becoming Glorvina's husband, it is intimated that the hero has in some way countered the horrors of corrupt landlordism. At the end of the text, H.M. is charged with the task of bringing back into 'renovating life' the 'national virtues' of the Irish. Yet, despite the optimism inspired by this symbolic marriage that represents an ideal fusion of English and Irish interests, it still remains open as to what kind of future this happy ending actually heralds. In the closing moments of the novel, the wild Irish girl is eclipsed by the distant prospect of the complete restoration of the ideals of Gaelic culture by this reformed Anglo-Irish landlord. She is transformed from a nightmare vision of the violence and losses of Irish history into a comforting and prophetic dream of a harmonious future. Glorvina becomes the cultural capital and symbolic reservoir for the romantic nationalism that Lady Morgan proposes. The ghostly traces and gothic horrors of the past will be converted into the spirit of an ideal future. However, the erasure of Glorvina from the final pages of the novel seems a measure of the absences and cancellations on which even this optimistic spectropolitical vision depends.

In *The Absentee* and *The Wild Irish Girl* Edgeworth and Lady Morgan produce political fictions that are at once enlightened, conciliatory and riddled with ambiguity. Their land-owning heroes define themselves in terms of their Irishness and of their responsibilities as governors of a colonial society. In addition, both texts insist that the work of achieving national harmony in Ireland is dependent on the mediating presence of women who precariously straddle the divide between Anglo-Irish landlords and their Irish tenants. However, in the final reckoning, the belief of these writers in a future which will be uncontaminated by the conflicts of the past is persistently undermined by the spectres of history which haunt their texts.

III

'Discourses of Difference': Women's Travel Writing

Anne Plumptre: An Independent Traveller

GLENN HOOPER

In 1812, Henry Lichtenstein, doctor of medicine and philosophy, and professor of natural history at the University of Berlin, published his two volume *Travels in Southern Africa*. In the preface to his work Lichtenstein considered the purpose of travel writing, and how the variety of accounts published for similar regions differed so widely; although the sole subject for many a writer, he concluded, 'seems to have been to make their works entertaining to their own countrymen, or at the utmost, to their contemporaries in general', he, himself, had 'avoided all attempts to embellish his descriptions, lest they might endanger the throwing [of] an improper shade over the whole of the picture'.[1] While Lichtenstein's self-analytical and ruminative tone may strike a note of cautious piety for many a reader, it also serves as a means of comprehending the various changes that were happening to the travel narrative form for this particular period. For example, in Mary Louise Pratt's *Imperial Eyes*, it is suggested that where eighteenth-century travel writers worked with a more factually based model, eschewing all temptations towards self-promotion or personal drama, the nineteenth-century writers moved in the direction of making their texts more entertaining, or autobiographical, or simply more imaginative than had been previously the case. According to Pratt, texts such as Mungo Park's *Travels in the Interior Districts of Africa*, first published in 1799, not only marked 'the eruption of the sentimental mode into European narrative ... at the end of the eighteenth century', but also transformed the way in which travel writing would be subsequently written and read.[2]

What makes Lichtenstein's text interesting for the purpose of my discussion, however, is not just its relationship to the various threads of a specifically Euro-American discussion concerning the complexities of the travel narrative form, but that his text had been translated into English from the original German by Anne Plumptre, novelist, mineralogist and traveller. Author of a novel, entitled *The Rector's Son* (1798), and a travelogue, *Narrative of a Three Years' Residence in France* (1810), Plumptre is not just an interesting narrator in her own right, but the quietly unobtrusive and, I believe, methodologically sympathetic figure behind Lichtenstein's work. In fine, her translation of his *Travels* reveals an affinity for a more scientifically based model, suggesting that Pratt's thesis of an end-of-century transformation of the travel narrative form is not necessarily true for all writers.

Born in 1760 to Anne and Dr. Robert Plumptre, President of Queen's College, Cambridge, Anne Plumptre received a good education and went on to excel in

---

1 H. Lichtenstein, *Travels in Southern Africa* (2 vols., London, 1812). 2 M. L. Pratt, *Imperial Eyes: Travel Writing and Transculturation* (London, 1992), pp. 74–5.

languages, in addition to developing an interest in drama and creative writing. In fact her linguistic and theatrical interests were to coalesce during the years 1799 and 1800 when she was given the opportunity to translate several of Augustus Von Kotzebue's plays from German to English. Poet Laureate and director of the Imperial Theatre at Vienna, Kotzebue was a hugely popular dramatist in his day, and Plumptre seems to have revelled in her duties as translator, completing his *The Count of Burgundy*, *The Virgin of the Sun*, *The Force of Calumny* and *The Horse and the Widow*, all within this two year period. In addition, she translated, also from German, *Letters Written from Various Parts of the Continent*, a series of observations published in 1799, in which several travellers offered their views on continental Europe at a time of intense and significant change. She spent the period 1802 to 1805 living and conducting research in France, and making preparations for the first of her travel narratives.

But in the summer of 1814, Plumptre made a trip to Ireland, remaining there until the following year. The results of her visit were written up and eventually published in 1817, under the title *Narrative of a Residence in Ireland*. Compared with many another travelogue, Plumptre's *Narrative* is an accomplished piece, blending together issues as diverse as science and architecture, politics and mineralogy, while showing little or no sign of plagiarism throughout.[3] In addition the narrator not only appears well-informed and genuinely interested in the subject of her inquiry, but seems drawn towards the sort of methodological procedures outlined by Lichtenstein. Divided into two parts, with many subsections and chapters, the text is concerned with two separate journeys; the first to Dublin and Wicklow, with an extensive visit to Antrim and Down where the author has the opportunity to indulge her passion for mineralogical inquiry, followed by a second journey, which also takes in Dublin and Wicklow but which then fans out towards the south and south-west. Although the itinerary is interesting in itself, particularly her northern route, a region ignored by many travellers, the issues I wish to address concern how Plumptre actually engaged with the country, how her writings differ, if at all, from those of men, and the predominant political and ideological pressures under which she wrote.

In Sara Mills's analysis of women's travel writing, it is suggested that it is the various travellers who moved across landscapes as investigators and scouts who should be credited with much of the colonial enterprise. Mills's efforts to map differing responses to dominant discourses, her assessment of recent criticism which has conceptualised colonialism in masculine terms only, and her preparedness to accept that women's writing had its own discursive and interpretive parameters, makes her text an important stage in our understanding of the relationship between colonial discourse and travel writing. For example, while she acknowledges Mary Kingsley's efforts at self-deprecation in her *Travels in West Africa* of 1897, Mills also points to the masculine adventuring hero position

3 For an overview of the extent to which plagiarism distorted the writings of many travellers, see P.G. Adams, *Travelers and Travel Liars 1660–1800* (New York, 1980).

adopted by Kingsley as well as the alignment of the narrator with colonial politics generally.[4]

Although Plumptre's text, like Kingsley's, evokes the occasional note of humour, relating, for example, a comical moment in which she is invited to christen an island off the west coast of Ireland by local inhabitants, the text is more interestingly read within the context of colonialist discourse. More specifically, the narrative can be related to the Act of Union of 1800, to the attendant 'double-think'[5] that affected many English commentators who travelled to Ireland in its aftermath, and to the way in which the Union inferred a relationship of parity and equivalence between the two countries. This equivalence, however, could only be partially satisfied within the parameters of epistemological desire. Many writers were obsessed with comprehending Ireland, not least because they linked an understanding of the country with an opportunity for greater control and more effective management. For example, in Sir Richard Colt Hoare's *Journal of a Tour in Ireland, A.D. 1806*, it is suggested that 'the island of HIBERNIA still remains unvisited and unknown', a condition he attributed to 'the want of books, and living information'.[6] In the preface to Plumptre's travelogue, we are told that it was 'the very flattering reception with which the *Narrative of my Residence in France* was favoured' that prompted the current engagement with Ireland.[7] However, a selective quotation from Spenser's *A View of the Present State of Ireland*, printed on the title page, in which the country is evoked as a deterritorialised landscape, suggests that a post-Union interest in the commodification of Ireland may have had some part in that decision.[8] Moreover, Plumptre continues:

> If we are anxious to be introduced to a knowledge of the face of their country, to understand its natural advantages and disadvantages, its customs and manners, its civil and political state, that we may be enabled to compare them with our own, and judge between them and ourselves, – a much deeper interest will surely be excited when these injuries, these comparisons, relate to an object so near to us as a SISTER.[9]

Like Hoare, Plumptre reveals a desire for information about the country, not just because a Union has been effected, but because that Union's chances of success are read in terms of epistemological gains and advantages.

On the one hand, Ireland is there to be discovered, so to speak, and to be made available to a readership full of anticipation in the wake of this recent legislation. On the other hand, Ireland is a vehicle by which Plumptre can assert her own

4 S. Mills, *Discourses of Difference: An Analysis of Women's Travel Writing and Colonialism* (London, 1991), pp. 153–74.   5 R. Foster, *Modern Ireland, 1600–1972* (London, 1988), p. 342.   6 Sir Richard Colt Hoare, *Journal of a Tour in Ireland, A.D. 1806* (London, 1807), ii.   7 A. Plumptre, *Narrative of a Residence in Ireland* (London, 1817).   8 'And yet it is a most beautifull and sweet countrey as any is under heaven, being stored throughout with many goodly rivers, replenished with all sorts of fish most abundantly, sprinkled with many very sweet islands and goodly lakes … ', ibid., title-page.   9 Ibid., preface.

independence and authority. By speaking about the political and cultural affairs of Ireland, in other words, she can present herself as a figure of decision, aligning herself with narrators as centrally placed, in canonical terms, as Edmund Spenser, while simultaneously presenting her own work as a contribution to that canon. Describing herself as the author of a well-received travelogue may reveal a pride and confidence in her ability to map the contours of Irish cultural and political life, but it also allows us to recognise something of the dominant manner and tone of the text itself. Bearing in mind that until 1857 women, on marriage, 'became civil minors and were not allowed to own property' helps establish the degree to which the text may be seen as radical in its assessments and strategies.[10] Indeed, it is possible to present Plumptre as a proto-feminist writer, since her attempts at political assessment, her observations, and her narrative style suggest an indifference to the contemporary discourses of femininity which affected, and frequently limited, the writings of many other women. As Mills has indicated, because women travel writers sought physical as well as intellectual freedom in which to prepare and then document their own experiences, they very often had to compromise themselves by incorporating into their texts gestures of ideological and discursive surrender. For example, Mills suggests that because the writer Fanny Parks wished to report on Thug militancy in India but realised that such a commentary and subject matter might be deemed 'unfeminine', she decided on a 'distancing strategy' that would help provide, and yet 'mediate the information' for her readers; in Park's case the best vehicle proved to be the 'letters from a friend' format.[11]

With Plumptre, however, things are rather different. There is no shirking or denying her responsibilities, and no efforts at self-effacement or denigration anywhere in the text. She confidently cites Richard Pococke and John Carr,[12] and by so doing not only establishes her familiarity with each of their texts, but manages a degree of almost institutional, certainly professional, compatibility between each of their works and her own. As to those aspects of women's writing which very often remain undeveloped entirely – like the adoption of a quasi-scientific voice – Plumptre has absolutely no reservations. Admittedly, the level of scientific assessment performed at the Giant's Causeway may come across as a little strained, certainly a little exhaustive, yet the description is not an isolated affair and, regarded in the context of the overall work, not at all unusual: 'The latter circumstance, in addition to the occurrence of basaltic fragments, in which a *sphere appears to be enveloped by a polyhedral figure*, suggested the hint for an opinion which I have been led to adopt – that a *compressible laminated sphere is the primitive figure* of each prismatic articulation.'[13] Supported by references to a paper originally published in the *Journal de Physique* and to an 'excellent paper in the Philosophical Transactions'[14] by Mr Gregory Watt, Plumptre's enthusiastic

10 Mills, *Discourses*, p. 95.   11 Ibid., p. 82.   12 Richard Pococke, *Tour in Ireland in 1752*, edited by G.T. Stokes (Dublin, 1801), and Sir John Carr, *The Stranger in Ireland* (London, 1806).   13 Plumptre, *Narrative*, p. 145, emphases in original.   14 Ibid., p. 146.

assessments, backed up by an indefatigable belief in her own interpretive self-worth,[15] have a very credible legitimacy and worth.

When Cora Kaplan writes of the way in which women are linguistically defined as 'segregated speakers' for whom 'the suppression and restriction of their speech'[16] is an internalised position into which they have been inscribed by the forces of patriarchal discourse, she writes for the majority of women. However, when we look at the narratives of women travellers to Ireland and, occasionally, elsewhere we are immediately confronted by a sense of ideological violation. In seeking access to cultures and landscapes quite alien, and certainly quite incompatible with anything like that sphere of the domestic with which they had institutional familiarity, many women were challenging social proprieties and expectations far in excess of anything previously imagined. Not all the women who travelled, of course, were like Plumptre. Many of them had to sacrifice themselves and their opinions in order to comply with the rubric of femininity that pervaded the social and ideological landscapes of the time, while many more of them masked or underplayed their intelligence so as simply to have their work accepted, even though to do so carried its own problems and penalties.[17]

Anne Plumptre was however something of an exception to these gendered limitations, writing confidently and unselfconsciously on a range of topics distinctly 'unfeminine'. Indeed, Plumptre's feminist credentials are very clearly displayed at several junctures of her text. For example, during the course of her travels she not only informs us of how she has procured a letter of introduction to Lady Morgan, whom she describes as that 'amiable authoress',[18] but she also meets, while in Dublin, with Sir William Betham, brother of Matilda Betham, author of the *Biographical Dictionary of the Celebrated Women of Every Age and Country*, which was first published in 1804. In instances such as these, Plumptre takes the opportunity to emphasise not only the range of her reading and the extent of her social contacts, but also her alignment with progressive, in some instances explicitly feminist, figures. For example, in Plumptre's private life she also happened to be a friend of Helen Maria Williams, the well known democrat, noted for her sympathy for the revolutionaries in France, with connections to Fanny Burney and Wollstonecraft; what might be said to have drawn Williams and Plumptre together was not just their travelling and respective residences in France, but their commitment to the kind of revolutionary politics current in Britain as well as continental Europe from the 1790s onwards. In addition, it is tempting to make a connection between Plumptre and Elizabeth Inchbald, who

---

15 'I am not aware that any theory ... I have never observed ... I am inclined to think ... I would now take a comparative view ... the most familiar examples with which I am acquainted ... ', ibid., pp. 146–47. **16** C. Kaplan, *Sea Changes: Culture and Feminism* (London, 1988), p. 77. **17** Mills's assessment is worth some consideration in this regard: 'However, as I have already noted, women writers are caught in a double-bind situation: if they tend towards the discourses of femininity in their work they are regarded as trivial, and if they draw on the more adventure hero type narratives their work is questioned', *Discourses*, p. 118. **18** Plumptre, *Narrative*, p. 9.

also worked on Von Kotzebue's plays, specifically *Lovers Vows*, which Inchbald was asked to fit for the stage at Covent Garden in 1798. All of these women wrote about women's issues, of course, but perhaps just as noteworthy for our purposes, is how many of them complement Plumptre's own philosophical and literary development. More specifically, while feminist politics appears to be the one theme that binds all of their texts together, many of them seemed to regard travel writing as an additional focus in their lives. For instance, when we remember that Mary Wollstonecraft published her *Letters Written during a Short Residence in Sweden, Norway and Denmark* in 1796, a text which was well received and went into several printings, we can begin to see how important was the travel narrative form for women of this period. Whether we might consider Wollstonecraft as laying the foundation, so to speak, for other women travellers of the time is debatable, but since Mary Williams also published a travel account, entitled *A Tour of Switzerland*, followed by Plumptre's travelogues of, firstly, France, and then Ireland, a tradition of politically enlightened female travel writing would appear to have been in the making for the last decade of the eighteenth, and the early years of the nineteenth centuries.

An interesting question to now pose is: in what manner did Plumptre deal with the subject of a female emancipatory politics while touring in a country recently in conflict with her own and, to what extent, and in what ways, did she deal with the politics and practicalities of colonialism? Sara Mills has suggested that many feminist analyses of women travellers tend to downplay any oppressive or unpalatable aspects to the women under discussion in favour of a critique that centres on their individuality or eccentricity.[19] Other lines of engagement have simply chosen to regard women as far too involved in their struggle against social convention to be interested in anything as alien as colonial policy or ethnicity and, of course, there are levels or degrees of interpretation for which analyses such as these have a certain applicability. But, in addition to delegitimising women as ideologically complex figures in their own right, there are further dangers with this type of assessment; dangers in seeking to see them as non-political and as uncontaminated by the experiences of so ethnographic an encounter. To be sure, problems existed for women which tended to make any ideological interpretations and pronouncements they might offer considerably more complex, like the pressures and parameters of a restrictive feminine discourse that foregrounded the individual over the racial, or the domestic and private over the public spheres, but women who were intelligent and privileged enough to travel (sometimes unchaperoned), as well as motivated enough to have their experiences later published, cannot be seen as uniformly apolitical.

For example, I suggested earlier that Plumptre's text was coloured by an Act of Parliament which constitutionally established the Union of Britain with Ireland. However, we must also remember that because that Act was brought about, in large part, by the revolutionary activities of the Irish themselves, its

19 Mills, *Discourses*, p. 3.

reception and interpretation by successive English travellers to Ireland was seen in distinctly uncertain and ambivalent terms. In fine, if Ireland was to be afforded the narrative luxury of parity and accommodation, then that narrative would have to exist alongside another, one of widescale nondenominational insurrection. Consequently Ireland, increasingly regarded by specifically English writers as a politically ambivalent and unpredictable terrain, came to be a source of inter-pretive difficulty for many of its visitors. With Anne Plumptre the tendency to double-think may not be so pronounced as that of, say, Sir Richard Hoare, but a brief examination of some of the issues raised by Plumptre reveals a more complex and politically aware narrator than might be supposed.[20]

In her assessment of nineteenth-century women's travel narratives, Shirley Foster makes the point that 'the woman writer often represents foreigners sym-pathetically, as individuals with whom she tries to identify rather than as symbols of an alien "otherness"'. The woman traveller/writer, she continues, 'blurs the demarcation between "them" and "us" and may be less assertive than her male equivalent'.[21] Sara Mills, while keen to stress the power differential that existed between women travellers and their 'subjects', gives qualified support to this thesis by suggesting that because the assessment of women and colonised natives was similar, ('simple, childlike, deceitful, passive, not capable of intellectual thought, and more closely allied to nature'), the representational efforts of some women were more sympathetic than those of men.[22] While this may well be the case for the texts analysed by Foster and Mills, it is not wholly the case with Anne Plumptre. For example, if we examine Plumptre's experiences at the Giant's Causeway we will find her description of the native Irish to be no less explicit than that to be found in male texts, and no less sure in its pronouncements:

> But the troop of guides by which the Causeway is infested are always upon the look-out to collect every thing they can find worth seizing ... Not-withstanding my peremptory rejection of their services, a whole flock of these cormorants would continue to follow me about the whole day, and then made their impertinent intrusion a pretence for wanting some remuneration at the conclusion.[23]

Dehumanising the Irish and translating them into an undifferentiated mass whose intrusive presence is one to be painfully endured by the visitor to Ireland is a central theme here. The Irish, Plumptre seems to suggest, are a hindrance and an obstacle to leisured and intellectual activity, their presence best seen as a fright-ening plurality of native and ethnic difference:

---

20 For an assessment of the difficulties that faced figures such as Hoare, see my 'Stranger in Ireland: The Problematics of the Post-Union Travelogue' in *Mosaic*, 28, 1 (March, 1995). **21** S. Foster, *Across New Worlds: Nineteenth-Century Women Travellers and their Writings* (London, 1990), p. 24. **22** Mills, *Discourses*, p. 92. **23** Plumptre, *Narrative*, p. 142.

> Scarcely can a carriage stop at a shop, or a well-dressed person enter one, but
> the door is immediately surrounded by a number of these miserable-looking
> beings [beggars], whose clamours and importunities exceed those of the English
> beggars in equal proportion with the wretchedness of their appearance ... to
> them working and being well kept, is greater misery than their rags and
> wretchedness, while indulged in their beloved indolence.[24]

What the language also establishes is the degree of representational compatibility
that exists between Plumptre and her male colleagues, showing, in particular,
how unconstrained is the narrator by the discourses of femininity that traditionally
bound women to specific areas of assessment and interpretation. Plumptre's
evocation of the Irish in these lines is no different in sentiment from a dozen
other male texts, in that the same enunciations of power seek to represent the
Irish as an uninvited and unwelcome presence.

However, Plumptre's choice of language also shows her to be influenced by
the quite specific issues of unionism, or at least by the sorts of quite radical and
problematic frames of reference which unionism inspired. For example, when,
towards the close of the text, she suggests, 'It cannot be denied but that the state
of the country calls loudly for some amelioration – that the situation of the
inferior classes among the Irish is lamentable, is affecting',[25] and writes that 'the
Irish are a kind and warm-hearted people, extremely disposed to show kindness
themselves, and no less feelingly alive to receiving it from others',[26] she shows a
level of tolerance and, particularly, in the latter instance, a level of parity between
herself and the Irish. In other words, for Plumptre Ireland can be the 'SISTER'[27]
island, with a relationship to England which is important, if at times a little unfortunate and unpleasant. It can also be a source of great interest to her, provoking
some serious reflection and, on one occasion, even a vigorous defence of it against
one of its better known critics:

> The writers of his time, then, taking their cue from the court, vilified Ireland
> in every way; and Mr Hume, at all times too much disposed to abandon his
> better judgement when personal or national prejudices interposed, has, without
> considering the inconsistency of what he says, suffered the impartiality of the
> historian to be overswayed by their designed and wilful misrepresentations.[28]

However, Plumptre's generosity towards the Irish is ambivalent throughout, and
one finds the country aligned with a deeply conflictual model of representation:
a model that cites their basic humanity, their poverty, or their congeniality one
moment, and their barbarous and marginalised state the next. Ireland has been
linked in union to Britain, Plumptre's narrative would appear to suggest, but that
Union looks like an extremely fragile one indeed:

24 Ibid., p. 44.   **25** Ibid., p. 338.   **26** Ibid., p. 337.   **27** Ibid., preface.   **28** Ibid.,
pp. 334–5.

The heads of the rebellion were crushed, but venom still rankled in the hearts. If in later times these things have been partially corrected; if by degrees something of the jealousy and asperity with which this rival sister was regarded has abated, too much has still been retained: till that be entirely eradicated, Ireland can never be other than a diseased limb of the body politic.[29]

In the course of reading Plumptre's *Narrative*, then, one encounters a rather curious blend of ideas. As I have indicated, Plumptre was interested in mineralogy and politics, historiography and architecture, and she wanted to believe that she was not only travelling into sometimes strange and dangerous terrritory, but that she was on a mission of discovery also. At Glenarm, for example, she tells of the following experience:

As if everything connected with the shores of this extraordinary corner of the globe was of a gigantic nature, I found marine plants of a size so enormous that everything of the kind, which before I had thought vast, were dwindled into pigmies; – they were besides of a totally different kind from any I had seen before. Part of the principal stem of a leaf which I picked up and carried away with me, but afterwards unfortunately lost, measured nearly four inches in circumference. I was not more fortunate with two immense leaves which I brought away, one measuring above three yards in length.[30]

But these acts of discovery, it seems to me, interesting or humorous though they may be, are a means of avoiding other realities also. Without being ungenerous to Plumptre, one of the sensations her text provokes is that she sometimes uses this older, more scholarly, Linnean tradition as a means of avoiding many of the specificities of recent Irish unrest: one type of language, in other words, used as a means of repressing other histories and other voices.

Although the concept of 'home' is usually regarded as signalling a realm of domestic fixity and permanence, Alison Blunt suggests that for women travellers, in particular, home is 'constructed in an arbitrary, retrospective way while the traveller is away, and, by necessity ... changes on the traveller's return'.[31] Between Britain and Ireland, the concept of home has always had a particular relevance, although it has frequently indicated confusion and loss as much as notions of ownership and possession. While many post-Union travellers were content to relate to Ireland in the context of epistemological realignment, others desired a state of renewal, unsullied by past memories of conflict and racial antagonisms. Anne Plumptre, trying desperately to avoid a confrontation with the past, found herself presenting Ireland's incorporation within the Union as a naturally occurring political reality, making Ireland home – the title of her text, *Residence*, suggests at much – while at the same time exoticising the country for the purpose

29 Ibid., p. 336.   30 Ibid., p. 107.   31 A. Blunt, *Travel, Gender, and Imperialism: Mary Kingsley and West Africa* (London, 1994), p. 114.

of professional satisfaction, even if such claims occasionally rang hollow and untrue. Unfortunately, trying to get such a balancing act right, trying to make Ireland sufficiently foreign to justify being there in the first place, but sufficiently amenable so as to complement the prevailing ideologies of the time, could make, as the following quotation suggests, for very uncomfortable writing indeed. Like some of her colleagues, Plumptre attempted to disengage from Ireland, to purify herself in the interests of ideological propriety, but occasionally the past, and past memories, would come back to trouble her:

> At Tipperary I first heard of the disturbances which just now commenced in these parts; only two nights before the Mail had been attacked on the other side of Cashel by a very desperate gang, and a soldier had been killed ... the object was not so much to get money, as arms ... I came to Cashel to see the celebrated rock and the venerable remains of antiquity with which it is crowned, but I could now see nothing except the increased sufferings which the country had prepared for itself; I became indifferent to everything else, and I thought only of quitting scenes which seemed surrounded with nothing but gloom and horror. I saw the rock and the ruins at a little distance, as I entered the town, and as I quitted it they presented but new ideas of devastation, and I passed on. Yet for one moment I felt an impulse to stop the carriage and ascend the rock. The rain had ceased in the night, the morning was fine, the sun was shining upon the mouldering towers and turrets, and they assumed an air of magnificence which methought ought not to be passed by. The next moment, however, the idea that though the heavens were bright and clear, all was gloom in the moral atmosphere, came too forcibly over my mind to be repelled, and I pursued my route. At present my feelings upon this occasion seem strange to me, they seemed so in a few hours after, but at the moment they were irresistible. I have often asked myself since, why I did not see the ruins of Cashel, – I could never answer the question satisfactorily.[32]

Setting Ireland into a framework by which it may be read as a place of racially inferior inhabitants, or effete antiquarianism, then, is not particular to male narrators, nor particularly unique come to that. Anne Plumptre's strategies may differ from many others because they are less ethnologically charged, or because they are born of a somewhat more liberal post-Union paradigm, and yet her text can converge with a quite radical form of engagement also.[33] She fitted in with many other writers of post-Union Ireland in that she inherited a certain unease about her relationship to the country, which was rendered all the more prob-

---

32 Plumptre, *Narrative*, pp. 310–2.   **33** Nicola Watson's assessment of Helen Maria Williams provides an interesting gloss to Plumptre: 'Later friends included Anne Plumptre, Amelia Opie, the Wordsworths, and Lady Sydney Morgan, all known for their "Jacobinical" opinions at one time or another', in Watson, *Revolution and the Form of the British Novel, 1790–1825* (Oxford, 1994), p. 29.

lematic in her case because of her natural sympathies with revolutionary politics. Above all else, though, the act of writing seemed a very affirmation of self for Anne Plumptre: a means of self-validation in the normal manner of things, but a gesture of revolutionary, specifically feminist, activity also. Aligning herself with a series of complex and frequently incompatible discourses, her writing showed a remarkably dense philosophical and literary inheritance, even if like Von Kotzebue, the dramatist who inspired her to a period of intense intellectual activity at the beginning of the nineteenth century, she has slipped quietly from our view.[34]

34 The institutional amnesia concerning Plumptre is all the more unjust when we consider that the originally unpublished tour-notes by Plumptre's brother, James Plumptre, written in the 1790s when he was travelling around Britain, were recently published. See James Plumptre, *The Journals of a Tourist in the 1790s*, edited by Ian Ousby (London, 1992).

Women's Travel Writing in Mid-Nineteenth Century Ireland

JOHN MCAULIFFE

In the 1840s, travel writing about Ireland proliferated. Its mostly English audience showed an increased interest in charismatic leaders like Fr Theobald Mathew and Daniel O'Connell, in Ireland's social problems, its attractions as a tourist destination, and the effectiveness of British government there. Obviously, English travellers approached Ireland from the point of view of colonial power, and, predictably, Edward Said's definition of such writing as 'that which disregards, essentialises, denudes the humanity of another culture' does apply.[1] But, since Said's ground-breaking, discipline-forming work appeared, a number of writers have granted colonial discourse a complexity which he had appeared to disallow.[2] Recently, Mary Louise Pratt and, particularly, Sara Mills, have written instructively of how women work with the traditionally colonial discourse of travel writing.[3]

The problem, a fruitful one, as they see it, lies in the difficulty women had in assuming the position of their male peers as masterful judges of their subject, given that Victorian England expected altogether different 'feminine' characteristics of its women writers. How did women writers respond to the conflicting demands of their audience? Pratt and Mills argue that women often resisted the generalising, demeaning perspectives of their male counterparts, that they took the sting out of the colonial traveller's tale. This essay will consider that argument in relation to three writers: two English, Lady Henrietta Chatterton and Mrs Frederic West, and one American, Asenath Nicholson. A New Yorker, Nicholson provides a useful contrast with the works of the English travel writers and she also consolidates the thesis that women's travel writing can be marked off by certain distinguishing features.

The first published of the three writers under discussion, Henrietta Chatterton wrote novels as well as travel books, which are dominated by an intense and precious religiosity.[4] It is interesting to note that Nicholson read Chatterton's

1 Edward Said, *Orientalism* (New York and Harmondsworth, 1978), p. 157.   2 In *Orientalism*, the traveller's production of the Orient is seen as the ally of official colonial power; it denies the native a voice in its own identity, keeps the Oriental in the object position, always available for evaluative description. For an outline of Said's subsequent thoughts on travel writing, see the introduction to Dennis Porter's *Haunted Journeys* (Princeton, 1991).   3 Mary Louise Pratt, *Imperial Eyes: Travel Writing and Transculturation* (London and New York, 1992) and Sara Mills, *Discourses of Difference: An Analysis of Women's Travel Writing and Colonialism* (1991; London and New York, 1993).   4 Chatterton later followed her husband into Catholicism, which may have prompted the eminent praise of John Henry Cardinal Newman for one of her novels. See George Smith and Sir Sidney Lee, (eds), *Dictionary of National Biography*, iv (London, 1930).

book, *Rambles in the South of Ireland*, while on her own travels. Finding it on her bedside table one night she tells us that it is unusual in that 'it is prettily and candidly written, free from sarcasm on Irish character and Irish manners'.[5] Nicholson then uses Chatterton as a springboard to attack travellers whose attempts to 'give a sentence a lively turn may fix a libel on a people which will be read and believed by many generations'.[6] Chatterton's innocence of this charge, however, is rooted in her inattention to the people who are supposedly her subject. The focus for her religious musings is landscape rather than its inhabitants.

Although comparatively new to travel writing about Ireland this emphasis on landscape is typical of many of her contemporaries. Most critics now recognise this as the later of two forms of nineteenth-century travel writing.[7] The first, which is often called the 'customs and manners' or scientific style, became less popular as the century progressed and is exemplified by travelogues which listed, and suggested improvements for, the country's institutions, use of mineral resources and agricultural methods. This project, tied up with colonial profit-making, was obviously underwritten by its subject's purported inferiority. As we will see, women travellers had difficulties adopting this perspective, but by the 1840s a different style of writing was in vogue. Scientific travel writing was replaced by, or mixed in with, what is generally called sentimental travel writing. This form of topographical writing was heavily influenced by ideas of the sublime and the picturesque, as popularised by the painters Salvatore Rosa and Claude Lorraine and by the Romantic poets.

At first, this kind of travel writing took Alpine scenery, especially, as its subject but the Napoleonic Wars quickly forced English tourists back from the Continent.[8] Travel writers soon found some compensation in their newly accessible sister island; travel books of the time are packed with exhortations to the tourist to look for the sublime closer to home.[9] Chatterton's *Rambles in the South of Ireland* takes this kind of writing to an extreme.[10]

What is most striking on first reading the *Rambles* is its excessive attention to landscape (and not the impartiality that Nicholson noted). Chatterton frequently depicts set-piece landscapes in painterly terms so that they are often 'highly varnished' or look 'freshly finished'. Like many of her peers, she has no time for artificial refinements. She divines only the Divine in Ireland's wild sublimity. Parallel to her landscape writing is her enthusiasm for Ireland's equally empty

5 Asenath Nicholson, *Ireland's Welcome to the Stranger, or an excursion through Ireland in the years 1844 and 1845 for the purpose of personally investigating the condition of the poor* (London, 1847), p. 333.   **6** Ibid.   **7** See Pratt, *Imperial Eyes*, p. 5, and Barbara Maria Stafford, *Voyage into Substance: Art, Science and the Illustrated Travel Account* (London and Cambridge, Massachusetts, 1984), p. 442.   **8** See the anthology *Strangers to that Land*, edited by Andrew Hadfield and John McVeigh (Gerrards Cross, 1994).   **9** Colleen Dube's *Enabling Institutions and Disabling Illustrations: Images of Connemara in Tourist Handbooks, 1850–1880* (unpublished thesis, University College Galway, 1994) shows the close links between tourism development and newly available modes of transport.   **10** Henrietta Chatterton, *Rambles in the South of Ireland* (London, 1839).

ocean and cloud scenery. Such thinking transforms Ireland into an uninhabited landscape, nature without culture, and strips or denudes the landscape of local and historical associations. Chatterton's 'libel' thus fixes her subject as an edenic magnet for the tourist and a land of undeveloped potential for the entrepreneur.

The Irish ruin, for Chatterton, is more likely to prompt thoughts of the author's own mortality than the processes which caused it. An incident from Mrs West's tour also exemplifies this outlook. When Mrs West's Kerry guide mentions Cromwell's campaign, she tells him that her own family's estate had fallen under his power. A curious alliance ensues and they curse the 'iron-hearted villain' together. In the next sentence, our attention is drawn to 'the sunbeams slanted down on Ross Castle, in one rich stream of golden light'. The guide recedes as West writes: 'I could not take my eyes off the picture.'[11] Chatterton is even more effusive when she declares her love for Nature. At dinner one night, she amuses her hosts when she drops her knife and fork, rushing from table to window to exclaim at the moon's brilliance. This sensibility which she displays is different to the simple colonial discriminations of 'scientific' travel writers but is equally removed from treating Ireland on its own terms.

Chatterton's work is, moreover, as much a product of the discourse of femininity as the discourse of colonialism. Her book about France and Spain presents the same obsession with Nature and national characteristics. Throughout both books, she avoids political and public issues. This general avoidance is commented upon by Nicholson who, again more self-conscious about her position, observes as she criticises the lack of hospitality shown to her at Derrynane, O'Connell's residence: 'hush! a woman must walk softly on political pavements'.[12]

Returning to the dining room for a moment, we see Chatterton at her favourite vantage point. At every turn of the road, at each new destination, Chatterton observes and sketches Nature and people from a room with a view. This concrete example of the importance of feminine reticence keeps even the traveller within the sphere of the domestic. Women of Chatterton's social class were rarely positively presented outside of certain narrowly ascribed roles, and women travellers faced corresponding typecasting. Mary Louise Pratt notes that in 1828, *Blackwood's Magazine* listed 'romantic female' as a type of travel writer, 'whose eyes are confined to a half-dozen drawing rooms and who sees everything through the medium of poetical fiction'.[13] The line thus drawn between acceptable male and female behaviour sets definite limits for women travellers.

Certainly, survival literature and navigational narratives, forms in which travel writing has its roots, contained no precedent for women travellers. Involving arduous journeys over hills whose heads touched heaven, and escapes from kidnapping slavers whose heads grew below their shoulders, these forerunners of travel writing set a number of ideas in the mind of the reading public. One such preconception was that the traveller's assertions must be subjected to incredulous and sceptical questioning. By the nineteenth century, this fantastic travel writing was less popular, but the woman traveller's credibility was still an issue. What audience could take seriously, or approve, a woman's claim to have made her way through O'Connell's Ireland unscathed? In response to such questioning, women's texts, as we shall see, developed distinct features. Mills and Pratt argue that one of the motivating forces behind the travel narrative's structure is the desire to convince its reader of its veracity.[14] Hence the first-person diary which all three writers use convinces the reader that the writing is rooted in the time and place it describes.

Women travellers also accord prominence to those who accompany them. Chatterton travels in a party, West with her husband. Significantly, West brings her husband to the fore when in difficulty: when they need food in Castleisland, when they go riding in south Kerry, and when they attend a Young Ireland meeting in Dublin. She also reports that she could not see Killary, or sketch a certain tower, because her husband insisted they make the most of their short trip and travel elsewhere. In stark contrast to this are the more famous tours of Thackeray and Henry Inglis.[15] Thackeray does not once mention his Irish wife's presence on the early stage of his journey, while Inglis' declaration in the final chapter that his wife had been ill in the middle of their tour is the first indication that she accompanied him.[16]

All three female writers determinedly assert their ill-health. Both of the English women suffered from neurasthenia and all three overexert themselves at some stage of their journey. It becomes almost a rite to restore the faith of contemporary audiences in their credibility. An incident from West's tour illustrates this point. In Limerick, West and her husband are taken by a guide 'through the filthiest alleys' to climb the Cathedral's bell-tower.[17] On a windy day her descent proves awkward:

> It is not always *facilus descensis* as of a surety I discovered, with a brain spinning round, encumbered with a weighty sketchbook. However, I reached *terra firma* at last, although the stiffness produced by this cramping of my whole person in my fright down those unusually steep stairs was such, I could not walk for three days without pain or flinching and suppressed ohs and ahs . . .[18]

This emphasis on the person and the personal is typical, but when West continues, 'It was thoroughly provoking to be baulked of my bird's-eye view, and lamed at once', a broader inference is possible. The bird's-eye view or monarch-of-all-I-survey scene is a commonplace of colonial travel writing, where the 'physical act of describing the landscape also masters it'.[19] West pictures herself as unfit for

---

14 Ibid., pp. 24, 113. **15** Thackeray, *The Irish Sketchbook* (London, 1843) and Henry Inglis, *A Journey throughout Ireland* (3rd ed., London, 1835). **16** Asenath Nicholson's frequent vaunting of her own independence shows how strong the prejudice was against unaccompanied women travellers. **17** West, *A Summer Visit*, p. 148. **18** Ibid., p. 150. **19** Mills, *Discourses of Difference*, p. 78.

that task in Limerick.[20] But, with some difficulty and a little help from others, she is able to muddle through, in her own way. Like Chatterton, she thereby conforms to an acceptable type without assuming the powerful, all-seeing role so common in the travel books of her male compatriots.

Illness served another purpose, and, in the forms of depression and neurasthenia, provided an original excuse for women to make their trips abroad. Male tourists, in contrast, felt no need to excuse their travels. Shaftesbury, Hume and Hutcheson had debated the value of travel in the early eighteenth century, but it was soon seen as part of a gentleman's education. More importantly, such debates constructed another image of the travel writer, that of a scientist in pursuit of knowledge. This travel writer's authority rests on his status as urbane, enlightened outsider seeing through the fog of local prejudice. He stays out of the frame in order to give the reader a clearer picture.

But, as we have seen above, women restore their credibility by introducing their physical presence into the text. Simultaneously, they undermine their own authority as commentators on Irish society. The pressure to present themselves in a favourably feminine light discouraged scientific generalisations *and* personal contact with their subject. A closer examination of Mrs West's 1845 tour shows how this 'catch-22' contradicts audience expectations of colonial travel writing.

West, unlike Chatterton, is more interested in antiquarianism than sightseeing. She writes that her first reason for visiting Ireland was to see the round towers. Here again the prerogatives of femininity control how she writes about her subject. Antiquarianism, for most travel-writers, is the scientific equivalent of Chatterton's depictions of the play of light and shade on a ruined castle. Examining Ireland's ruins, antiquarian travellers generally speculated on the possible origins of the Irish race, often separating the ruin from its culture. On West's arrival, the debate was centred on the purpose of the round towers. Other travellers conjectured wildly on their use. But West only quotes authorities, 'abler heads than mine', before adding her 'humble belief in their eastern and pagan origin' and referring the reader to the RIA's proceedings.[21] She also includes them in her engravings of picturesque landscapes, but her unease with the scientific discourse of her contemporaries is obvious. On the same theme, Nicholson writes, after overhearing two passengers on her stage coach discuss astronomy: 'So sorry was I when the lecture ended that had it not been presuming for a woman to know that the moon is not a pot of curds and cream, I should have proposed a question or two.'[22]

The narrow range of interests expected of them forces these writers to approach traditional subjects differently. The Irish economy is presented as more

20 West has less difficulty in conventionally picturesque spots like Killarney and Glendalough.   **21** West, *A Summer Visit*, p. 19.   **22** Nicholson, *Ireland's Welcome*, p. 230. On the antiquarian perspective on Ireland, Nicholson is more cutting: 'Had the object of my visit to Ireland been to have rummaged castles and abbeys, old graveyards and bridges, for antiquities to spread before the public, the public (to say the least) must have said: "We have caught nothing."'

than the price of potatoes and a day's work. Women travel writers, present in the text, discuss the prices they pay for travel, guides, accommodation and food. This transfer of emphasis is also evident in West's sole encounter with Irish politics. She mentions in passing that she and her husband were turned away from the door of a Young Ireland meeting. West draws our attention to a fellow outcast. She writes: 'He says, "well it won't be on account of appearance they refused you", looking at my own small individuality.'[23]

This turn away from explicit political comment is echoed in Asenath Nicholson's *Ireland's Welcome to the Stranger*. On the evening of O'Connell's release she abandons a rowdy Clonmel to tour the local area's attractions. On her way she loses her spectacles and is forced to stumble back to her noisy inn's lodgings. Nicholson, for all her independence, did not see fit to take an active interest in the political developments taking place around her. She regrets this early on her travels:

> When leaving New York, a friend said to me, 'Give us all the information you can, but don't touch politics. That is miserable work for a woman.' But I soon found in Ireland that it was a great misfortune that I had not acquainted myself more with at least the technicals of the different parties; many egregious blunders might have been saved.[24]

Nicholson is silent on her allegiance to political parties, yet she never fails to speak out strongly for the Irish poor. Her relation to them is far more intimate than West's and Chatterton's. The English writers do not look farther than their guides and although West, in particular, presents these men as more than types, they are still removed from the context of the Irish poor, who are mostly pictured as parts of the quaint scenery, a fate worse than the awful brogues which most writers inflicted on their guides. The anthropologist, Johannes Fabien has coined the phrase 'denial of coevalness' to describe such a perspective.[25] Nicholson is exceptional in avoiding it.

She uses her American background to enter Irish society at a level untested by English travellers. Her American accent makes her welcome where her Douay Testaments do not. Accordingly, her subject is the people, not the landscape. On this rare occasion, the Irish are shown as a working people, compatible members of society, contemporaries of the author. In Kilkenny, she visits the families of her New York servant girls. In a Cork convent, she talks American politics. She meets a child whose parents tell her he has been baptised Yankee Doodle. Most of the cabins she stays in have people in America. Some of the labourers she meets 'know and abhor American slavery'. Another man tells her: 'I passed three pleasant years in New York and left it with great reluctance. I am quite attached to its customs and people in many respects especially their hospitality to strangers and their politeness to females.'[26] Fabien's denial of coevalness is inapplicable to this

---

23 West, *A Summer Visit*, p. 189.   **24** Nicholson, *Ireland's Welcome*, pp. 63–4.   **25** Johannes Fabien, *Time and the Work of Anthropology* (Chur, 1991).   **26** Nicholson, *Ireland's Welcome*,

kind of writing. The contrast between Nicholson's and any other English travel writer's depiction of the Irish is stark.

All three writers possess a self-awareness which is most clearly present in Nicholson's text. Parts of her account are dominated by her acute awareness of the undue attention accorded her by the local people. This unaccompanied woman, with her spectacles, exotic clothes, strange luggage paraphernalia and vegetarian diet, was plagued by inquisitive locals. To a lesser degree, Chatterton and West note the same problem. Chatterton writes of the country people staring at her party's zealous sketching. West writes: 'the men watch the unwonted passing of our carriage till we were out of sight'.[27] Nicholson, on the other hand, is outspoken about the supposed novelty of women travel writers.

In a curious role reversal, the unaccompanied Nicholson becomes the object of the locals' gaze. In the same way as representations of the Irish as types place them in a powerless position, Nicholson is cast in one of two marginal roles. The poor cast her as a penitent and saint. She writes: 'The notices made of me in their papers brought me before the public so prominently that I begged them to desist. I had wished to go through Ireland as unobservedly as possible, asking no honorary attentions.'[28]

The other role in which she was cast is less favourable and more persistent. The *Achill Herald* reported that 'the singular course which she pursues is utterly at variance with the modesty and retiredness to which the Bible gives a prominent place in its delineation of a virtuous female ... (she must be) the emissary of some democratic and revolutionary society'.[29] Nicholson closes her brilliant book with another lament for the travesties of religion which wield so much power over the Irish before forecasting that before their heart-rending misery ends, 'there must be an explosion of some kind or other'.[30] She attempted to speak outside, or against, the discourses of colonialism and femininity which dominated the works of her contemporaries. Subsequent notice of her work concentrated on casting her in the role of an eccentric whose views are more amusing than worthwhile. Thus the editor of the 1927 abridgement remarks, 'it is not difficult to smile at the vagaries of this early Victorian woman.'[31]

Again, these notices were coloured by preconceptions about women's abilities or lack of them: what has been referred to as the discourse of femininity. West and Chatterton, faced with a different set of preconceptions, produced deviations from typically colonial travel writing about Ireland, but did not even aspire to the plain talking of Nicholson. Constrained by gender and nationality, their approach

pp. 98 and 53.   **27** West, *A Summer Visit*, p. 48.   **28** Nicholson, *Ireland's Welcome*, p. 235.   **29** Quoted in Nicholson, *Ireland's Welcome*, pp. 437–8.   **30** Ibid., p. 442. **31** Nicholson, unlike the English writers, is still, barely, visible to the reader of Irish literature. One of Brendan Kennelly's most anthologised poems, 'My Dark Fathers', takes a line from her as its epigraph, and in the recent Field Day Anthology, excerpts from her 1850 work, *Lights and Shades of Ireland*, are included. See also Margaret Kelleher, 'The Female Gaze: Asenath Nicholson's Famine Narrative' in Chris Morash and Richard Hayes (eds), *'Fearful Realities': New Perspectives on the Famine* (Dublin, 1996), pp. 119–30.

to traditional subjects is hesitant and unreliable; drawing back from a generalising, essentialising tone, they wrote books which still retain a degree of individual flavour. The three writers asserted that they were trying to change their audiences' minds about Ireland, but Nicholson alone does not conjure up an Ireland of waterfalls and charming simply-dressed guides as an alternative to savage wildness. She is most conscious of the positions a travel writer may take, and of the consequence of her own writing. As a result, Nicholson successfully shows her subject at a level which was beyond the ken of Chatterton, West and their compatriots.

Isabella Croke: A Nurse for the Catholic Cause during the Crimean War

MARY ELLEN DOONA

Dedicated to the memory of Sister M. Albeus (Nora Russell 1910–95) who made available the Croke Diary and who now lies beside Sister M. Joseph (Isabella Croke) in the Charleville Convent graveyard.

Fully confident of its essential place in modern health care, nursing has turned to the past in search of its founders. The focus of this article is Isabella Croke and the diary that she kept during her stint of nursing in the Crimean War (1854–56).[1] Croke's diary transforms the nature of the evidence upon which the history of Crimean War nursing is based and throws new light on gender issues in nineteenth-century Ireland.

Background

Isabella Croke (1825–1888) had been a Sister of Mercy for seven years when the Crimean War (1854–1856) began. She entered the convent in Charleville, County Cork in 1847 at the height of the Great Famine, which reduced the population of her town from 4,472 in 1845 to 2,862 in 1850. Among its victims was Croke's twenty-eight year old brother, the Reverend William Croke, who picked up a fever while caring for his famine-stricken parishioners.[2]

Death was very much a part of Croke's life. Her father William Croke had died when she was nine years old, leaving his wife and eight children in Dromin, Castlecor, Co. Cork in desperate straits. His widow Isabelle (Plummer) Croke was an Anglo-Irish Protestant and a descendant of the Fitzgerald Knights of Glin in Limerick. She had been alienated from her family when she married William Croke, a Catholic from Tralee, Co. Kerry. Nor did their attitude change when he died seventeen years into their marriage.[3] Indeed, had they not been rescued after his death by his brother, the Reverend Thomas Croke, William's wife and family might have fallen into the poverty which was such a feature of nineteenth-century Ireland. Instead, Thomas Croke settled the family in Charleville, Co. Cork, where he was parish priest. The older boys lived with their uncle in his house and the girls and younger boys lived with their mother in a house on the Limerick Road

1 Sr M. Joseph Croke, *Diary of Sister M. Joseph Croke*, Catherine McAuley Museum Archive, Charleville, Co. Cork.   2 Mark Tierney, *Croke of Cashel: The Life of Archbishop Thomas William Croke, 1823–1902* (Cork, 1964).   3 Ibid.

around the corner from the Catholic Church. This arrangement reflected more than convenience, for in mixed marriages like the Croke's, boys were often raised in the religion of their father and girls in that of their mother.

Three of the boys became priests: William served in Charleville until he died during the famine, James served in the foreign missions in California and Oregon in the United States, and Thomas, named after his uncle, became Archbishop of Cashel. The two girls converted to Catholicism and entered the Sisters of Mercy convent in Charleville.

Their uncle, Thomas Croke, had persuaded Catherine McAuley to establish her Sisters of Mercy in Charleville. McAuley and four of her nuns arrived there on 29 October 1836, when Isabella was nine. In December 1838 McAuley returned again for the laying of the cornerstone for a purpose-built convent in Charleville's main street.[4] Little is known of Isabella's life, and much of that is known only through her brothers' biographies. So it is a matter of conjecture as to whether she attended the school which the Sisters of Mercy established in Charleville. There can be no doubt, however, that she was aware of their work as teachers and carers for the sick in the locality. Perhaps the most significant public event which Isabella may have witnessed as she grew up occurred in May 1845 when Daniel O'Connell spoke at a Monster Meeting in Charleville. Afterwards he dined with Isabella's uncle and the town's leading men.

Isabella Croke becomes Sister Mary Joseph Croke in 1847

In 1847, at the age of twenty-two, Isabella Croke became one of the hundreds of women who were to enter a convent in nineteenth-century Ireland. She became a Sister of Mercy, serving under a religious superior and being guided by the principle that 'the act of one was the act of all'.[5] As Sydney Woollett, Isabella Croke's Jesuit chaplain in the Crimea, said, 'In religion you become part of a body, no self-seeking allowed there, mind that.'[6] If ever Isabella chafed at having to submerge her own will for the good of a common mission, she had only to remember the words of Mother McAuley that the superior symbolised Christ, and when she obeyed that superior she was, in spirit, following Christ.[7]

Yet for all their organisation and internal self-determination the Sisters of Mercy were not autonomous and had to take account of the wishes of the clergy. Of all those who took vows in the Church priests, brothers, monks and nuns, nuns were in many respects the least powerful.[8] If Isabella did not have much

4 Mary Teresa Austin Carroll, 'Foundation at Charleville' in *Leaves from the Annals of the Sisters of Mercy* (4 vols; New York, 1881–1895), i, p. 148.   5 Catriona Clear, *Nuns in Nineteenth-Century Ireland* (Dublin, 1978), pp. 34–5.   6 Sydney Woollett, 'Obituary', Crimean War Papers, Archives of English Province of the Society of Jesus, London. 7 [No Author] *Rules: Familiar Instructions of Rev. Mother McAuley* (St Louis, 1927), p. 41. 8 See Clear, *Nuns in Nineteenth-Century Ireland.*

independent power as a Sister of Mercy she gained both prestige and the opportunity to use her talents for the good of others when she became Sister M. Joseph Croke. Indeed, other women, among them Florence Nightingale, envied convent careers and women's useful place in the Roman Catholic Church. The Church of England, noted Florence Nightingale, gave her neither work to do, nor education for it.[9]

As Isabella made the transition into Sister M. Joseph Croke, she walked in the steps of her foundress Catherine McAuley and all the Sisters of Mercy who had preceded her. She visited the sick. She instructed the ignorant. She helped the poor. She raised the status of women: educating them and teaching them skills by which they could become self-sufficient. As the famine spread, Croke and her sisters in Charleville, as indeed Sisters of Mercy throughout Ireland, fed the starving, nursed the sick in the fever hospital, prayed with them and prepared many for death. There was not much that could be done for the sufferer as typhus, typhoid fever, relapsing fever and scurvy overwhelmed their wasted bodies. This experience provided the young nun with a nursing education, honing skills that in 1854 propelled her into political prominence.

Even as the famine prepared Croke for nursing during the Crimean War, it sharpened in her a healthy scepticism of British policy. The thinking that rationalised famine deaths as divine providence, the retribution of a just God against Irish popery, came from the same cast of mind that a few years later permitted British soldiers to perish in the pestilential hospitals in the East. Many of them were Irish boys and men who had joined the army only to die of the same diseases that had claimed their country men, women and children at home.

'There are no nurses'

The first battle of the Crimean War in September 1854 found the British unprepared to care for the wounded and the sick. War correspondent William Russell asked, 'Can it be said that the Battle of Alma has been an event to take the world by surprise?' His demand for answers grew: 'Has not the expedition to the Crimea been the talk of the last four months? ... And yet, after the troops have been six months in the country, there is no preparation for the commonest surgical operations!' As a result, he informed his London *Times* readers,

> Not only are the men kept, in some cases, for a week without the hand of a medical man coming near their wounds; not only are they left to expire in agony, unheeded and shaken off, though catching desperately at the surgeon whenever he makes his rounds through the fetid ship, but now, when they are placed in this spacious building [the Barrack Hospital at Scutari] where we

9 Florence Nightingale to Edward Manning in C. Woodham-Smith, *Florence Nightingale* (London, 1954), p. 98.

were led to believe that every thing was ready which could ease their pain or facilitate their recovery, it is found that the commonest appliances of a British workhouse are wanting.

There were no nurses to care for the men when they arrived in Constantinople from the Crimea,

> without having been touched by a surgeon since they fell, pierced by Russian bullets, on the slopes of Alma. The ship was literally covered with prostrate forms ... The worst cases were placed on the upper deck, which, in a day or two, became a mass of putridity. The neglected gunshot wounds ... the putrid animal matter ... the stench ... [the] misery ... The men attend to each other or receive no relief at all ... The sick appeared to be attended by the sick, the dying by the dying.[10]

Russell's frequent dispatches to the *Times* were read by a shocked public and his columns were flanked by the names of the dead and wounded. Never before had the civilian population of Britain known war with this immediacy, and never before had so many British soldiers perished as a result of injury, disease and lack of organisation. As a result, demand grew for a nursing service for British soldiers to compare with that provided for French soldiers by the Sisters of Charity.

If Russell, the Irish-born war correspondent, had changed the way war was reported, his dispatches also effectively inaugurated female military nursing in the British army. Competent nurses, not Sairey Gamps[11] nor the do-gooding Ladies Bountiful, were needed, it was argued. The War Office turned to the Anglican Sisters of St John's and the Sellonites but they were too few in number to meet the demand and silence the public uproar. At this point, Florence Nightingale offered her services as a 'real hospital nurse'. She was not, of course, but she was trying to distinguish herself form the Ladies Bountiful. She knew a lot *about* nursing, but had little – almost no – experience *in* nursing. As most women did, she had cared for family members. She had observed at the Kaiserweth Deaconness Institution in Germany for three weeks and returned for a three month stint of direct work, but found that 'the nursing there was nil'.[12] Then for just over a year, she had administered the Harley Street home for gentlewomen in distress. This 'hospital nurse' took charge of the nursing experiment with its contingent of nurses, nuns, both Anglican and Catholic, and civilians – forty people in all. Soon after the party had arrived in Constantinople, Florence Nightingale claimed that 'about ten of us have done *the whole work*. The others have only run between our feet and hindered us'.[13] The Battle of Inkermann on

---

10 *Times*, 12 and 13 October 1854.   **11** Charles Dickens, *Martin Chuzzlewit* (1844). **12** Woodham-Smith, *Florence Nightingale*, p. 91.   **13** Florence Nightingale to Sidney Herbert, 10 December 1854, in S. Goldie (ed.), *'I Have Done My Duty': Florence Nightingale in the Crimean War, 1854–56* (Iowa, 1987), p. 47.

5 November 1854 had brought shiploads of sick and wounded to the hospitals, filling them to overflowing with more than three thousand men. It was evident though that the need for nursing care far outran the capacity of Nightingale and her colleagues to supply it. The War Office then turned to the Irish Roman Catholic Church and to the Sisters of Mercy.

Service to the Catholic cause

The superior at the Mercy Convent at Baggot Street, Dublin, responded to the appeal for nurses. She wrote to her brother, Monsignor Robert Whitty, the Vicar General at Westminster in London, offering her nuns as skilled nurses, who could speak the Irish language and sympathise with the habits and feelings of the Irish soldiers.[14] 'Attendance on the sick,' wrote Sister Vincent Whitty, 'is … part of our Institute; and sad experience among the poor has convinced us that … many lives are lost for want of careful nursing.'[15] The offer was keenly supported by clergy in Dublin and London as being for the good of the 'Catholic cause'. For the newly-resurgent Catholic Church in Britain, in particular, it was an opportunity to demonstrate that Catholicism was compatible with patriotism.

If the dilemmas of the British Government and the Catholic hierarchy propelled the nuns into prominence, it was a position of prestige which was full of danger. Indeed two nuns would die in the Crimea, one of cholera, the other of typhus. Several others nearly lost their lives from infections they contracted while caring for their patients. Croke herself almost died from Crimean fever, the same typhus that had claimed her brother, the Reverend William Croke, though then it had been called 'famine fever'.

By means of skilful planning the Irish Sisters of Mercy who went to nurse the soldiers kept themselves as a distinct organisation, under the leadership of Mother Francis Bridgeman of Kinsale, County Cork. First the Irish Sisters of Mercy signed a contract with the War Office that established them as a separate unit. They agreed to provide corporal care to all soldiers but spiritual care only to Catholic soldiers. However, they insisted that their group have its own chaplain. The continuing public outcry about the conditions of the soldiers made the War Office amenable to such a demand. Their contract gave the Sisters a good deal of freedom for their sixteen months as military nurses. It was a freedom of which they took full advantage.

Croke and her fourteen fellow Sisters of Mercy knew 'the eyes of the whole world would be on the poor nuns'.[16] But nothing could have prepared them for

---

14 Sister M. Vincent Whitty to 'My dear Reverend Mother', 20 October 1854 in Carroll, *Leaves from the Annals*, i, p. 144.   **15** Sister M. Vincent Whitty to Monsignor Robert Whitty, 18 October 1854, Crimean Papers, Mercy International Archives, Dublin. **16** Sister M. Vincent Whitty to 'My dear Reverend Mother', 20 October 1854 in Carroll, *Leaves from the Annals*, i, p. 144.

the reception they received on 17 December 1854 when they arrived at Constantinople.[17] Grateful for surviving the rough sea voyage and eager to be at work, Croke and her sisters were taken aback when Florence Nightingale sent word to their ship that they were 'not wanted'. What is more, she had no room for them. Then she said, 'The Sisters are assigned ... to the Inspector General, not to me.'[18] This effectively released the nuns from their contract to serve under her in matters of nursing. However, once their chaplain, the Jesuit William Ronan from Gardiner Street in Dublin, confronted Florence Nightingale, 'things were much better' and there was plenty of work for the nuns.[19] Within a few weeks, Croke and nine of her fellow Sisters of Mercy were working independently of Florence Nightingale and successfully implementing the McAuley system of organised nursing at the Koulali Hospitals which were under the sponsorship of Lady Stratford de Redcliffe, the wife of the British ambassador to Constantinople.

The remaining five nuns worked at the Scutari Hospital with Florence Nightingale's group. She had made room for them by sending five nuns in her party back to England, thus keeping constant the numbers of Protestant and Catholics. At first she assigned them to the kitchen and linen room to prevent them from 'intriguing' for their church, but a fresh outbreak of cholera soon ensured that these experienced nurses were called on to tend to the sick and wounded.

'One mind appears to move all'

Confident about the success of their nursing, Croke and her sisters became concerned about accusations that they were proselytising Protestants. When they were accused of proselytising, they demanded an open and fair hearing and proof of the charge. This had a way of silencing the uproar, but only until the next accusation was made. When pressed for details one woman retracted her accusations that the nuns had distributed Catholic pamphlets to Protestant soldiers. The matter seemed resolved but flared up again when this same woman took her charges to other more sympathetic listeners.

The 'Protestant howl and the Roman Catholic storm' got so vehement at the Koulali Hospitals that it was decided to organise the wards along religious lines, separating Catholic patients and Catholic nurses from Protestant patients and Protestant nurses, though this worried some Protestant patients. 'I care not for creed or difference of opinion', one patient told Croke's nuns, 'To me, you are all angels of mercy.'[20] Though often done with difficulty, Croke kept nursing in

---

17 Contemporary accounts and Croke's diary give this date for their arrival at Constantinople while works about Florence Nightingale state 15 December 1854.   **18** M. Francis Bridgeman, *An Account of the Missions of the Sisters of Mercy in the Military Hospitals of the East, Beginning December 1854 and Ending in May 1856*, Archives of the Sisters of Mercy, Silverspring, Maryland.   **19** William Ronan to 'My dear Reverend Sir', 22 January 1855, Cullen Papers, Dublin Diocesan archives.   **20** Carroll, *Leaves from the Annals*, ii, p. 173. By this time two nuns had returned home and one had died.

perspective. Mindful of her patients' need for the restorative powers of sleep, Croke sought to silence 'a *pious* orderly' who read 'at the very top of his voice a chapter of the Bible for the good of the would-be sleeping patients'. She begged he would do her the 'pleasure of closing his mouth if not his book'.[21] On another occasion Croke was at the receiving end of the confrontation about religion. She became involved in a dispute with one of the Protestant clergy about dispensing Catholic booklets. But she and he were able to resolve the matter. She was eager not to offend the man because she and her sisters 'like[d] the minister very much [because] he is straight forward and acts on principle'.[22]

An atmosphere of smoothing differences and arriving at new understandings was even more to the fore at Balaklava in the Crimea itself. When the work at the Koulali hospitals became 'slack' the hospital was given to the allied Sardinian troops. At this point the nuns offered their services for the hospitals at Balaklava which were still filled with patients. The British military leadership went out of its way to be amenable to the Catholics. For example, the senior officers invited the English Jesuit Sydney Woollett to dine with them. During these dinners, Woollett answered their questions about the Society of Jesus. Such discussion tended to correct some of the misinformation about the Jesuits that the officers had gained from reading contemporary novels. Out of such interchange came an increased tolerance for Catholics and regard for their sensibilities. The officers also acknowledged how offensive it could be to Catholic soldiers to be read the Bible and Protestant tracts by the Protestant clergy. And they stopped soldiers from burning the pope in effigy on bonfire night, 5 November 1855. The disparities in salaries, however, with the Protestant clergy earning twice that of the Catholic clergy, remained unchanged.[23]

Woollett paved the way for Croke and her sisters who arrived from Koulali to take charge of the Balaklava Hospitals. There were few obstructions to their access to patients. One of the doctors, in admonishing Croke, acknowledged how her nursing care softened the harshness of military practice. 'Sister,' he said, 'you must not listen to the patients when they ask you for any thing. It will be impossible to get them out of the Hospital, they will be so petted.' Croke countered, saying that Sisters of Mercy always listened to their patients.[24] Indeed, sickened by the cries she heard from an orderly being flogged she appealed for one of her patients, a prisoner scheduled for flogging, and was 'kindly answered'.[25]

Irritated by their success, Florence Nightingale, 'the sweet songstress' as Croke ironically referred to her, tried to undermine the growing reputation of Croke and her sisters. She, too, used the religious issue, saying Croke and her sisters were teaching Catholic doctrine to Protestant patients. But her claims were found to be just as unreliable here as they had previously been in Constantinople. Next she railed against the expense of the nuns' system of care, though a governmental

21 Croke, *Diary*, pp. 62–3.   **22** Ibid., p. 92.   **23** Sydney Wollett, *Crimean War Diary*, English Jesuit Archives, London.   **24** Croke, *Diary*, p. 73.   **25** Ibid., p. 114.

study was to find against that charge as well. In fact the twelve nuns were fifty per cent less costly than the seven nurses who had preceded them. Moreover, the study concluded:

> The superiority of an ordered system [of nursing] is beautifully illustrated in the 'Sisters of Mercy', – one mind appears to move all; – and their intelligence, delicacy, and conscientiousness, invest them with a halo of confidence extreme [*sic*]; the Medical Officer can safely consign his most critical cases into their hands; – stimulants or opiates – ordered every five minutes, will be faithfully administered, though the five minutes labour were repeated uninterruptedly for a week. The number of Sisters, without being large, is sufficient to secure for every patient needing it, their share of attendance; a calm resigned contentedness sits [on] the features of all – and the soft care of the female and the Lady breathes placidity throughout.[26]

Among the more remarkable features of the work of the Irish nuns was their continuing of care for their patients throughout the night. Fearful for her nurses' moral protection, Florence Nightingale would not allow nurses to be on the wards after 8.30 p.m. Croke and her sisters, however, made their rounds throughout the night 'up and down the wards every half hour with [their] little lamps'.[27] What is more, Croke and her sisters were on their own as they tended to the soldiers in the hospital huts spread over the Balaklava hills.

One of the first things the nuns did on taking over the hospital at Balaklava was to relieve the hospital orderlies of the job of giving out wine and brandy. This reduced the drinking among the orderlies and ensured that those most in need of it received the alcohol and felt its numbing effects. Croke reported that the orderlies were 'not at all pleased at the prospect of being soon deprived of their happiness of giving "spiritual consolation" to their patients'.[28]

The Sisters of Mercy depended on their Jesuit chaplains – William Ronan in Constantinople and Sydney Woollett in the Crimea – to speak for them with the military officials and to conduct religious rituals. Often their paths crossed those of the chaplains who were also on the hospital wards hearing confessions and praying with those near death. Although Croke and her sisters tended to the spiritual needs of their patients as did the Jesuits, there was no sharing of power with the chaplains. The nuns depended, too, on the female network of support they had created with and for one another as they continued their convent careers while in the East. Daily Mass and meditations, enhanced by periodic spiritual retreats, continued the usual routines of convent life, while evening recreations provided respite from work on the hospital wards. But neither the oversight of the Jesuits nor the nuns' caring for one another eliminated the anxieties Croke and her sisters experienced. They were within a ten-mile march of the battlefront

---

26 'The Confidential Report' in Goldie, *'I Have Done My Duty'*, p. 301.   **27** Croke, *Diary*, p. 41.   **28** Ibid., p. 46.

and the cannon roar was part of the rhythm of each day and night. Croke swore she saw the flash of the cannon but knew her sisters would refute such a claim as the work of an inflamed imagination. During their leisure hour, however, they joined Croke 'amazing [them]selves by going in idea to Siberia as prisoners of war'.[29] The nuns had more to fear from the rats that scampered over them as they slept in their huts than they had from their imagined Russian captors ten miles away. Unknown at the time, these rats spread the Crimean fever (typhus) which had almost carried off Croke herself.

Conclusion

Croke's career as a military nurse came to an end with the signing of the peace treaty on 30 March 1856. Two weeks later she left the Crimea for Ireland, exclaiming in her journal that 'Every heart beat light – Going home! Alive after such scenes! And going home, *alive!*'[30] All in Charleville 'were in the greatest joy' at her return, and for a long time thereafter she entertained her fellow sisters during evening recreations with tales of her 'Eastern Campaign'. Within six years of her return, the bishop of the diocese appointed her the superior for her community, a position she subsequently was elected to for six terms. She was a 'large-minded, generous, warm-hearted Mother' who led her community in the care of Charleville's poor. Towards the end of her last term, after eighteen years of governance, on 7 November 1888, 'calmly, consciously and peacefully' at the age of sixty-three, Croke died in her own bed.[31]

29 Ibid., p. 105.   30 Ibid., p. 138.   31 Annals of Charleville Convent, Catherine McAuley Museum Archives, Charleville, County Cork.

IV

Private and Public: Social and Religious Institutions

'A Lightness of Mind': Gender and Insanity in Nineteenth-Century Ireland

OONAGH WALSH

The Connaught District Lunatic Asylum (CDLA) was opened at Ballinasloe, Co. Galway in 1833, the first public institution for the care of the insane in the west of Ireland. Although the asylum accepted paying patients, at a rate of between £12 and £25 per annum,[1] the majority of the residents were labourers, and skilled and unskilled tradespeople, drawn from the counties of Galway, Roscommon, Sligo, Leitrim and Mayo. The CDLA was originally built to house 150 patients, but within twenty years of its opening had expanded (with very little additional construction) to accommodate more than double that number. Within the asylum, as with all such public institutions, men and women were strictly segregated, occupying initially separate dormitories and cells, and eventually separate wings. In the later nineteenth century, the two sexes were also fed at different times in the asylum refectory, to ensure that boundaries were fully maintained. Transgressions did occur, including a number of elopements, but ironically the first such scandal involved not two patients, but rather the asylum physician and one of his charges.[2] In 1848, he tendered his resignation because he had made a young patient pregnant. Although he had signed a certificate stating that she was recovered from her psychiatric illness the week before the board of governors received his resignation, they refused to release her, and actually referred the case to the government (the asylums were under the direct control of the lord lieutenant). This incident was something of an exception to the normal running of the asylum, however.

When the CDLA began to accept cases, there were two principal means of admitting alleged lunatics to asylums in Ireland. The first, which accounted for a large majority of admissions to Ballinasloe between 1840 and 1860, was through the use of the Dangerous Lunatics Act of 1838, which allowed any two justices of the peace to commit a person 'apprehended under circumstances denoting a Derangement of Mind, and a Purpose of committing some Crime' to prison. From gaol, they were removed to a lunatic asylum by order of the Lord Lieutenant. Although a medical opinion could be sought by the justices, it was not actually required by law. What left the act open to particular abuse was the fact that the justices could act on 'other proof' to make the committal, usually a statement by a third party alleging insane behaviour on the part of the proposed patient. This evidence did not have to be corroborated, and neither did the statement have to

1 Board of Governors Minutes, Connaught District Lunatic Asylum (hereafter CDLA), 2 September 1835. 2 Ibid., 31 March 1848.

be sworn. Strenuous objections were raised to the act, but not necessarily through concern for the lunatics. Rather, the inspectors of gaols complained that lunatics confined in prison on their way to the asylum were having a disruptive effect on the sane prisoners.[3] (In the early years of the act, lunatics were routinely confined in gaols for up to a year after their committal, before being transferred to the district asylums.) When the act was amended in 1867, it did little to protect the alleged lunatics. A medical examination was now required, and evidence provided by the person seeking committal had to be given on oath, but the patient could be sent directly to the asylum, which had no power to refuse cases (apart from lack of space). If a patient was deemed a dangerous lunatic, he or she was automatically confined.

The repercussions of a far-reaching act such as this were felt in Ballinasloe. Admissions rose sharply, with a greater number of relations seeking direct access to the asylum for their charges, and a significant number of workhouses attempting to transfer inmates whom they found disruptive within their own institutions to the asylum. It is from this period onwards that female admissions rise. Although one could interpret this increase as an instance of male authority over women in nineteenth-century Ireland, since it was fathers in the majority of cases who sought the admissions, it does need to be placed against a background of enormous increases in asylum populations generally, both male and female. Also, there is a significant difference in the patterns of male and female histories prior to admission. Women were far more likely to have been kept at home during the initial stages of an illness, and admitted when they became uncontrollably violent. The history provided by the father of a twenty-year-old woman in 1887 was not untypical:

> He states this is the first time for her being insane. The present attack is more violent than any of the former. She is under no restraint, out in the fields, and she says she would sooner commit suicide than to be always suffering. She must be constantly watched and she is violent.[4]

Another married woman, committed two years previously following the death of one of her children, was taken home by her husband, but her condition deteriorated. She was readmitted after relatives and friends feared she was going to harm her remaining children.[5] Male patients on the other hand were more often committed on their first attack, and were less likely to be taken back by families voluntarily, unless they appeared quite cured. Part of the reason for this difference in male and female patterns may be the fact that women were physically easier to control than many men, and families could cope to a greater extent with them, even in periods of violence. In addition, an apparent reluctance to commit women to the asylum may be an indication of their importance to

---

3 Board minutes, CDLA, 18 April 1846.   **4** Form of Admission (hereafter FOA), 3 April 1887.   **5** FOA, 30 March 1867.

the rural domestic and agricultural economy. This pattern, and also a greater degree of reassimilation of women back into the family after discharge from the asylum, was also echoed in England during this period.

This is not to say however that the asylum was not used as a means of disposing of wayward female relations. The board of governors kept a careful check on recently admitted patients, and in 1842 they discharged an eighteen-year-old woman whom they noted in the register was 'Not insane. Admitted in a pregnant state.' Similarly the asylum would often refuse to accept mentally handicapped patients, if they had previously been cared for at home, on the grounds that they were incurable cases.[6] It was less from private citizens however that the asylum received blatantly false applications, but rather other government institutions, particularly the workhouses and gaols, who saw in the expansion of the asylum system a perfect opportunity to rid themselves of long-term or troublesome inmates. In 1867 for example, Tuam workhouse sought the admission of a fifty-year-old woman whom the Matron claimed was insane.[7] The evidence provided was that 'she is restless and constantly crying and wandering about the ward at night attempting to climb the Boundary wall'. This behaviour might more rationally be attributed to an understandable desire to get out of the workhouse, rather than symptoms of insanity, and the asylum refused the case, on the grounds of insufficient room.

The asylum registers cast some interesting light on perceived causes of lunacy amongst men and women in nineteenth-century Ireland. Although it was clearly recognised that insanity could take many forms, attribution was a very generalised affair. Until the 1880s, patients at Ballinasloe were almost without exception diagnosed as suffering from mania, or occasionally monomania. The exceptions were those labelled epileptic or idiotic, both conditions which were classed as diseases in the nineteenth century. This does not mean that analysis of cases did not take place. On the contrary, the detailed case books and notes for each patient indicate a high level of engagement with the various manifestations of psychiatric illness, but a distinct lack of an appropriate vocabulary to describe and comprehend it. The records reveal an anxiety to tie, clearly, aberrant behaviour to a specific cause, in an understandable desire to explain otherwise incomprehensible states. In the nineteenth century, the causes of mental illness were broken down into two main categories, moral and physical. Physical afflictions included mental handicap, as well as physical damage to the brain. Moral reasons for insanity covered a huge range of possibilities, but could broadly be categorised as stress related illness in one form or other. There is a striking split between men and women with regard to which category they were judged to fit. For example, an analysis of the reasons for admission to the Central Asylum at Dundrum indicated that 70 per cent of the total women admitted in 1861 were judged insane as a result of moral causes.[8] Insanity amongst men, on the other hand, was believed

6 Board Minutes, CDLA, 7 September 1836. 7 FOA 26 June 1867. 8 Parliamentary Report of Inspectors-General on District, Local and Private Lunatic Asylums in Ireland, 1861.

to be caused by physical reasons in almost 60 per cent of cases. In examining the breakdown of causes within the moral category, 30 per cent of the women were believed to have become ill as a result of 'grief, fear and anxiety', and a further 21 per cent because of 'poverty or reverse of fortune'. The corresponding figures for men are 19 and 21 per cent respectively. These are proportionate percentages – the actual numbers of men and women in the moral category are 368 men and 532 women. Given the later nineteenth-century emphasis within psychiatric medicine upon the supposed links between women's physiology and mental illness, it is interesting to note that only 14 per cent of women were admitted as a result of the effects of 'love, jealousy and seduction', and that this figure is almost matched amongst the male group at 11 per cent. The only entry within the moral category in which men outnumber women is that of 'religious excitement', which accounts for 26 per cent of the men, and 16 per cent of the women.

In the physical category, the so-called 'idiots' were included, as well as those who had suffered injuries to the brain, or been brain damaged by fever. However, the largest single physical cause of insanity in this category occurred amongst men, and was attributed to 'intemperance', accounting for 48 per cent of all male patients. Alcohol abuse remained the main reason for admission of males to the Ballinasloe Asylum until the mid-twentieth century. The figure for women was far lower, at 18 per cent. An interesting category within the physical causes was that of 'climate'. This was applied almost exclusively to soldiers, and in fact, under cause of admission in the registers, 'climate' is entered practically without exception, regardless of the actual history of the individual soldier concerned. Of course, these categorisations apply only to those patients for whom the asylum received case histories. As the nineteenth century progressed, greater attention was paid to the maintenance of comprehensive patient records, but in the 1860s, on average less than half of those admitted had anything more than the most cursory of details regarding their illnesses. Those inmates who had been transferred from gaols were least likely to have any useful information provided for them, apart from their name, county of origin and perhaps their age.

When the Connaught District Lunatic Asylum was in its planning stages, it was believed that the institution would cater mainly for curable and convalescent cases. As a result, the buildings were constructed along hospital lines, with no barred windows and with wooden rather than flagged floors. As soon as the asylum opened, and the prison governors began passing their lunatic inmates to Ballinasloe, the asylum buildings were found to be unsuitable. In 1837, they underwent extensive reconstruction, based on the manager's report of that year. He noted that: 'No portion of the building [is] properly adapted for very violent and refractory cases ... no cells, day rooms or corridors [exist] wherein the windows are above the reach of patients ... [There are] no flagged day rooms for wet and filthy patients.'[9] The adaptations which were made to the institution also mark the moment of recognition by the board of governors that the resident

9 Manager's Report, Board Minutes, CDLA, 7 June 1837.

asylum population differed substantially in fact from the type of short-term, curable cases they had originally envisaged. In 1835 the board had written to the Lord Lieutenant asking for funds to expand the accommodation for incurable cases. They stated that of the 146 patients presently in the asylum, eighty-six of whom had been long-term inmates in the various county gaols, approximately thirty, or just over 20 per cent, were potentially curable cases.[10] The asylum then was rapidly resigned to tending for many patients on a life-long basis. However, the experiences of male and female patients regarding how long that life might be, and the circumstances under which they might eventually leave the asylum, often differed radically.

In Ballinasloe, as in the other district asylums in Ireland, male patients formed the majority of the inmates. This majority varied throughout the nineteenth century from 73 per cent in 1837 to a more balanced 57 per cent in 1861.[11] In the early years of its establishment, men were more likely to die prematurely in the asylum than women, although as a long-term resident body developed, and a greater aged female population emerged, the number of female patient deaths increased. It consistently remained below that of men, however. It was also the case that when an unusual element was added to asylum life, men were more vulnerable to its effects than women. One example is the cholera outbreak of 1849, but more startling is the impact of the Great Famine and its allied diseases on male and female death rates in the asylum.

The Connaught District Lunatic Asylum had in literal terms nothing to do with the famine, in terms of relief administration or tending to victims in any way. However, the scale of the disaster, particularly in the west of Ireland, made a significant impression on the asylum residents. Once famine hit, admissions to the institution rose sharply. If we focus on just one year, 1847, we find that 113 patients were admitted, an increase of 53 per cent on the previous year. Men account for almost 60 per cent of this 'surplus' admission. The reason for this huge jump in new patients is unclear. 78 per cent of these patients were received from the county gaols under the Dangerous Lunatics Act, an increase of almost 30 per cent in such admissions from the previous year. There are two possible explanations. One is that the families who had been caring for mentally ill members at home were no longer able to do so, and the scarcity of food caused them to seek admission for their charges by swearing to their violent state before a Justice of the Peace. Another explanation is that the so-called 'lunatics at large', the generally harmless wandering population, were being admitted to the asylum in increasing numbers as a result of the famine. These people had traditionally depended upon the charity of individual households for their survival, but famine conditions eliminated this form of support.

One would logically expect chronic overcrowding in the asylum as a result of the new influx of inmates. This did occur, but ironically the institution was

10 Register of patients, CDLA Schedule 1, January 1846 to December 1860.   11 General Registers, CDLA, 1837–1861.

saved from collapse by a sudden rise in the death rate. In 1847, ninety-five out of a total asylum population of 340 died.[12] At over a quarter of all the patients, this actually exceeded the proportionate death rate at the Ballinasloe Workhouse and Fever Hospital combined. Before and after the famine, deaths ran at an average rate of 20 per year.[13] Given the fact that the group in the wider population normally most vulnerable to famine, children, were largely absent from the asylum (there were a few children, those designated 'congenital idiots' or 'idiots born', but their numbers never exceeded seven or eight in any one year), the 1847 death rate was particularly high. Men accounted for 72 per cent of the dead.

When one analyses the causes of these excess deaths, they appear even more surprising. A total of sixty-eight were attributed to Marasmus, which literally means wasting, and was usually associated with starvation as opposed to disease. A further eleven cases were designated Pthisis, which was also associated with wasting but appears to have tubercular associations and which is accelerated by malnutrition. Another death was attributed to dropsy, or an accumulation of fluid, a condition often confused in this period with famine oedeama, or swelling. Thus in 1847, only five patients died of what could be described as natural causes (gangrene, aneurism and apoplexy), or at least deaths which had no direct association with the famine.

The average age of those who died is also interesting. This stood at thirty-seven, and again there is a higher representation of men than women. However, this male age group represents the third least vulnerable group in the wider population, after adolescents and adult women.[14] The asylum physician's explanation for this phenomenon was that 'the patients have been all of a most wretched class, and chiefly afflicted with chronic disease. No great improvement can be effected even under the best treatment. The destitution and neglect in which they are found to be in on being first brought to the asylum, is frightful in the extreme.'[15] This is indeed a valid explanation for many of the deaths which took place shortly after the patients' arrival at the asylum, and a small number of deaths are in fact marked 'admitted in a dying state' in the register. These patients tended to live for only a few weeks or months at most. However, the majority of those who died in the asylum during the famine were long-term residents. The average length of stay before death was actually five years and five months, with those resident for under one year averaging almost six months in the asylum before death.[16] In other words, the huge jump in deaths cannot be attributed to recently admitted patients who were also famine victims when outside the asylum. In addition, the asylum inmates received three meals per day by law. Their diet, consisting mainly of bread, milk, oatmeal, and, before famine struck, potatoes, was described by the asylum inspector as 'sufficient and wholesome'.[17] Although

12 Register of Patients for 1847.   13 Register of Discharges and Deaths, CDLA, December 1844 to December 1853.   14 Mary Daly, *The Famine in Ireland* (Dublin, 1986), p. 100.   15 Parliamentary Report, 1847.   16 Registers of Discharges and Deaths, CDLA, to 1847.   17 Appendix to the Report of the Inspectors-General on District, Local and Private Lunatic Asylums in Ireland, 1845.

it seldom varied, nutritionally it was more than adequate. When famine was at its height, and the population outside of the asylum literally had not eaten for days, the inmate's diet could be described as positively sumptuous. There is no indication from the asylum accounts or from the board of governor's minutes that the patients' diet was cut significantly during the famine years. How then did a relatively well-fed and housed group succumb in such large numbers?

In a sense, escape from famine-associated death within the asylum depended upon a combination of genuine severity of psychiatric illness, and gendered assumptions regarding the innate characteristics of men and women in the nineteenth century. These two factors combined to determine where each patient was housed within the asylum buildings. Although males and females were increasingly segregated in asylums through separate male and female wings, their separate accommodation was not identically planned or allocated. The women, although housed for the most part in dormitories similar to the men, had greater access to uncrowded rooms within the asylum buildings during the daytime. When the asylum was constructed, it was hoped that the female inmates would produce clothes for the patients, and a large workroom at the top of the main building was stocked with the various necessary materials, including two quilting frames. Recuperative female patients who demonstrated a docile temperament were encouraged to work there, thereby taking them out of the often oppressive dormitories during the day. The female day room was also at the top of the main building, and was described by the Inspector in 1845 as 'present[ing] a very busy scene and pleasing appearance'.[18] The male day room, on the other hand, was small and dark, with no occupation or diversion for the patients. In addition, those cases which were considered dangerously violent, or clearly incurable, were kept in the basement and ground floor wards and cells, and were frequently confined by day as well as night. Once a patient, and particularly a male patient, acquired a reputation for being difficult, the asylum staff were slow to revise it. The following case, described by the Inspector in 1847, was typical:

> I found a patient ... locked up in his cell, lying on a straw bed placed upon the ground. He was represented as being subject to occasional attacks of great excitement, bordering on violence. On questioning him, he expressed a wish to be allowed out about the corridor and airing-yard, which request I got the Manager to comply with. I saw him in the airing yard afterwards; he appeared to conduct himself properly, and was quite tranquil.[19]

On the same corridor, the inspector visited a ward in which ten patients were confined to bed with dysentery. 'This ward was evidently overcrowded, and the air at night must consequently be rendered foul and highly injurious to the patients; and to add to the evil, we find that, from want of an infirmary, the sick and healthy classes are obliged to be accommodated in the same apartment, which

18 Ibid.   **19** Parliamentary Report, 1847.

is very objectionable, but at the same time unavoidable under existing circumstances.'[20] The spread of disease in these conditions was accelerated by the fact that the inmates spent between ten and twelve hours out of twenty-four locked in their dormitories. The state of a patient's health was therefore significantly determined by, literally, their level of occupation within the hospital buildings, and in 1847, men constituted a majority amongst the lower strata, along with the incurable females. When describing the three basement wards, the Inspector conjured up a monstrous picture:

> It is truly melancholy to behold the number of unfortunate inmates who are destined to spend so great a portion of their lives in these underground apartments. The excitement, noise, and confusion which occurred amongst this class on my first entrance was most distressing to behold; and it struck me that there was evidently not a sufficient number of intelligent or active nurses to superintend a class labouring under the severest and most appalling forms of insanity, and which require, above all others, the most vigilant care and attention.[21]

Outside of moments of crisis such as the famine, men also tended to have less occupation than their female counterparts. The board of governors, along with the administrators of the other district asylums in Ireland, recognised the therapeutic value of manual work for patients. As the majority of inmates at Ballinasloe, both men and women, were designated 'from the labouring classes', it was considered important that such work be provided for them. However, the original grounds surrounding the asylum were quite small, with only eleven acres of farm land, so there was always a shortage of work for able-bodied men. In 1863, the asylum manager reported to the board of governors that he could find work within the asylum grounds for only twelve labouring men, out of a total male patient population of 178. Another four men were at work indoors, occupied in tailoring and repairing shoes. Women patients, on the other hand, fared rather better. Sixty-one of them were employed, twenty-seven at needlework and knitting, nineteen in the laundry, and a further fifteen in cleaning the asylum.[22] Thus, although the women were literally unskilled, their domestic training, and their gender-specific roles within society as house workers, allowed them greater scope for occupation within the asylum. For the remainder of the patients, there was literally nothing to do all day long. As many were unable to read, the small library purchased by the manager in 1845 of 'light amusing books, such as have been approved by the National Board of Education' was of little use.[23] The board fretted about the adverse effects of prolonged inactivity, particularly on the male convalescent cases, but were hampered by a lack of trained staff, equipment and finances to alter the situation.[24]

---

20 Ibid.   **21** Ibid.   **22** Parliamentary Report, 1863.   **23** Board minutes, CDLA, 8 January 1845.   **24** 'The Medical Officer and Manager feel considerable embarrassment in not being able to have the inmates put to any other occupation, consequently a great

The overall picture of the experiences of men and women within the Connaught District Lunatic Asylum is a varied one, but it would appear that women fared somewhat better than men in terms of frequency of discharge, lower death rate, slightly better living conditions and the eventual possibility of being released permanently. Residence in the asylum undoubtedly carried a significant degree of stigma in nineteenth-century Ireland, but what is most surprising, in Ballinasloe as in the other district asylums, is the enormous expansion within the system throughout the century. From the administrators' point of view, the asylums offered a refuge and sanctuary to the mentally-ill population which raised them above anything they had previously experienced. The Inspector in 1862 declared of Ballinasloe:

> Its inmates – at least, the great majority – belong to the humblest classes of the rural population, and are in every way most carefully attended to; indeed were we to adduce an instance of the benevolent and liberal spirit which pervades the management of Irish District Asylums, we would most appropriately refer to that at Ballinasloe, where patients, hitherto living in a destitute condition, are afforded food, raiment, lodging, and other domestic comforts previously unknown to them.[25]

Whether the residents would actually have agreed with this assessment of the asylum is open to question; however it is true that the institution had a significant impact not merely in the immediate area, but throughout the whole of the province of Connaught for the nineteenth century.[26]

part of the time which these unfortunate individuals spend in the Asylum, is of that monotonous and listless nature as to operate injuriously upon them.' Parliamentary Report, 1845.   **25** Parliamentary Report, 1862.   **26** My thanks to the staff of St Brigid's Hospital, Ballinasloe, for their help in the preparation of this paper.

The Irish Police: Love, Sex and Marriage in the Nineteenth and Early Twentieth Centuries

BRIAN GRIFFIN

This essay explores a neglected area of the lives of rank-and-file members of the Royal Irish Constabulary (R.I.C.) and Dublin Metropolitan Police (D.M.P): the various ways in which membership of these two forces affected policemen's roles as fathers, husbands, and lovers. It is well known that the R.I.C. and D.M.P. had wide-ranging codes of rules and regulations which prescribed, in minute detail, the procedures to be followed by policemen in a myriad of situations likely (or even not very likely) to be encountered in their daily round.[1] These procedures involved not only the prevention and detection of crime; considerable attention was also devoted to outlining what constituted appropriate police behaviour in areas such as personal hygiene and daily life in barracks. Less well known is the extent to which the codes' regimentation governed the most intimate areas of policemen's private lives, including family life.

In 1836, when the Irish Constabulary was established as a uniform organisation, recruits to the force had to be bachelors or widowers without children. If a policeman wanted to marry, he had to receive permission from his county inspector and from the inspector general. In every instance the fiancée's background was examined by the man's officer to ensure that she and her family were 'respectable'. When a man married, he was forbidden from serving in his wife's native county, or in any county where she had relatives or where her relatives had business interests. Because of this rule, marriage was one of the major causes of transfer within the R.I.C.. This was part of the constabulary authorities' effort to ensure impartial policing by their force, or at least to ensure that its members were not placed in situations that might give rise to suspicions that they were favouring their in-laws. A similar desire to ensure acceptance by the local community lies behind the rule forbidding wives from keeping shop or taking in lodgers: it was feared that established shopkeepers or guesthouse-keepers might resent the competition from constabularymen's wives and that this might diminish the efficiency or popularity of the force.[2] In contrast to the constabulary, the D.M.P.

---

1 For a good account of the genesis of the Royal Irish Constabulary's code of regulations, see Gregory J. Fulham, 'James Shaw-Kennedy and the Reformation of the Irish Constabulary, 1836–38' in *Eire-Ireland*, xvi, 3 (1981), pp. 93–106.   2 *Royal Irish Constabulary and Dublin Metropolitan Police. Appendix to Report of the Committee of Enquiry, 1914. Containing Minutes of Evidence With Appendices* H.C. 1914–16 [7637] xxxii 359, pp. 140–1, 157, 192.

at first allowed married men with children to join, although unmarried recruits were preferred. Even men who had been dismissed from the Irish Constabulary for marrying without permission were initially accepted into the D.M.P., thus weakening the constabulary's efforts to curb that breach of regulations. It wasn't until Inspector-general Duncan McGregor complained to the D.M.P. chief commissioners in 1842 that the D.M.P. stopped accepting men from the sister force who had been dismissed for marrying without leave. Also in 1842 the rule was introduced that no married man with more than one child would be accepted as a D.M.P. recruit, and in the 1850s it was decreed that all men had to be unmarried when joining the force.[3]

All policemen who wanted to marry had to have several years service before permission to wed was granted. The length of this service varied. For most of the R.I.C.'s period of existence a minimum of seven years was required.[4] The D.M.P. minimum period of service also varied, but generally a constable was expected to prove that he and his fiancée had enough money saved to secure a modestly comfortable house. In the 1850s, £40 was the usual sum required, which, it was estimated, took from five to seven years to save; in the 1880s a rule stipulating a minimum period of five years service before marriage was introduced.[5]

It was not uncommon for an R.I.C. man to get married with permission and to be dismissed when his wife gave birth less than nine months after their marriage. Inspector-general McGregor pointed out in 1852 that he considered it an offence for police to engage in 'criminal intercourse' – sex before marriage – and that he punished every known instance with dismissal. This was McGregor's policy despite appeals from clergymen and other influential figures to adopt a less harsh attitude.[6]

3 Chief Commissioner George Browne, D.M.P., in a letter to Inspector-general Duncan McGregor of the Irish Constabulary, 11 April 1842, Public Record Office, Kew, HO 184/111; *Return of the Income and Expenditure of the Dublin Metropolitan Police, for the Two Financial Years 1856–57 and 1857–58; Copies of Notices or Proclamations Issued From Time to Time to Procure Recruits for the Force; Statement of the Annual Pay of Each Class of Officers and Men; Number of Superintendents, Inspectors, and Men of the Force on 1st January 1858, With the Proportion of Each Professing the Protestant, Roman Catholic, and Presbyterian Religions; and Number of Resignations and Dismissals From the Force Since 1st January 1856* H.C. 1857–58 [430] xlvii 815, p. 5. In 1838, Duncan McGregor, then a lieutenant colonel in the British army, was appointed to the position of inspector general of the Irish Constabulary. McGregor was knighted in December 1848, and retired from the Irish Constabulary in 1858.   4 For details of the various regulations regarding the length of service required by R.I.C. men before they could marry with official permission, see Brian Griffin, 'The Irish Police, 1836–1914: A Social History' (unpublished Ph.D. dissertation, Loyola University of Chicago, 1991), pp. 552–4, 559–60.   5 Sir Francis B. Head, *Fortnight in Ireland* (London, 1852), p. 105; *Report of the Committee of Inquiry Into the Dublin Metropolitan Police; With Evidence, Appendix, and Maps* H.C. 1883 [c.3576] xxxii 1, p. 39.   6 Memorial of Mrs Anne Browne to the chief secretary for Ireland, Lord Naas, 22 October 1852, National Library of Ireland, Mayo Papers, MS 11018 (21); Inspector-general McGregor in a letter to Lord Naas, 25 October 1852, National Library of Ireland, Mayo Papers, MS 11018 (21). See also R.I.C. circular of 17 October 1876, Public Record Office, Kew, HO 184/115.

It frequently occurred that R.I.C. men got married secretly,[7] most probably because their girlfriends were pregnant and the policemen knew that it was a waste of time asking for official permission to wed. In December 1838 McGregor offered an amnesty to all secretly-married policemen who came forward and admitted their married status, and warned that after that date every policeman who was secretly married was to be dismissed.[8] Until the 1890s 'criminal intercourse' and marrying without leave were the only breaches of regulations to be invariably punished with dismissal. Men who married without leave were refused permission to re-join the force in striking contrast, for instance, with drunken policemen, who were often allowed to re-join after being dismissed.

Despite their superiors' disapproving attitude, policemen continued to marry secretly and sometimes remained undetected for years.[9] It is difficult to believe that colleagues and the local community did not connive in keeping such cases from the knowledge of officers. The most tragic incident involving a clandestinely-married man was probably that which occurred in Dungannon in December 1859. Earlier in the year Constable John Holden, who had served for over fourteen years, applied for permission to marry. On his officer's investigation of Holden's fiancee's background, it turned out – or was alleged – that the couple were already married and had a son. Holden denied that he was married but he admitted being the father of the child, and persisted in his request for permission to marry. Not only was this refused, but Holden was reduced to the rank of sub-constable and ordered to be removed to Newtownstewart. Holden held a colleague, Sub-constable McClelland, responsible for informing their sub-inspector about the details of his case, so in December 1859 he shot and killed McClelland and attempted to kill his sub-inspector. Holden was hanged for murder in August 1860.[10]

7 Bishop Thomas Plunket, *Special Report of a Government Investigation Into the Conduct of the Constabulary at Tuam, Upon Charges Preferred by the Right Hon. and Right Rev. the Lord Bishop of Tuam* (Dublin, 1859), p. 32.   8 Irish Constabulary circular, 20 December 1838, Public Record Office, Kew, HO 184/111.   9 See, for instance, the case of Sub-constable John McLernon of Derry, who was dismissed for being irregularly married in August 1855 – he had been married in 1849: Irish Constabulary disciplinary cases July to September 1855, National Archives, Dublin, 1/492.   10 The details of Holden's trial are in *Belfast Newsletter*, 26–28 July 1860. Holden was not the only secretly-married Irish policeman to commit murder. In January 1864 Luke Charles, an ex-member of the Irish Constabulary and a member of the Preston police, was executed at Kirkdale Gaol for murdering his wife. During his trial it transpired that, in December 1854, Charles, while stationed at Heath in Queen's County, had secretly married. While at Heath he also 'formed the acquaintance' of a young woman named Ellen Ford, from whom he kept his marriage secret. Indeed, Charles continued to reside in barracks apart from his wife, due to the secret nature of their matrimonial state. Charles proposed to Ford and was accepted, and promised to marry her at some unspecified time in the future. Eventually, in 1861, he emigrated to England with his wife and joined the Preston police. Subsequently his wife disappeared and was later found murdered. In the meantime Charles had returned to Ireland in order to bring Ford over to England for the purpose of marrying her. The details of Charles's secret marriage and his proposal to Ford were enough to convince the

By the turn of the century, the constabulary authorities adopted a somewhat less harsh attitude towards secretly-married men. This is exemplified by the case of Constable Edward Robinson. In 1896 Robinson married without permission after just two-and-a-half years of service. This did not come to the inspector-general's notice until May 1904 – some eight years later – and even then only because Robinson's wife wrote to him, complaining that her husband would not ask for official permission to marry. In this instance Robinson was not dismissed but merely given an unfavourable record and transferred.[11] This more humane approach was typical of that adopted towards many, but not all, cases of secret marriage after 1894. One exception occurred in December 1898 and involved a Constable Prendergast of Cahir. Prendergast, who was secretly married, requested permission from the inspector-general to marry according to police regulations. When this was refused the constable killed himself on 22 December 1898.[12] As late as 1914, Inspector-general Chamberlain stated that he knew of twenty-eight secretly-married R.I.C. men. These were not dismissed; however, their wives were not officially recognised as policemen's spouses, which meant that their husbands received none of the privileges normally granted to married R.I.C. men, the wives and children were not entitled to any pension should the husbands be injured, and the families received no lodging allowance.[13]

The harsh treatment accorded to secretly-married policemen, or to those who wished to marry pregnant girlfriends, contrasts markedly with the comparatively lenient punishments imposed on men who frequented prostitutes. In November 1844, Inspector-general McGregor ordered that all policemen who had to undergo hospital treatment for venereal disease be stopped 10d per day from their pay until they were cured. This followed complaints from several county inspectors that many policemen 'have brought disease upon themselves by their own vice, thereby imposing additional duties upon their well-behaved comrades'.[14] Upon their cure, these constabularymen were usually allowed to re-join the R.I.C.. Instances exist of uniformed R.I.C. men getting drunk in brothels and being punished with fines or demotion rather than dismissal.[15]

Within the D.M.P., men who frequented prostitutes were also treated more leniently than those who married without leave. From January 1838 to January 1857, some 121 D.M.P. men were reported for being in brothels. Only twenty-two of these men were dismissed or compelled to resign. Most of the other cases, even of men found drunk and in uniform in brothels, were punished merely with fines, the largest amount being the £2 imposed on a detective in 1850.[16] A report

jury at his trial that he had sufficient motive to murder his wife. For details of Charles's trial see *Irish Liberator* (London), 16 January 1864.   **11** *Hansard*, fourth series, cxxix, 8 August 1904, *c.*1359.   **12** *Freeman's Journal*, 24 December 1898.   **13** *Royal Irish Constabulary and Dublin Metropolitan Police Enquiry, 1914*, p. 14.   **14** Irish Constabulary circular, 11 November 1844, Public Record Office, Kew, HO 184/111.   **15** See Griffin, 'The Irish Police,' pp. 558–9.   **16** Chief Commissioner Browne in a letter to Chief Secretary Herbert, 25 January 1858, National Archives, Dublin, Chief Secretary's Office Registered Papers, C.S.O.R.P. 10934 on 1858/11753.

from the D.M.P.'s medical officers in 1848, explaining the high rate of venereal disease cases in the force, stated that most recruits came from rural areas, 'where none of the temptations peculiar to a great city exist', and 'finding themselves surrounded on their beats with vice and infamy, under many attractive forms, they were probably unable to restrain themselves from the influences brought to bear upon them'.[17] D.M.P. sufferers from venereal disease were discharged until cured, and then were re-accepted into the force. For most of the organisation's existence, it appears to have been accepted as a fact of life by the D.M.P. authorities that some bachelor policemen, at least, were going to pay prostitutes for their services. David Neligan records in his memoirs that D.M.P. instructors carefully avoided discussing the seamier aspects of Dublin's night life with recruits, despite the problem of policemen frequenting brothels. He explains that he was put off the idea not by his instructor but by two of his uncles, who were already in the D.M.P.. They took him in tow during his training, and, according to Neligan, 'The hair-raising stories they told me about night-life in the city frightened me so much, that for several years I was afraid to even look at a woman!'[18] Towards the end of the force's existence the authorities decided to actively discourage recruits from consorting with prostitutes: in one strategy, trainee policemen were taken to a Lock Hospital and shown the terrifying effects of syphilis and gonorrhoea.[19]

Once a man got wed, even with permission, police regulations still intruded on his married life. Married R.I.C. men were often required to live in barracks, a rule which was obligatory for all the unmarried men. Official statistics show that in 1881, some 1,412 of the R.I.C.'s 3,513 married men lived in barracks.[20] According to R.I.C. regulations, only one married man's family was allowed to reside in each barracks: these families enjoyed the considerable benefit of rent-free accommodation, but they also had to obey the stringent regulations laid down for the running of police barracks. There were quite minute rules as to when wives were to wash clothes and sweep married quarters, and concerning the use of barrack furniture. When officers inspected barracks they also examined married men's quarters to ensure that their families obeyed barrack regulations. Wives and children had to be clean, they were obliged to attend Sunday worship, the children had to be respectably clad and those aged between four and twelve had to attend school daily. If a man's wife quarrelled with her husband or with any other policeman residing in barracks she had to reside away from her husband.[21] The D.M.P. went even further in curbing 'troublesome' wives: if a wife

17 *Report of the Medical Officers of the Dublin Metropolitan Police, for the Year 1848, With Returns in Connexion Therewith* (Dublin, 1849), p. 4.   **18** David Neligan, *The Spy in the Castle* (London, 1968), p. 38.   **19** Kevin C. Kearns, *Dublin Tenement Life: An Oral History* (Dublin, 1994), p. 178.   **20** *Report of the Committee of Inquiry Into the Royal Irish Constabulary; With Evidence and Appendix* H.C. 1883 [c.3577] xxxii 255, p. 470.   **21** *Standing Rules and Regulations for the Government and Guidance of the Constabulary Force of Ireland; as Approved by His Excellency the Earl of Mulgrave, Lord Lieutenant General and General Governor of Ireland* (Dublin, 1837), p. 49; Irish Constabulary circular, 22 December 1837, Public Record Office, Kew, HO 184/111; *Standing Rules and Regulations for the Governance and Guidance of the*

quarrelled with her D.M.P. husband, he was liable to be dismissed. Recruits were warned, in general terms, that the chief commissioners would 'remove from the service any constables whose wives conduct themselves improperly'.[22] Some further insight into the pervasive nature of official interference in the married lives of D.M.P. men may be gleaned from an examination of the surviving disciplinary records of the force. These show that D.M.P. men were disciplined not only for marital quarrels but also for such offences as not having their residences adequately furnished, for residing in unhealthy dwellings, for failing to ensure that their children attended regularly at school, and for falling into arrears with rent payments.[23]

At first four children – nicknamed 'Peeler's brats' or, if they misbehaved, 'Peeler's pups'[24] – were allowed to live in constabulary barracks with their parents. In the early decades children, and especially daughters, had to move out of barracks when they reached the age of fourteen-and-a-half years. Inspector-general McGregor explained that this rule had the effect of

> compelling the parents to send their daughters to service or other regular employment, which many of them are reluctant to do, & of guarding the young females themselves against the ruin in which some of them have been involved, by constantly living in a confined barracks, with none but single men as their companions.[25]

It was probably to avoid similar scandals with the female barrack servants that regulations stipulated that the servants had either to be old women, or married.[26]

Policemen's families residing in their own lodgings away from barracks were not entirely free from the scope of police regulations. For instance, policemen's houses had to be within a quarter of a mile from the local barracks; this made suitable accommodation difficult to find, especially in rural areas, and placed families at the mercy of unscrupulous landlords who were aware of the quarter-mile rule. Houses had to be kept as orderly as barracks, and were also subject to officers' inspections.[27] In addition, men living out of barracks had to keep the same hours as colleagues residing within barracks. Where there were several married men stationed at one barracks, the privilege of sleeping at home was enjoyed on a rota basis. In the 1870s only one man at a time was allowed this privilege, which lasted for a year; in 1888, the period of indulgence was reduced to three months.[28] This

Royal Irish Constabulary (3rd ed; Dublin, 1872), pp. 50, 61–2, 142.   **22** *Instruction Book for the Dublin Metropolitan Police* (Dublin, 1865), p. 18.   **23** Griffin, 'The Irish Police', pp. 571–3.   **24** F.J.M. Scully and R.J.K. Sinclair, *Arresting Memories: Captured Moments in Constabulary Life* (Coleraine, 1982), glossary.   **25** Inspector-general McGregor's report on the duties and training of the Irish Constabulary, 10 December 1847, National Archives, Dublin, Official Papers, Miscellaneous Assorted O.P.M.A. 145/8.   **26** *1837 Irish Constabulary Standing Rules and Regulations*, p. 49; *1872 R.I.C. Standing Rules and Regulations*, p. 67.   **27** *1872 R.I.C. Standing Rules and Regulations*, pp. 64–5; *1882 R.I.C. Committee of Inquiry*, p. 115.   **28** *1872 R.I.C. Standing Rules and Regulations*, pp. 64–5; Sir Andrew

was probably the most irksome of all the rules affecting married R.I.C. men and their wives. Sometimes the exigencies of police service obliged husbands to reside away from their wives, and when this happened it was not unknown for the men to take out their frustrations on their colleagues. For instance, Jeremiah Mee records in his memoirs the example of the head constable of Collooney barracks in 1913, whose wife and family resided in Dublin. Mee felt that the head constable's enforced isolation from his family was at the root of his strict enforcement of barrack regulations. The stringent regime resulting from the head constable's frustration proved so oppressive that the men spoke in whispers and there was a depressing atmosphere throughout the barracks.[29] Mee contrasts the situation in Collooney with that in Geevagh, where the sergeant resided with his family and a 'laid-back' atmosphere prevailed:

> During the day each man went out on patrol at the appointed time but where he went was his own affair and his own responsibility. The sergeant did his patrols, tilled his garden, helped the children with their school-lessons, repaired their shoes and asked no awkward questions.[30]

Why did thousands of Irishwomen marry policemen if there were so many intrusions in their private lives? Apart from the obvious reason – love – one can point to many material advantages which outweighed, or at least helped make more bearable, the various restrictions imposed by police regulations. Policemen's wives generally came from a similar background to that of their husbands: they were mostly the daughters of tenant farmers or small shopkeepers.[31] For these women, marrying a policeman was a step up the social ladder, just as joining the R.I.C. or D.M.P. was a step up the same ladder for a farmer's son. Because a policeman had permanent employment, usually had good wages and had the prospect of a pension on retirement which he often supplemented by purchasing a small farm or keeping a shop or public house, he was regarded in a favourable light by unattached Irishwomen. Numerous sources attest to the fact that in rural areas R.I.C. men were regarded as 'good catches'.[32] In the late nineteenth century, an official of the Local Government Board noted that public houses in the west of Ireland were doing a brisk business in a home-made perfume called 'White Rose'. This was a concoction that was sold to young women keeping company with policemen. The official was told by a carman that 'The girls do be puttin'

Reed, *The Constabulary Manual; or, Guide to the Discharge of Police Duties* (Dublin, 1888), p. 74. In March 1866 Sub-constable Patrick O'Connell of Limerick resigned because he was refused permission to sleep at home. See Irish Constabulary general register, Public Record Office, Kew, HO 184/11, p. 137.   **29** J. Anthony Gaughan, *Memoirs of Jeremiah Mee, R.I.C.* (Dublin, 1975), pp. 33–4.   **30** Ibid., p. 37.   **31** Griffin, 'The Irish Police,' pp. 617–18.   **32** In 1901 a Longford district inspector noted of young women in his area that 'They look upon the police as the best catches in the country. All the girls in the country are going after them'. See *Royal Irish Constabulary. Evidence Taken Before the Committee of Enquiry, 1901. With Appendix* H.C. 1902 [Cd. 1094] xlii 313, p. 59.

it on their handkerchers … if they're goin' walking out with the police … [I]t takes
the smell of the turf out of their hair and clothes and gives them a great charrum.'
The official had a sniff of the 'White Rose' and found that it had a 'rank powerful
odour of shaving-soap and hair oil'[33], hardly the most attractive of perfumes!

It is worth mentioning here that young men who were not in the police often
enviously reported the greater pulling power of policemen when it came to
courting. One of the best examples occurs in James Comerford's autobiographical
account of his young days in Co. Kilkenny early in the twentieth century.
Comerford, a farmer's son, contrasted his lot unfavourably with that of young
R.I.C. men:

> As they patrolled the roads in rural Ireland they attracted the favourable
> attention of the girls. They were the envy of the young sons of farmers who
> plodded daily, except on Sundays, with heavy boots caked with clay when
> working in ploughed fields with or without horses for eight or nine hours a
> day, who sweated in the meadows making hay for twelve hours a day in hot
> summer weather until twilight, or who slogged along on a wet day through
> the fields while feeling wet and cold, but still doing essential farm work.[34]

As stated earlier, one of the attractions of the police, in the eyes of young women,
was that marrying them represented an improvement in one's social standing.
Policemen – especially sergeants, but not only men of that rank – stood high in
the social pyramid in rural areas.[35] It is no coincidence that police families were
preoccupied with their social status. This was reflected in parents' enthusiasm for
educating their children. Although most policemen and their wives received only
a National School education, they often insisted on secondary education for their
children. In their own childhood they had probably been accustomed to hard
physical work and frugal living standards, but they were determined to provide
a higher standard of living for their children. Sean O'Faolain, the son of an R.I.C.
constable, records the sacrifices made by his parents to obtain a good education
for their children. The family rented rooms over a public house in Cork city, but
most of the rooms were let to lodgers, while the children slept in the attic.
According to O'Faolain, 'This was a token of the thrifty principle that dominated
all our lives – my father's and mother's constant anxiety to give their three children
a good education'.[36] Numerous other accounts are available of R.I.C. men paying
extra to have their sons attend Christian Brothers schools, and of policemen's
sons and daughters attending Civil Service academies along with the children of
comfortable farmers and shopkeepers.[37] David Neligan writes of policemen's

---

33 Sir Henry A. Robinson, *Further Memories of Irish Life* (London, 1924), pp. 41–2.
34 James J. Comerford, *My Kilkenny I.R.A. Days, 1916–1922* (Kilkenny, 1978), p. 146.
35 Ibid., p. 144; Robert Lynd, *Home Life in Ireland* (London, 1909), p. 83; John D. Brewer,
The Royal Irish Constabulary: An Oral History (Belfast, 1990), pp. 4, 23, 27, 30.   **36** Sean
O'Faolain, *Vive Moi! An Autobiography* (London, 1967), p. 52.   **37** Recollections of

children that they 'got good education, and at one time ran the Civil Service, religious orders, and many other professions'.[38] While this overstates the role played in Irish society by policemen's children, it shows that contemporaries were aware of the special efforts made by policemen and their wives on behalf of their offspring.

Yet, although the evidence suggests that married men committed fewer breaches of discipline than single men, as far as the superior officers of both forces were concerned, bachelors were preferred to married men. It was felt that a bachelor, living in barracks, was freer of local attachments than a married man and, above all, that it was easier to transfer him than his married counterpart. This was a particularly important consideration for the R.I.C., whose men were liable to be sent on 'detachment duty' – duty at elections, evictions, and the Northern anniversaries – at short notice. Unmarried men were considered more suitable for this type of duty. Similarly, in the D.M.P., bachelors were preferred to married men, despite the fact that married men posed considerably less of a disciplinary problem. In 1882 Chief Commissioner Talbot stated that it was absolutely neces-sary that at least two thirds of his force be unmarried and living in barracks, as this facilitated sending the men to scenes of trouble. Talbot opposed granting a lodging allowance to married men, as he felt that this would put a premium on marriage and hamper the mobility of the force.[39]

Married men, in both forces, were viewed as potentially ill-fitting cogs in the police machine. Their presence was often seen as an inconvenience, as the constabulary and D.M.P. authorities had to go to special lengths, when stationing their men, to ensure that married men and their families had access to respectable housing and above-average education. Some R.I.C. county inspectors felt that married men 'usurped' the best town stations, and that they were an encumbrance because they were less likely to be transferred, or to serve on the frequently dangerous detachment duty, than single men.[40] Indeed, in the 1880s the county inspector for Tyrone expressed his hostility towards married men by adamantly refusing to allow them to serve in Omagh, the most important station in Tyrone, if they were accompanied by their wives.[41] The married status of many D.M.P. men posed particular challenges for the general administration of the force since practically all married policemen resided in private accommodation, the only exceptions being married sergeants or acting sergeants whom superintendents might occasionally require to reside in barracks.[42] For instance, the statistical returns for the year 1844 show that the vast majority of constables in Dublin's A, C and D divisions were married, while the vast majority of those in the B, E

Martin Nolan, R.I.C., Department of Irish Folklore, University College Dublin, MS 1264, pp. 254–61; Siobhan Lankford, *The Hope and the Sadness: Personal Recollections of Troubled Times in Ireland* (Cork, 1980), pp. 71–2; *Royal Irish Constabulary and Dublin Metropolitan Police Enquiry, 1914*, pp. 34, 57, 288.   **38** David Neligan, *Spy in Castle*, p. 31. **39** *1883 D.M.P. Committee of Inquiry*, pp. 39, 185–6.   **40** *1883 R.I.C. Committee of Inquiry*, pp. 305, 321, 331, 355; *1901 R.I.C. Committee of Enquiry*, p. 140.   **41** Recollections of Martin Nolan, R.I.C., Department of Irish Folklore, University College Dublin, MS 1264, pp. 245–6.   **42** *1865 D.M.P. Instruction Book*, p. 60.

and F divisions were unmarried.[43] That most police in the latter divisions were bachelors probably reflects the fact that they contained the more exclusive areas of Dublin with inevitably higher house rents: the chief commissioners obviously took this into consideration when posting married men.[44] In another instance involving special consideration being accorded to married D.M.P. men, this time in the 1870s and 1880s, married men, many of whom were in straitened financial circumstances, were unofficially allowed to break the rule which stipulated that policemen should eat well in order to be fit for police duties. Indeed the D.M.P. surgeon often allowed undernourished married policemen to go on the sick list for several days to recuperate their strength.[45]

In conclusion, given the frequently hostile attitude on the part of superior officers towards married policemen, and the nature of the regulations regarding marriage, it is not surprising that the D.M.P. and R.I.C. had a higher proportion of bachelors than any other police force in the United Kingdom. In 1864 only 32 per cent of the D.M.P. were married, and the R.I.C. had an even smaller proportion of married men; in marked contrast, only one of the 75 county or borough forces in England and Wales, that of Staffordshire, had a majority of unmarried men. Even Staffordshire's police force contained a considerably higher proportion of married men than the two main Irish police forces since some 47 per cent of the Staffordshire force were married.[46] Yet, while it is true that, at any given time, most R.I.C. and D.M.P. men were bachelors, this does not tell the full story; the longer policemen served, the more likely they were to marry. The available statistics show that most men who were entitled by regulations to wed eventually did so.[47] An interesting difference within the Irish forces is also indicated by this

43 Initially four D.M.P. districts existed: south of the Liffey, the A or southwest division and the B or southeast division, and north of the Liffey there were the C or northeast division and the D or northwest division. In 1840 the police district expanded to include the E or F divisions. The E division stretched from Crumlin to Ringsend, and included Rathmines, Rathgar, Milltown, Donnybrook, Sandymount and Irishtown. The F division stretched from Booterstown to Killiney and Ballybrack and included Blackrock, Stillorgan, Galloping Green, Kingstown (Dun Laoghaire), Kill-O-Grange and Dalkey. In 1844 the G or detective division was established.   44 *Statistical Returns of the Dublin Metropolitan Police for the Year 1844* (Dublin, 1845), p. 49; Chief Commissioner Browne in a letter to the under secretary for Ireland 2 February 1857, National Archives, Dublin, Chief Secretary's Office Registered Papers, 10932 on 1858/11753.   45 *Report of the Commissioners Appointed by the Lords Commissioners of Her Majesty's Treasury to Inquire Into the Condition of the Civil Service in Ireland on the Dublin Metropolitan Police: Together With the Minutes of Evidence and Appendices* H.C. 1873 [c.788] xxii 1, pp. 3, 5; *1883 D.M.P. Committee of Inquiry*, p. 196. 46 *Return of the Number of Soldiers Quartered in the United Kingdom; Giving Comparative Numbers of Married and Single Men; Number of Days' Absence From Duty During a Period of One Year, Distinguishing the Married and Single Men, and Stating Respectively the Percentage of Those Absent From Duty on Account of Ordinary or Particular Illness: and, Similar Return in All Respects of the Police Force of the United Kingdom* H.C. 1864 [409] xxv 599.   47 Griffin, 'The Irish Police', pp. 560–61, 575. R.I.C. men appear, on average, to have waited for several years after the regulation seven-year service period before contracting marriages.

data, with a higher rate of marriage among R.I.C. men entitled to wed than was
the case in the D.M.P.. In 1901, for instance, 52 per cent of eligible D.M.P. men
were married, compared to 62 per cent of eligible R.I.C. men, a difference which
reflects the greater isolation of the average D.M.P. man from the community he
policed and the greater popularity of the R.I.C. during most of the period.[48]
The history of marriage and bachelorhood within both the D.M.P. and the R.I.C.
thus provides a unique perspective on the intersections of public and private life
during the nineteenth and early twentieth centuries; a policeman's occupation
clearly governed all of his social interactions, its influence extending to the most
private sphere.

For instance, an examination of the force's general register shows that the recruits who
joined in 1851, and married with permission, did so after an average of over thirteen years'
service, while those who joined in 1861 married after almost thirteen years' service on
average. In contrast, the men who joined in 1871, 1881 and 1891 and who married served
for an average of just over eleven years before ceasing to be bachelors. Data from (Royal)
Irish Constabulary general register, 1851, 1861, 1871, 1881, 1891, Public Record Office,
Kew, HO 1848, 14–15, 19–20, 28–9.   **48** *1901 R.I.C. Committee of Inquiry,* p. 218; *Dublin
Metropolitan Police. Evidence Taken Before the Committee of Inquiry, 1901. With Appendix* H.C.
1902 [Cd. 1095] xlii 227, p. 20. For a discussion of the unpopularity of the Dublin
Metropolitan Police see Brian Griffin, '"Such Varmint": The Dublin Police and the Public,
1838–1913' in *Irish Studies Review,* 13 (winter 1995–6), pp. 21–5. A more extensive
examination of the relations between the R.I.C. and D.M.P. and their respective publics
is provided in Griffin, 'The Irish Police,' pp. 625–802.

'Equal Sinners': Irish Women Utilising the Salvation Army Rescue Network for Britain and Ireland in the Nineteenth Century

GRÁINNE M. BLAIR

> There is neither Jew nor Greek, there is neither male nor female for ye are all one in Christ Jesus (Gal, 3: 28).

The development of the Salvation Army Rescue Network and its utilisation by Irish women in the nineteenth century form the subject of this essay. Since the Salvation Army considers the British Isles as one complete Salvationist Territory and, prior to this research, no real separation of Irish and British data existed, I will begin with an outline of the origins and development of the Army Rescue Network in the British Isles Territory, commencing in London, and the subsequent development into Ireland. Once a woman made contact with the Salvation Army and requested help, she became part of this rescue network.

This research provides the first study of Irish women who utilised the Salvation Army Rescue Network throughout the British Isles Territory during the nineteenth century. The sample of 233 Irish women was obtained from unpublished Salvation Army Receiving House Statements and Rescue Home records.[1] (See Table 1) Documentary research was also carried out on the Annual Reports of

---

1 Five record books from the London 'Lanark House' register, 1886–1892, were the primary sources for this research. Information on all women giving an Irish birthplace was extracted and analysed. (During the course of my research it became apparent that this Salvation Army register was incorrectly labelled as 'Lanark House', because 'Lanark House' did not become Salvation Army property until after the period, 1886–1892.) The records in the so-called 'Lanark House' register refer to three Salvation Army Rescue Homes: the Chelsea Rescue Home until October 1886; subsequently for the Dalston No. III Rescue Home, at 44 Navarino Road; and afterwards the London No. III Rescue Home, at 183 Amhurst Road, Hackney (*The Deliverer*, June 1896, pp. 185–7). The other record books were, London Book I, Final Reports, 1886–88; London Book II, Final Reports, 1887–1890; Country Book I, Final Reports, 1887–1890; and Country Book II, Final Reports, 1890–1892. The London records deal specifically with the London Receiving Homes while the Country records deal with the Houses in the rest of the Army's British Isles Territory. It should be noted that there are changes in the information requested on the official forms and in the information given by the Salvation Army over time, so the amount of information available on each Irish woman was not always consistently recorded.

Table 1: Source of Records of Irish Women who used the Salvation Army Rescue
Network of Ireland and Britain, 1886–1892

Source used	Lanark House N=	London I N=	London II N=	Country I N=	Country II N=	Total N=
Total records entered	487	1003	397	501	503	2891
Total multiple entries entered	3	6	5	3	5	22
Total Irish records★	6	17	6	142	72	243
Actual Total Number (less multiple entries):						233

★ The total number of Irish records in this table refers to all Irish women's records entered,
including the 22 multiple entries for 10 women. The Actual Total Number, cited subsequently, is 233.

the Salvation Army between 1886 and 1900, and on various Salvationist journals
and published works. The Annual Reports, although not acceptable as objective
historical statements, nevertheless serve to pin-point certain events, offer evidence
of the Army's public progress and provide the basis for further exploration of its
methods and mission. Furthermore, they provide valuable, collaborative background information to the hand-written reports of these women's lives. They are
also a valuable resource tool in providing a list of the Receiving Homes and Rescue
Houses and their uses.[2] Finding information about the early work of the Salvation
Army in Ireland proved more difficult. Every Corps was required to record the
main events locally, in what is called the Corps History Book, but because of the
absence of a central collection or archive, many have been lost over time; this is
similarly the case in Ireland. No specific history of the Salvation Army in Ireland
has been written to date.[3] While the scope of this paper does not lend itself to
an in-depth examination of the work of the Salvation Army in Ireland, I hope
it may stimulate interest and further research.

'It is easy to see the importance of history to feminism', Mary Cullen has
observed, 'and why a feminist historical perspective begins with a search for the

2 R.G. Moyles' *A Bibliography of Salvation Army Literature in English 1865–1987* (New
York/Canada, 1988) is an invaluable source both for Salvationist publications and anti-
Army critiques. In the section entitled 'The Salvation Army Throughout The World',
bibliographies are subdivided by territory. Although there are two Salvationist entries for
Scotland and one for Wales (p. 28), Moyles does not mention Ireland.   3 For information
regarding the Army's activities in Dublin, see Sr Katherine Butler, R.S.C., 'Dublin's
Hallelujah Lassies' in *Dublin Historical Record*, xlii (1989), pp. 128–46.

historical identity of women.'[4] This study endeavours to portray the 'historical identity' of the Irish women involved in the Salvation Army rescue network in Britain and Ireland in the nineteenth century. In the course of my work, it became apparent that much of the Salvationist and general literature, as well as some of the present-day feminist literature available on rescue work, assumes that all rescued women were 'prostitutes', without always challenging the language that defined them as such. 'Rescue work' was associated in the nineteenth century with 'prostitution' and with 'unmarried mothers'; the language used about these women is often specific and damning. 'Fallen' women were those who had 'fallen' from the virginal or maternal high altar of respectability into the murky under-belly of a society which operated on a 'double standard'. The use of such terms to describe women is a significant illustration of nineteenth-century social and cultural constructs.[5]

I

Against the backdrop of the decades of reform and colonial expansion in nine-teenth-century Britain, the Salvation Army marched to its particular War. Popular papers reported the sensational finds and victories of the time, emigration to the far flung corners of the exotic empire was encouraged, and the battle against 'foreign control' had begun. In their study of the development of the English middle class, Davidoff and Hall argue that the 'powerful combination of religious, commercial and scientific ideologies' appealed to 'people carving out a destiny'; these images were in turn enhanced by 'the glory of war ... although the seriously religious, committed to Christ's Army, were uneasy in its unqualified celebration'.[6] The Salvation Army was thus, to some extent, a product of its time, exciting, expan-sionist, and sensational.

The state of the churches in Britain was the first battlefield into which this Army marched. William and Catherine Booth's avowed mission was to the 'churchless' working classes.[7] By the first half of the nineteenth century, it was clear in Britain that abstinence from religious worship was commonest amongst the working classes, the landless poor. A common practice of the time was to rent pews, with the further exclusion of the working classes because of lack of suitable

4 Mary Cullen, 'Telling it our way' in *Personally Speaking* (Dublin, 1985), p. 255.   5 See Lucy Bland, *Banishing the Beast: English Feminism and Sexual Morality, 1855–1914* (London, 1995); Nancy F. Cott, '"Passionless": A Reinterpretation of Victorian Sexual Ideology, 1790–1850' in *Signs*, 4 (1978), pp. 219–36; Pat Caplan, *The Cultural Construction of Sexuality* (London, 1987); Susan Kingsley Kent, *Sex and Suffrage in Britain 1860–1941* (London, 1990); Michael Mason, *The Making of Victorian Sexuality* (Oxford, 1994); Judith Walkowitz, *City of Dreadful Delight: Narratives of Sexual Danger in Late Victorian London* (London, 1992). 6 Leonore Davidoff and Catherine Hall, *Family Fortunes, Men and Women of the English Middle Class, 1780–1850* (London, 1987), pp. 97–9.   7 Catherine Bramwell-Booth, *Catherine Booth* (London, 1970), p. 194.

dress as they sat in the few available free seats at the back or in the corner of the church.[8] The repeal of anti-Catholic/Dissenter legislation from the mid 1770s, culminating in the granting of Catholic emancipation in 1829, significantly altered the religious balance of power. However it was not until the 1860s that it became clear that the Anglican church could never hope to re-instate itself as the national church. The period then was one of increasing secularism. Continental free-thought was invading England and advances in science contributed to growing scepticism. Protectionism versus free trade, and the notion of linking colonialism with employment were attractive ideas to many people and carried weight at a time when there was considerable concern in Britain about what was called 'the social problem' – a generic term for the desperate condition of London's poor, when strikes and riots and outrages were frightening the middle classes and colonies appeared one very obvious way to relieve poverty.

Catherine and William Booth, both dissident Methodists,[9] were appalled by the misery of London's slum-dwellers. They were determined to 'wage war' on behalf of the 'submerged tenth'[10] of English society. The Salvation Army was successful and popular partly because of its military style. By the end of the nineteenth century, it had achieved the reputation of being one of England's leading social reform agencies and had extended its work world-wide. Public notoriety and controversy, through the Booths' social and political activities, also ensured the Army's success. In particular, its well-known social services developed as a natural result of Catherine and William Booth's belief that it was a waste of time to preach to a 'congregation' who were cold and hungry.

The East London Revival Society, led by William Booth and later called the East London Christian Mission, was the forerunner of the Salvation Army and one of the several organisations of the time combining some social service with religion. The Religious Worship Act of 1855 allowed the use of secular buildings for religious services, so now large crowds could be attracted to local halls, tents

8 Christine Ward, 'The Social Sources of the Salvation Army 1865–1890' (1970, Unpublished M. Phil Thesis, History, Bedford College, University of London), p. 29. 9 William Booth had been associated with the Wesleyans, the Reformers and the Methodist New Connexion. He was expelled from the Wesleyans in 1851, and became a minister for the Reformers in 1851–54. He joined the New Connexion in 1854 and resigned in 1861 when he was refused permission to be a travelling evangelist. He then worked as a free-lance evangelist until he became a missioner of the Christian Revival Society from 1865, which became the East London Christian Mission in 1867. Catherine Booth preached publicly for the first time in Gateshead in 1860. 10 William Booth, *In Darkest England and the Way Out* (London, 1890), pp. 21–3. Using Charles Booth's recent survey of four London boroughs, *Life and Labour of the People of London* (London, 1889), as his guide, William estimated that one in ten of the population of the country was living in destitution, i.e. 'the submerged tenth'. William's calculations may be open to criticism, as he estimated the probable destitute population for the whole of London and then the rest of the country. William also referred to other authorities, taking a moderate figure from their opinions and calculations. See also Christine Ward, 'Social Sources', p. 192; Kathleen Woodroofe, *From Charity Work to Social Work* (London, 1962).

and theatres. The inception of the Army took place in 1878 when William, already aware of how difficult it was to make decisions by committee, was perusing the *Annual Mission Report* entitled *A Volunteer Army*. Conscious of the poor reputation of the volunteer forces of the day, he replaced the word 'volunteer' and brought the 'Salvation Army' into being with a stroke of his pen. He became the first General of that Army and remained so for the next thirty-four years, until 1912, when he was succeeded by his son Bramwell, later deposed in 1929. Evangeline Booth, William's daughter, initially commanded a large London Corps, then was Commander of the United States Territory, and later became General of the Army, like her father and brother before her, from 1934 to 1939. A member of the Booth family was thus at the helm during the formative years of the Army. World-wide Territorial decisions and ideology were formulated in the London Headquarters and were directly influenced for many years by Bramwell who effectively ran the Army from 1881 as Chief of Staff and by his wife, Florence Booth, who developed women's social work.

Catherine Mumford Booth is described by W.T. Stead, the well known editor of the *Pall Mall Gazette*, as 'the prophetess of the new movement' who 'saw it afar off': 'She was glad she was a socialist of the heart, full of passionate sympathy with the poor and the oppressed of every land and clime; full too, of fierce indignation against all who did them wrong.' Stead goes on to say that the distinct beliefs and ethos and enduring work of the Salvation Army were due more to Catherine 'than to any other human being'.[11] During Catherine and William's courtship, William had suggested to Catherine that man 'was her superior in regard to intellect'. Catherine replied in Wollstonecraftian terms, arguing that 'woman is, in consequence of her inadequate education, generally inferior to man intellectually, I admit. But that she is naturally so, as your remarks seem to imply, I see no cause to believe'.[12] The courtship survived as William admitted equality and they subsequently had eight children who from an early age were all involved in the expansion of the Salvation Army. From then it became an essential element of their creed that in Christ there is 'neither female nor male' and 'that the gospel combined with nature to place both on a footing of absolute mental and spiritual equality'.[13] This fundamental acceptance of the importance of women's equality with male colleagues was demonstrated by the Army's deliberate decision to exclude communion and have women lead the Meetings. Unfortunately this equality did not extend into comparative salaries until the twentieth century.

As early as 1865, Catherine Booth was aware that there were women 'ready to perish' for a variety of reasons, and that they 'would willing enter a home if one were available'.[14] Florence, her daughter-in-law, visited other rescue homes in order to educate herself as she strove to develop an ethos for the Army's Rescue Homes. She was horrified by what she found:

11 *War Cry*, 8 November 1890, p. 9.   12 William Booth Bramwell, *These Fifty Years* (London [1929]), pp. 83–6.   13 Ibid.   14 *Wesleyan Times*, 27 March 1865.

Women were kept in these places for one, two and even three years, and if they failed to run well, were never given a second chance. Bolts and bars, bare, dismal rooms, high walls, no occupation but that of laundry work, seemed to explain this discouragement. I could not imagine myself becoming any better for a long stay in similar circumstances.[15]

Catherine and Florence clearly understood 'that what these woman most needed was a real home, for they were homeless, and that they needed support in their first efforts to earn their own living and return to respectable society'.[16] It was their genuine belief as 'Salvationists'[17] that they were equal as sinners with those they were rescuing; this was the real strength behind the development of this early rescue work.

The Army's Women's Social Services evolved out of the practice of individual Salvationists, around the world, taking 'penitent'[18] 'fallen' women into their homes. On 22 May 1884, the Hanbury Street Women's Refuge opened in London's Whitechapel district. This was the official start of the Salvation Army women's social work. Sewing and washing paid the rent and fed the women and, within months of opening the Refuge in Hanbury Street, the demand for places was overwhelming. From the beginning the provision of suitable employment and lodgings for women alone, without friends or family in the city or towns, was a very important feature in the development of the Salvationist social services.

Florence Bramwell Booth was put in charge of the new Refuge and, assisted by Adelaide Cox, expanded the Army's rescue work to 117 homes in Britain during the next thirty years, thus earning the Army the reputation of being one of the largest, most effective, and, to some extent, most innovative rescue organisations in Britain and world-wide. Florence encountered daily the prevalent 'double standard' when she heard from young girls, just in their teens, 'the stories of their destruction' and wrote of her horror on discovering

that if they were thirteen years of age, or if there were reason to believe they had reached that age, the men who destroyed them could not be punished; that for these outcast women there seemed left no place of repentance on earth, and the majority, even if they wished to return, were cast out of their homes and no one would give them employment; I felt this was a mystery of iniquity indeed.[19]

In 1884 General Booth outlined a scheme for rescue work which included three target classes: prostitutes, young girls in danger of falling into sin, and 'girls who have been ruined and forsaken but who are opposed to leading an immoral life'.[20]

---

15 *Sunday Circle*, 18 March 1923.   **16** Ibid.   **17** 'Salvationist' is a term used for work done or published by a member of the Army which expresses the ethos of the organisation; this term is still used today.   **18** Those who came to the Penitent Form (a stool or a bench) at the Army Meetings and made a public declaration to change their lives.   **19** *Deliverer*, July 1904, p. 2.   **20** *All the World*, iv (1888), pp. 64–8.

The latter clearly included unmarried mothers, who were often described as having taken only the first step on the 'downward path'. But it was Florence again who was probably responsible for the Army's entrance into a relatively new area of rescue work, caring for pregnant single women, and women with illegitimate infants. The 'double difficulty' of being both a 'fallen woman' and a mother shaped the direction of the Army's social work in this area as very few other rescue homes allowed a mother to bring her child with her.

Thus Ivy House in England was established in 1890 for 'girls who previous to their fall, have led respectable lives, and who have been betrayed by the so-called men to whom they have been engaged and whom they loved not wisely, but too well'.[21] Such was the situation of Sarah, an Irish born woman who, according to one Salvation Army House's Receiving Statement, 'whilst in our situation became engaged to a young man, a member of the Brethren, who seduced her, and then went to America. Sarah was with us until just before her baby's birth, returned to the House with her baby when well enough, and until she met with work. She is doing well and brings the child to see us sometimes. Sundays she always spends with us'.[22] Sarah clearly represented one of the group of whom Florence Booth stated 'no class of women for whom we have worked has yielded such uniformly encouraging results'.[23] The high success rate claimed by the Salvation Army was not that surprising, considering the lack of alternatives for unmarried pregnant women. Loss of respectability, homelessness and unemployment, aligned with pregnancy and responsibility for the child, obviously limited their options and made them more obviously dependent on charitable assistance than other 'fallen' women. Because they were mothers and had therefore reached the pinnacle of Victorian society, by 'foul' means rather than fair, they were at the zenith of 'fallen' women – if one accepts a hierarchical structure operated in the rescuing of these women – once they chose to enter the rescue network.

The Women's Social Services, graphically described as the 'Cellar, Gutter and Garret Brigade', responded to the changing needs of those they were rescuing. Slum work began in 1884, and developed into small social care agencies ministering directly to the needs of the poor in their own neighbourhood. Other Salvationist facilities used by Irish women were the shelters and metropoles,[24] 'eventide' and servants' homes, maternity hospitals, district nursing, alcoholic rehabilitation, crèches, adoption homes and children's homes, a help and enquiry department and servant registries.

As Table 1 illustrates, the Salvation Army unpublished records for the British Isles Territory show twenty-nine Irish women staying in the London Army Houses and two hundred and fourteen outside London, i.e. in the rest of the British Isles Salvation Army Territory, between 1886 and 1892. Where information

---

21 *Saved in Time: Annual Report of the Women's Social Work for 1892–93*, p. 11; *Deliverer*, September 1890, p. 42.   **22** Final Reports of the Salvation Army Receiving House Statements, Country Book I, 1887–1890.   **23** *All the World*, xiv (1894), p. 111.   **24** The Metropoles charged a small accommodation fee.

is recorded by the Army, seventy-two Irish women stated Ulster, with forty-one specifying Belfast, as their point of entry to the rescue network and a further thirty-eight women originally entered through the Dublin rescue network. Sixteen entered in London, and a further twenty-two entered from England, Wales and Scotland. It is clear from the Army records that once a woman entered the rescue network, she could be sent anywhere within the British Isles Territory, dependent on her needs as assessed by the Army.

II

> Ireland – a land heretofore all uninvaded – by methods of evangelisation so downright and outspoken as ours. Just as well, perhaps, that simple women, utterly ignorant of all the countless political and religious complications of the country, pioneered it! [25]

Women were continually involved as leading missionaries and administrators for the developing Salvation Army programmes. Salvationist women raised and administered the necessary funds for the Women's Social Services which operated independently from the rest of the Army. Women were also involved in the evangelical revival that spread across the Army's British Isles Territory. Caroline Reynolds was one of those women who, according to the *War Cry* of 4 September 1886, joined what was known as 'The Female Band' – a company of Whitechapel soldiers who went about to different parts of London and caused 'a great sensation in London'.[26] It was Caroline Reynolds who undertook the 'invasion' of Ireland, arriving in 1880; in the next twenty-eight months she opened sixteen stations, beginning in Belfast and Derry. By 31 May 1888, when the first Corps in Dublin was set up in South Richmond Street, there were twenty-eight Corps already established in Ulster. Although Ireland was part of the British empire, local customs and beliefs were different, to say the least, and unfortunately the Salvationists were not well prepared. As Captain Reynolds woefully remarked in 1886:

> No one will ever know what we went through. The Army colours given for Ireland had a green corner with the harp and no crown. We did not know that this was treason. Then we had orange hymn books. The Orangemen gloried in that, and the Catholics were wild at it! There were always crowds of Roman Catholics in our open-air meetings. They won't stand songs about fighting, but anything about the Cross or the Blood they will listen to.[27]

Once Belfast was better established, Major Reynolds moved on to Derry where, as was the norm in establishing Corps elsewhere, she initially faced strong opposition, with five days of riots. On their first afternoon there, they had no people

25 *War Cry*, 4 September 1886, p. 4.   26 Ibid.   27 Ibid.

to join in the hymns and she tells how they had 'only sung one verse when young men came running from all sides – regular Fenians! I thought, here's a beautiful lot of people to get saved!'[28] Undaunted the Salvationists held a meeting, and afterwards the police escorted them to a safe house. Despite the local difficulties, by the time the General visited Belfast in October 1886, 10,000 people were present at the meeting. Two years later, Catherine Booth saw 1,500 soldiers on the march.

In 1887, 'The Irish Rescue Home' was situated in 63 Great George Street, in Belfast described as 'a locality in which abound the class of girls we are seeking to save'. In order to off-set the expenses incurred by the rescue home, the Salvationists, as was common with other homes, began to take in some work. In Belfast this was 'the top-sewing of linen and handkerchiefs for one manufacturer, and the finishing of shirts for another'. Fulton's warerooms and laundry, located in Fountaine Street, provided the home with sewing and also provided employ-ment to three of the women when they left the rescue home.[29] The poverty of the women is clear from the Salvationists' request for cast-off clothing for the girls to wear as 'most of the girls came in barefooted, with a shawl over their heads'.[30] Major Adelaide Cox tells us that by 1889

> Two hundred and fifty-five cases had been admitted into the [Belfast] Home, a large proportion of which have been successfully dealt with, many have been sent into situations, and others – long-lost daughters – have been taken home to their parents.[31]

Opposition to the newly formed Salvation Army came in many forms in the nineteenth century, both in Ireland and England. The 1880s was a period of particular physical violence towards the Army throughout Britain, especially from a group of thugs called 'the Skeleton Army'; this group also threatened the newly formed Church Army and moral reformers such as Josephine Butler. Vicious attacks on the Army's processions were not confined to the adult soldiers. The *War Cry*, 5 January 1882, states that by that time twenty-three children had been injured in various 'battles'. Some people were killed in these attacks, among them women and children. Salvationists themselves were jailed for a variety of reasons during this time, including preaching by women and, even, disorderly conduct. As was common world-wide, these early Salvationists were attacked physically and verbally, with what ever came to hand, and so it was in Dublin. A 1901 edition of the *War Cry* describes Dublin as a city 'whose women are said to be treated with a courtesy unsurpassed in any other part of the world – strange to say, the sight of a woman wearing an Army bonnet in the streets acts upon the crowd like a red rag to an infuriated bull'.[32]

28 Ibid.   **29** Final Reports of the Salvation Army Receiving House Statements, Country Book I, 1887–1890.   **30** *War Cry*, 26 February 1887, p. 6.   **31** *Deliverer*, 15 September 1889, p. 27.   **32** *War Cry*, 13 July 1901, p. 12.

In the case of Ireland, both in Derry and in Dublin, their respectability was not doubted, just the Army's 'corybantic religion'. Belfast, on the other hand, welcomed the sight of these 'respectable warriors'. Ireland in the nineteenth century became polarised between Catholics and Protestants through religious consolidation, socio-economic, political and regional separation. Evangelicals were anathema to the re-establishing Catholic Church.[33] So to the majority of Catholics in Ireland the Salvation Army may have symbolised the oppressor, the British Protestant proselytising overlord. However, that did not stop some Catholic and other religious groups recognising the innate goodness and equality that the Army espoused. The strength of opposition to the Army in Dublin was fuelled no doubt by fear and ignorance as to the real nature of their work, at a time when the Catholic church was trying to establish its own charities and warning against proselytism. Catholics appeared frightened that their children would be 'captured in the war for souls', a 'battle' well-established in Ireland before the Salvation Army entered the fray.[34] The Army in contrast described themselves in the following words:

> We have no politics, and therefore cannot enter into discussion or arouse enmity ... on that point. We do not contend with other religious bodies or attack their creeds. We are not a sect, but an Army of peace, whose one duty is to preach the full, free, uttermost salvation of Jesus Christ to the souls of the people and to care for their bodies. We are aggressive against the devil and sin in all shapes and garbs, and that aggression should appeal to the militant spirit of the Irish. We are full of fire and life, so are they. Our religion is plain, practical, happy and bubbling over with songs.[35]

However, some ranks in Dublin were unable to wear their uniforms in public. One woman was advised not to wear her bonnet publicly by the Captain. 'Not a bit of it!' replied the girl, staunchly, as the *War Cry* of 13 July 1901 reported: 'I have always worn my bonnet and I shall continue to do so. I am not going back on my principle.'[36] This principled soldier was followed on her first Saturday night in Dublin by

> a howling crowd of men, women and children ... until she reached the door of her mistress's house in Grafton Street. The following Sunday evening, however, a gang of rough lads were waiting about for her; they followed her

33 K. Theodore Hoppen, *Ireland since 1800: Conflict and Conformity* (London and New York, 1989).   **34** Jacintha Prunty, 'The Geography of Poverty, Dublin 1850–1900: The Social Mission of the Church, with Particular Reference to Margaret Aylward and Co-Workers' (Unpublished Ph.D Thesis, Geography, University College Dublin, 1992); Joseph Robbins, *The Lost Children – A Study of Charity Children in Ireland, 1700–1900* (Dublin, 1987); Desmond Bowen, *Souperism: Myth or Reality, A Study in Souperism* (Cork, 1970). **35** *All the World*, September 1902, p. 471.   **36** *War Cry*, 13 July 1901, p. 12.

through the streets, hustling and pushing her, while respectably-dressed men and women encouraged them, and hurled their hisses and maledictions at the bonnetted Salvation lassie. The ensuing battle by the crowd for her bonnet, failed, but the onward rush of the crowd drove the defenceless girl's head through the glass panel of the door, [of her Mistress's home] and soon her face was bleeding profusely. The mob then turned its attention to smashing the windows of the house and continued this little entertainment until dispersed by the police.[37]

III

Who were these 233 Irish women who used the Salvation Army rescue network in Ireland and Britain between 1886 and 1892? The majority were born or lived in Ulster, and worked in either domestic service or the textile industry, possibly both. Eleven came from Cork and thirty-five were born in Dublin or its environs. A few came from a rural background. As stated earlier, for seventy-two women Ulster was their point of entry, and Dublin for thirty-eight others. Most of them were unattached and aged between fourteen and twenty-nine when they became involved with the Salvation Army. The majority of these women stated that they had lost their parents and partners through death and desertion. They came because they were homeless, sick or pregnant, in debt, afraid or at risk. Many of them had travelled a lot, a few to places as far away as New York, Canada or France, others all over Ireland and Britain. They spent, on average, four months in an Army refuge. They used other institutions like hospitals and refuges frequently. For all of these women life was hard, society unwelcoming.

Twenty per cent of the 233 Irish women in the British Isles Territory were recorded by the Salvationists as having 'fallen' due to 'bad company'. One hundred and seventy-one women were single or engaged, and pregnancy was not a major cause of entry to the network as 57 per cent of the single women aged between fourteen and thirty-nine had never given birth. It is often assumed that rescue work in the nineteenth century was particularly designed for pregnant unmarried women, and that women who entered such rescue networks did so due to pregnancy. In fact the highest attributed factor for entry to the Army's British Isles Territory rescue network was 'women at risk', recorded as 18 per cent.

Since the Salvation Army in Ireland was more established in Ulster between 1866 and 1892 than in any other part of Ireland, it is not surprising that the majority of Irish women were from that area. This would also have influenced their employment opportunities, as this was the one area in Ireland in the late nineteenth century where employment prospects were good, even if the wages were not. Although categorisation of social class was in its infancy in the 1880s, the 1881 Census attempted a division of the population into six different social

37 Ibid.

class categories. Using that categorisation' and from the information available, it does not appear that the women in this study initially came from very poor working class backgrounds.[38]

Applying the 1881 census categorisation to the details recorded by the Army of the former occupations of the 233 Irish women in this sample, the greatest number, 72 per cent, fell into Class II, i.e. domestic service, followed by 22 per cent in Class V, i.e. industrial workers, prior to entry to the rescue network. These figures dropped to 43 per cent for Class II, and rose to 25 per cent for Class V, for the women on leaving the Salvation Army network. These women were then at a low ebb, trying to survive on little or no wages. The social class of the father only defined the world in which women lived as long as their fathers were alive and employed, or as long as she lived under his care. For many women the death of a father or partner caused an immediate change for the worse in social class, and loss of old support networks as the Irish women moved downwards in the social scale.

Depending on the individual case of the women passing through the Salvationist rescue network, it became apparent that not all women were suitable for domestic service, and so some other form of alternative employment had to be found. In England bookbinding was operating in Devonshire House, Hackney and in Whitechapel by 1888. This was considered appropriate employment as 'it is sheltered, it is fairly paid, it is quickly learned, and it requires a concentration of thought and attention which is an invaluable shield and discipline'.[39] The *Deliverer* shows that knitting, text washing, upholstery and needlework were all industries undertaken within the rescue homes.[40] Laundry work was undertaken in 1891, when Florence Booth finally agreed to the establishment of a Salvationist laundry in Stoke Newington. The initial group were 'twenty-three women coming from the slums, the shelter, the rescue homes and stray workers who came on their own account'.[41]

A detailed examination of the 233 Irish women cited in this study reveals that 16 per cent or thirty-eight women stayed for a period of four months in the Army's rescue network throughout the British Isles Territory. Overall, 192 women or 82 per cent were recorded as staying between one and ten months. Only 6 per cent remained within the rescue network for a period between fourteen months and under three years. In general, these were women who entered the

---

38 Report of the Census of Ireland, 1881; Table 2 in Grainne Blair, '"Equal Sinners", Irish Women Utilising the Salvation Army Rescue Network for Ireland and Britain in the Nineteenth Century: An Analytic Portrait' (Unpublished M.A. Thesis, Women's Studies, University College Dublin, 1995), p. 63.   39 *All The World*, February 1888, pp. 64–5; Jenty Fairbanks, *Booth's Boots: Social Services Beginnings in the Salvation Army* (London, 1983), p. 105.   40 *Deliverer*, September 1891, p. 45; January 1892, p. 120; August 1891, p. 24; October 1891, p. 56. According to one Annual Report, religious texts or mottos, 'on red ingrain cambric with white linen letters firmly stitched on, are made in one of our Rescue Homes' ('Harvest Sheaves', Annual Report , 1888–1889, London).   41 *All the World*, July 1891, p. 504.

network early in their pregnancy, and stayed until a situation could be found for them and arrangements made for their child. Others in this category were women who were particularly ill and needed to convalesce, or were unsuitable for employment outside the network, and chose to work and live with the Salvationists.

Records also show that 56 per cent (131) of the Irish women were admitted to non-Salvation 'refuges', on a total of 208 occasions. Women who stayed in these other refuges were destitute, homeless, estranged from their families or orphaned, some syphilitic, institutionalised, pregnant or otherwise at risk, and for the most part were considered unrespectable or 'fallen' in one way or another. The Salvationists offered a different type of 'refuge' trying to give a 'fresh start' to many:

> For the methods of The Salvation Army are essentially movement, life, activity – light and colour and noise – the exchange of destructive excitements for these which are, at all events, harmless, when even not life-giving. And for women who have lived in the lurid glare and wild uproar of vice, this is better than the gloomy retribution of penance and penitence.[42]

Inmates of non-Salvationist 'refuges' were largely involved in laundry or sewing, and the work was a vital source of income for the refuges. This latter point was in direct contrast to the beliefs of Florence Booth who resisted the 'laundry work' despite its financial gains for a long time, as she preferred the 'opportunity for more personal influence over the girls'.[43]

One particular type of 'refuge' used frequently was Magdalene Asylums. Women were committed to these asylums for a variety of reasons. Many women stayed in these places for two or three years and even longer, until pronounced 'fit to attain their proper station in life'. In contrast, Irish women stayed in the Salvation rescue network from a few days to over two years, and were much freer within these institutions, bringing their children and friends with them, allowed to leave to get their belongings unaccompanied, and in general treated as an equal adult women.[44] Yet, despite the harshness of the regime of many of the non-Salvationist refuges, many women had no choice but to avail of these particular institutions. A visitor to the Army's women's shelter in Hanbury Street emphasises this difference, describing how the rollicking and rousing evening service, accompanied with banjos, tambourines and general noise often struck a right chord:

> the conscience vibrates in unison with the appeal, outcast sinners rise redeemed as penitent Magdalens. For such as these The Salvation Army has ever a glad welcome ... and, we venture to add, a more rational way of dealing with them than is to be found in the strict seclusion and dull monotony of many penitential homes.[45]

42 *Deliverer*, September 1891, p. 45.   43 *War Cry*, 6 February 1886.   44 Fairbanks, *Booth's Boots*, p. 9.   45 *Deliverer*, September 1891, p. 45.

The personal contact that the Salvationist rescue network provided to Irish women was also in marked contrast to many other institutions at that time. The Salvationists understood the lack of self esteem in the women who presented themselves for help. Society judged harshly women who had 'fallen' and expected them to continue in the 'fall'; the women themselves defined themselves as 'bad' and 'evil' and could see no way out of the downward trend. As Florence Booth observed,

> Now she is expected to be good; and, as a rule she is good. Considering the shattered nerves, the habits of drinking, the craving for excitement, the restlessness of mind and body with which a women who has been for any length of time leading a sinful life come to our homes, we could sometimes wonder ourselves as pronouncedly as they do others at the large percentage who have been permanently reclaimed therein.[46]

The Salvation Army presented an opportunity for these Irish women to attain 'respectability', by becoming a soldier or even through a personal commitment to the Army's ethos. It provided shelter, training and retraining, employment, personal development and a new support network of friends and a larger family group, if requested, thus responding to the perceived needs of the 'congregation' they were helping. Yet the Salvationists' primary task was to evangelise the masses, and the women's social work was a method of doing this. This work involved a clear recognition of the economic inequalities and the vulnerability of all women. Similarities did exist between other rescue societies of the time and the Army; in particular, the Salvationist belief that fornication outside a legal union was sinful, reinforced contemporary whore/madonna dichotomies. A significant difference however, was their belief that everyone was entitled to help – no matter how black the sin; in fact as far as the Salvationists were concerned, the blacker the better, as the saving would be all the greater.

The nature of the Salvationist work with women as I have examined it, shows clearly their genuine belief in their ability to identify with the Irish women that they were helping. In 1865 the *Wesleyan Times* described Catherine Booth in the following words: 'She identified herself with them as a sinner, saying that if they supposed her better than they, it was a mistake, as all sinners were sinners against God.'[47] Within this philosophy these women were equal with their helpers; in this the Salvation Army had something unique to offer the women it strove to save.

46 *A Brief Review of the First Year's Work* (London, 1891), p. 117.   **47** *Wesleyan Times*, 27 March 1865.

V

Expanding the Canon: Late Nineteenth-Century Literature

Women's Education, Edward Dowden and the University Curriculum in English Literature: An Unlikely Progression

CHRISTINA HUNT MAHONY

The higher education of women in Ireland, an exclusively extra-mural under-taking for most of the nineteenth century, can be viewed as an important part in the continuum of educational reform which resulted in English Literature being considered a suitable subject for degree examination. Furthermore, since the education of women continued to be a segregated, unrecognised process, lectures and courses for women, not subject to university and degree-related strictures, became the proving ground for early canon formation in the literature of a language which, in Ireland, had only become the majority vernacular a generation or two earlier. This anomaly, the periphery (female and Irish) informing and altering the establishment (male and British), was the result of the cohesion of a number of forces and factors – but an examination of a group of public lectures devised for women seems an appropriate place to start.

The Dublin Afternoon Lectures on Literature and the Arts were held every spring from 1863 to 1868. They were delivered by most of the prominent men in the city, but were geared, most unusually, toward an audience comprised of gentlewomen and male civil servants. These lectures became an important link in the chain of nineteenth-century educational enfranchisement. The Afternoon Lectures had, as their subjects, material which would not become canonical for another generation or two, yet was considered not too 'high brow' for the sisters, daughters, wives and mothers of the small coterie of educated men who brokered cultural power in Dublin in the 1860s. To best understand, however, the impact and the origin of the Afternoon Lectures in Dublin, it is necessary to begin earlier in the century and in England.

In British cities, from as early as the 1820s, well-intentioned groups of educated men tried to lessen the educational gap which existed between themselves and the working classes. Later such experiments, of a lasting nature, like Birkbeck College of the University of London, institutionalised these efforts; and these are well-documented. However, less well-known are the many individual, recurring or fleeting series of lectures devised for working men in the decades between 1820 and 1860. These lectures usually had one of two general purposes. The first was a focus on practical skills and vocational training. Topics ran from the supremely practical ('How to Plan a Productive, Balanced and Sightly Vegetable Garden'), to the self-improving ('How to Learn Telegraphy'). The latter type of lecture was often a well-intentioned 'come-on' to working men who paid, often quite dearly, for their lectures. Posters for these lectures were remarkably similar to those seen in advertisements today offering the promise of lucrative jobs to those willing to train or to retrain as computer 'programmers'.[1]

But it is the second category of public lectures in the latter half of the nineteenth century that is of greater import to anyone interested in either women's education or literary canon formation, the public lecture which aimed at the development of cultural awareness. Suitable subjects would have included an introduction to the works of Dante, Shakespeare or Goethe. Cultural lectures could also be serial, an attempt in some cases, at giving the lie to their facility – 'Italian Renaissance Frescoes in Four Weeks', for instance.

The British model for such public lectures transplanted well to Ireland, but only to parts of Ireland. Cities west of the Shannon, although they initiated series of public lectures, failed to see such efforts take root. In part, this failure to thrive, particularly in pre-famine Ireland, was due to the public lecture being English in both its language and ethos. But in Dublin, parts of Kilkenny and Tipperary, Drogheda, Dundalk, Belfast and several smaller urban centres in what is now Northern Ireland, the English-speaking working population adapted readily to the public lecture format.[2] In Dublin, specifically, there were very successful evening series of lectures sponsored by another thriving import, the working men's societies, including the St Ann's Working Men's Club and the Mechanics' Institute, located in Abbey Street.[3]

The Dublin Mechanics' Institute was typical of self-improvement organisations of the era, including a strong emphasis on moral education for the working man, or more specifically the artisan classes, those with good basic skills, and a certain amount of disposable income. Today's equivalent employment sector in Ireland would be, perhaps, members of crafts unions. Working men paid disproportionately large amounts to become members of its library at ten shillings a year and to take training and/or scientific courses. But they also paid their money to acquire a middle-class veneer with French lessons and dancing classes.

It is not surprising, then, that the range and stellar quality of the public lecturers at the Mechanics' Institute attracted much attention in Dublin, particularly in the contemporary press. But, and here is where the evolutionary process begins, it seems the Mechanics' Institute's lectures, which ended in 1860, three years before the Afternoon Lectures began, had failed to fulfil the specific needs of a large and hitherto neglected group in mid-Victorian Dublin – the ladies.

The preface to the first series of *The Afternoon Lectures* (1863) acknowledges this gap:

1 J.F.C. Harrison, in his important book *Learning and Life 1790–1960* (London, 1961), devotes considerable attention to the pitfalls and tragedies of such self-improvement efforts through the years.   2 Seamus Duffy, '"Treasures Open to the Wise": A Survey of Early Mechanics' Institutes and Similar Organisations' in *Saothar*, xv (1990), pp. 39–47.   3 Two valuable sources on Mechanics' Institutes are Kieran Byrne's 'The Mechanics' Institute in Ireland 1825–50' in *Proceedings of the Educational Studies Conference*, Dublin (1979), pp. 32–47

Experience has shown that books are often laid aside by those to whom oral teaching is very acceptable; and while the libraries of Mechanics' Institutions have been comparatively neglected, the evening lectures of 'Young Men's Societies' have been thronged. No city has witnessed more happy results from these lectures than Dublin; [but] large numbers have had reason to regret that the hour and the place have been such as practically to exclude them ... [Thus] It was considered essential that the new lectures should be delivered in some suitable building of unsectarian or neutral character, on the south side of the city, and at an hour when ladies could conveniently attend, and when the daily occupations of persons engaged in the law courts and the public offices should have ceased.[4]

Thus the Afternoon Lectures were born, delivered in the theatre of the Museum of Industry on Stephen's Green, later the site of the Loreto Convent. As the building was very near the spot where Alexandra College for Women would open its doors midway through the Afternoon Lectures series, its female audience became assured. The Afternoon Lectures were given, for the most part, by members of Trinity College, but also by prominent clergymen, barristers and such notables as Samuel Ferguson and John Ruskin; and the lecturers' chosen subjects were scrutinised by a diligent committee, overseen by the Lord Chancellor and, at times, by the Provost of Trinity College. The committee did not, it seems, view its role as being merely to rubber stamp submissions. They continued to maintain a very paternalistic stance, similar to that exercised by the committee which administered the Mechanics' Institution, and indeed membership of the two committees overlapped significantly. Material deemed frivolous in nature or found lacking in sufficient moral rectitude was withheld as being unsuitable for the ladies, just as it had been considered to be inappropriate for presumably equally-impressionable working men. English Literature was to be the focus, although in some years the range was opened to include 'The Arts', thus allowing Ruskin, for instance, to speak on Architecture, and a returned civil servant to introduce 'The Native Literature of India'.[5]

In general the lectures were scheduled annually in spring so as to encourage large attendance in the mild weather and the longer April and May evenings. Lectures were designed to offer detailed information on subjects already somewhat familiar to the audience; and they were given by men whose names were recognised by all in the small world which was Dublin's middle to upper classes. There was a decided social quality about the material too, which was often introduced with a clever, well-rounded and gentlemanly preface, accompanied

and R.G. Morton's 'Mechanics' Institutes and the Attempted Diffusion of Useful Knowledge in Ireland, 1825–79' in *Irish Booklore*, ii, 1 (Spring, 1972), pp. 59–74. **4** *The Afternoon Lectures on English Literature*, 1st Series (London and Dublin, 1863), preface. **5** The civil servant was Captain Meadows Taylor. See *The Afternoon Lectures on English Literature*, 2nd Series (London and Dublin, 1864), pp. 103–49.

by the sort of feigned apology, either for the speaker's lack of expertise or the dryness of his subject, which is a feature not only of the period, but of the specialised dynamic between male speaker and largely female audience.[6]

Thus, although the very first Afternoon Lecture, delivered by the Reverend Edward Whately on the writings of John Foster, speaker of the Irish House of Commons in 1800, got the lectures off to an atypical start, the audience was described in the *Irish Times* of 6 May 1863 as 'highly fashionable'. After the success of the first lecture, subsequent offerings were usually first described as having drawn a 'crowded and fashionable attendance';[7] and the presence of prominent men and women was duly noted.

But perhaps the coverage in the *Freeman's Journal* of J.K. Ingram's subsequent lecture on Shakespeare was more insightful, and helped to point the way toward the future of lectures such as these.[8] Here the writer applauds the choice of English literature by the organisers as fit subject matter, and at that point still rather a novel choice for a public lecture. The *Freeman* reporter, in a paragraph which makes the late-twentieth century reader realise just how removed we are from Ingram's audience, bemoans the fact that everyone was familiar with the classics, but so many were ignorant of literature in their own language. (It is interesting to note here that this report is written early enough that there is no modern Irish 'angst' as to just exactly which language is being referenced.) The reporter also congratulates Ingram for delivering a simple and organised lecture which, though not above the capability of his audience, was also sufficiently elevated to display his own talents. Later the lecture is described as 'intellectual thinkings aloud' – a phrase offered completely unself-consciously, and with a positive connotation which it could never carry today. Perhaps more pertinent to the occasion, however, were Ingram's observations on Shakespeare as author of vibrant and authentic female characters:

> In the painting of female character Shakespeare is especially admirable. No one has more exquisitely delineated those qualities of the heart which may be called the essential and fundamental constituents of that character in its worthy types – modesty, purity, tenderness, self-forgetting devotion. Nor has any one done fuller justice to the true merits of the female intellect, its delicate grace, its fine sagacity, its quick-glancing intuition. And his female portraits are marked by the same nice discrimination as those of the other sex.[9]

A month later the *Freeman* reports more negatively of a survey of literature offered in the series by Professor Rushton of Queen's College Cork: 'It was no small journey, even in this age of special trains and electric telegraphs, to go from Geoffrey

6 See Professor Arthur Houston's self-deprecating remarks which introduce his lecture on English drama, as reported in the *Irish Times*, 27 May 1863.   7 *Irish Times*, 3 June 1863.   8 *Freeman's Journal*, 16 May 1863.   9 J.K. Ingram, 'Shakespeare' in *The Afternoon Lectures*, 1st Series, pp. 109–10. The lecture was also reprinted in detail in the *Irish Times* of 16 May 1863.

of Monmouth to Wordsworth in Cumberland in an hour, and to stop at all the stations.'[10] Thus the *Freeman* gives voice to a recurring criticism of self-improvement lectures in the past: their tendency to sweeping subject. Yet the Afternoon Lectures, a cut above the rest, were in part designed to avoid this flaw.

In the same series there is an informative lecture, very typical of the age and striving to be canonical, delivered by the Reverend James Byrne and entitled 'On the Influence of the National Character on English Literature'.[11] This Arnoldian theory, as set out by Byrne, divides peoples ethnically into the quick-witted, pyrotechnical types which include Celts, and the slower-witted, more careful types which include Anglo-Saxons. After a long series of divisions, into those who deal with the world objectively or subjectively, and other rather arbitrary categories, Byrne constructs a familiar English literary genealogy from Spenser, through Shakespeare, Dryden, Cowper, and Burns to Wordsworth, and then proceeds to make the list contemporary with the inclusion of Tennyson as heir to an unbroken English tradition which he has just assembled. Byrne's list is somewhat idiosyncratic, however, because it removes Milton, whom he considered to be too big and universal to be an English author; but Burns, whose Scottishness is conveniently minimised, becomes English because he favours detail, and that, according to Byrne, is an irrefutable English characteristic. Canonisation has, one fears, always been a suspect undertaking. The following excerpt from Byrne, which proceeds from his assertion that Shakespeare is the most English of English authors primarily because of his favouring of details, gives valuable insight into the racial and ethnic theories of the era and their rhetoric:

> In Milton, on the contrary, there is a striking absence of English characteristics. There is no elaboration of details, no deficiency of general effect. His characters indeed are admirably drawn, and his descriptions shine with the light of genius, but we are struck rather with the poetry and truthfulness of the whole than with the life and fidelity of the particular touches. He had in common with all the born kings of human thought, the divine gifts by which they hold their universal and eternal dominion over the soul of man, but in him those gifts were specialised not as national but as individual.[12]

What the 1863 Afternoon Lectures illustrated, finally, however, was that English literature was not, as yet, a distinct discipline. As a case in point, its final lecture, on English drama, was delivered by the Professor of Political Economy at Trinity, Arthur Houston, one of many specialists from other disciplines who contributed to this literary series. Indeed in subsequent years the range of literary lecturers and the scope of their primary disciplines continues to impress: a Q.C. on Sheridan, a dean on Wordsworth, an archbishop on the sonnet, and a professor of Civil Law on eighteenth-century German literature.

10 *Freeman's Journal*, 3 June 1863.   11 Reverend James Byrne, 'On the Influence of the National Character on English Literature' in *The Afternoon Lectures on English Literature*, 1st Series, pp. 3–40.   12 Byrne, 'On the Influence of the National Character', p. 24.

Focusing somewhat differently, the second series of Afternoon Lectures, in 1864, featured Joseph Napier on 'The Influence of Women on Literature' – a stance obviously made attractive to most of the audience by his citing a long list of mythical and historical women who inspired great characters in literature, like Helen of Troy and Cleopatra.[13] Napier also examined the tradition of the popular female writer from Felicia Hemans to Anna Jameson to Elizabeth Barrett Browning, whom Napier had interviewed immediately before her death. His argument seems a particularly modern one at times:

> We have had Woman sketched by our greatest poets, from Shakespeare to Tennyson, but woman's account of Woman must be her own revelation. The song of the Troubadour, the romance of Chivalry, and many a tale has told of woman's love and woman's devotion, but we must have in her own living words, the sympathy, the tenderness, the self-sacrifice of her nature; the weakness that is strong, the gentleness that is earnest; the intensity of emotion, the quick and delicate perception of the true and right that is peculiarly her own.[14]

The prevailing Victorian myths regarding women return, however, when Napier continues:

> She is a help meet for man in the household, for the training of the young and the tender, and in all the offices that sanctify human affection; meet in the intercourse of life, to refine and chasten feeling; meet in both, to give to humanity its designed completeness. Therefore has she her proper sphere in literature, the character of which she has helped to purify and exalt in its leading departments.[15]

But the lecturers' subjects in 1864 did not pander entirely to the predetermined tastes nor did they coddle the sensibilities of the largely female audience. John O'Hagan, for instance, offered a rather demanding lecture on Chaucer as the common starting point in English literature even for non-specialists; but in an approach which was also common to the era, then proceeded to censor the *Canterbury Tales* for a female readership.[16] While devoting much time to an examination of Griselda's role in 'The Clerk's Tale', and to praising the characterisation of Chaucer's Prioress, O'Hagan disposes of the Wife of Bath peremptorily, as she is 'drawn with too free a pencil to permit me here to dwell upon it'. The Wife of Bath, he warns his female audience, is 'not only of the earth earthy, but with a thorough and undisguised contempt for anything but the earthy view of life', and thus not suitable for reading nor for discussing in a public, and largely female, assemblage.[17]

13 Joseph Napier, 'Opening Address' in *The Afternoon Lectures*, 2nd Series, pp. 3–26. See detailed and sympathetic report in the *Freeman's Journal*, 31 March 1864.   **14** Napier, 'Opening Address', pp. 8–9.   **15** Ibid.   **16** John O'Hagan, 'Chaucer' in *The Afternoon Lectures*, 2nd Series, pp. 247–77.   **17** O'Hagan, 'Chaucer', pp. 261–2.

Several years later, in 1867, when the young Edward Dowden took his turn to deliver his Afternoon Lecture, he had already begun to serve as the first Professor of English at the newly-established Alexandra College for Women around the corner in Earlsfort Terrace. He was also to begin his Professorship at Trinity College within a few months. Dowden's choice of topic for his Afternoon Lecture – 'Mr Tennyson and Mr Browning' – was typical for him at this stage of his career, being a contemporary choice.[18] It was also a rather typical choice for the somewhat avant-garde Afternoon Lectures, which had included Arnold and Dickens as subjects deemed worthy for the largely female and totally non-degree-oriented audience. It should be noted, however, that none of these choices for lecture would have been considered appropriate within the Academy at the time, and here is where I would suggest that the girls meet the boys.

Tennyson and Browning, Dowden's choice for the Afternoon Lecture series, were also subjects of his lectures at Alexandra College. In addition, Dowden lectured there on Walt Whitman whose poetry he loved, and Swinburne whose poetry he would grow to loathe. These latter choices were considered universally to be audacious, but especially so for female audiences. In fact the choice and range of lecture material on offer at Alexandra, as at the Afternoon Lectures, were considerably more modern and flexible than the syllabus Dowden was to create soon after at TCD. In this regard, however, the lecture series and the women's college should not be considered as being in the forefront of liberal educational reform, but rather as remaining in Dowden's mind, and in that of establishment Dublin of the time, part of the adult education movement; later, they were to prove a preliminary stage in the eventual granting of degrees to women, a concept to which Dowden was vehemently opposed. (Although he lived to see, in his words, 'lasses as well as asses in my classes'.)[19] In contrast to the variety offered the ladies at the Afternoon Lectures and at Alex in the 1860s, the gentlemen at TCD, for many generations, received lectures only on very major figures from Chaucer to Milton, some Shakespeare, and little else, as little else was considered worthy of degree study.[20] In Trinity, Dowden, who had a predilection for broadening the range of reading and study of students to include modern and contemporary authors, was subject in part to the very strong and universal academic preference for the classical and the linguistic. Dowden did have difficulties establishing his discipline's legitimacy against the charges of the classicists and antiquarians who held power in the college, but unlike some modernists at Oxford in the next decade or two, he never played the scientific/quantitative/linguistic card to validate

18 The 1867 and 1868 series of lectures were published together, in 1869, by London's Bell & Daldy.   **19** This jocular remark is made in a letter to a former student, William McNeile Dixon, who later held the Chair of English Literature at the University of Glasgow. See TCD MS 2259 McNeile Dixon Collection, no. 18, 18 December 1902. **20** Although Tennyson, Arnold and Ruskin were eventually included on the syllabus, there were no questions on any novels set for examinations, and only after 1905–1906 did any drama other than Shakespeare appear. See Terence Brown, 'Edward Dowden: Irish Victorian' in *Ireland's Literature* (Mullingar, 1988), p. 47n.

his discipline. Thus at Trinity, and eventually throughout Ireland, there was preserved in English Departments a more literary, rather than linguistic focus. Instead of the syllabus in English emerging, as it did in Oxford, from within the university, and developing philologically, the Irish model can trace its origin, in part through Dowden, to the extramural lecturing tradition established first for working men, and later co-opted by women. This literary continuum, adapted for degree study, would in turn colour the curriculum choices made by the more than thirty former students, all male, whom Dowden lived to see appointed to chairs throughout the English-speaking world before his death.[21]

Dowden was a pioneer then, though hardly a feminist. Involved in educational forces outside the academy as a young man, he was never entirely in step with the establishment, literary or other, even from his early days teaching young women; and a study of his aberration from the norm in this regard gives a stronger understanding of what was the mid-Victorian norm in literary taste. Dowden also provides the literary historian with an interesting link in the formation of the canon – a link in which women's education, with its unlikely origins in the educational reforms geared toward working men, eventually links with a TCD-educated diaspora influential in canon formation, or at least in the formation of the academic curriculum in the United States, Canada, Australia and New Zealand or, in short, the English-speaking world outside England.

Dowden would continue throughout his long life to offer lectures, both within and outside his college, on recent and living authors. He also lived long enough to see included on the academic syllabus several of his favourite modern writers – like Shelley. At first these new authors and their works would appear, ironically enough, on the exam papers set by Dowden, only for the next generation of civil servants, not for those reading English in university. Eventually, however, writers like Shelley and Whitman and Swinburne would be considered suitable for study by all degree candidates, even the ladies, whose grannies, had they been among those young ladies who had attended the Afternoon Lectures or Alexandra College in the eighteen sixties, would have considered the modern academic syllabus in English literature to be decidedly 'old hat'.

21 Brown, 'Edward Dowden', p. 40. Dowden's correspondence, especially with NcNeile Dixon, confirms his detailed involvement in the choice of various appointments to chairs of English from Cork to New Zealand. TCD MS 2259, McNeile Dixon Collection, especially from 1894–1904.

Far from Silent: Nineteenth-Century Irish Women Writers

ANNE COLMAN

Nineteenth-century Ireland has been portrayed as a silent period in Irish women's literary history. Excepting a few, major female voices, the nineteenth century has been known as an era dominated by male writers. In reality, however, this was a fertile period for Irish women writers who were actively publishing for an eager audience. Between 1800 and 1900, in excess of five hundred women were writing and publishing, throughout all genres.

Researching the lives and works of these women presents gender-specific problems, the most basic of which is establishing the author's identity. Women writers offer a host of possible names for the researcher, beyond the expected mix of married and maiden names. Women were more likely to seek anonymity when publishing their literary efforts, and their pseudonyms incorporated placenames, initials, social status ('by a Lady') and men's names. Miss Carew, for example, was particularly ambiguous about gender, publishing as both Frank Pentrill and Mrs Frank Pentrill during her career. When Lady Dufferin's husband objected to seeing his wife's name appear in print, she simply began publishing her verses under a pseudonym, or using her sister's name, Lady Caroline Norton. Cecil Frances Humphreys Alexander published under the pseudonym of 'X?' for a time. Some women added to the researcher's potential misery by publishing under the initials of their pseudonyms. Those women belonging to religious orders pose further challenges by publishing under their names in religion or as an anonymous member of a specific religious order. When these gender-specific pseudonyms are connected to the paucity of detail regarding women's biographies, the frustrations for researchers become clear.

The volume and context of women's publications

Simply the statement that there were in excess of five hundred Irish women writers during the nineteenth century should dispel the belief that women were silent. Just how far from silent these writers were becomes evident from examining the publishing records of some female authors. Elizabeth Thomasina Meade (1850–1915) wrote approximately 280 volumes, beginning circa 1875 and concluding with works published posthumously in the 1920s. Katharine Tynan Hinkson published 184 volumes during her career. The publishing output of Meade and Tynan-Hinkson is unusual, yet the overall publishing records of nineteenth-century women frequently indicate over twenty volumes by an individual. The extent of multi-volume publishing is demonstrated by the following sample of women authors: Mary Sweetman, or 'M.E. Francis', who published fifty-eight volumes, Lady Rosa Mulholland Gilbert's fifty volumes, Lady Norton's thirty volumes, Mrs S.C. Hall's twenty-five volumes, and Kathleen O'Meara, 'Grace Ramsey', who published twenty-one volumes. Yet these women and the number of works they published are only a representative sample of multi-volume publishing by Irish women. The number of female authors who each published up to twenty volumes prohibits a listing of individuals. Suffice it to say that Irish women were publishing in significant numbers and volumes.

Irish women writers of the period had a variety of publishing opportunities. The major publishing centres were Dublin and London, with smaller publishing firms in Belfast, Cork, Tuam, Dundalk, Londonderry and Larne. Newspaper printers occasionally functioned as book or pamphlet publishers. Pamphlet publishing was a viable option, particularly for writers interested in political or social causes. Subscriptions for forthcoming volumes were commonplace and women frequently printed their works 'for private circulation', especially in the early nineteenth century. Monthly magazines also flourished and encouraged women to submit pieces in all genres: poetry, serialised novels, essays, tales, short stories, travel pieces, religious articles and non-fiction pieces. The *Irish Monthly*, edited by Father Matthew Russell, was especially diligent in promoting writing by women and in recording biographical information about the women published. For some of these writers, Russell's 'Nutshell Biograms' constitute the only biographical source.

Contemporary interest in nineteenth-century women's writings and in what we now call feminist collections of literature and biography was very substantial, evidenced by the collections of writings by and about women. In 1877 Elizabeth Owens Blackburne Casey ('E. Owens Blackburne') published a two-volume set of biographical information entitled *Illustrious Irishwomen*. Casey's chosen subjects include authors, actors, political figures and famous beauties of the day. Elizabeth Sharp (Mrs William Sharp) published a feminist anthology, *Women's Voices; an Anthology of the Most Characteristic Poems by English, Scotch and Irish Women* (London, 1887). Miss C.J. Hamilton published two separate studies pertaining to literary women: *Women Writers: Their Works and Ways* (London, 1892) and *Notable Irishwomen* (Dublin, 1904). Some years later, Helena Walsh Concannon produced two volumes with feminist concerns: *Women of Ninety-Eight* (Dublin, 1919) and *Daughters of Banba* (Dublin, 1922).

Literary Families

Far from being isolated in their efforts, an examination of genealogical connections indicates a web of family support for women writers. Of particular note in this regard were a number of sisters who wrote and published simultaneously. The four Sweetman sisters pursued literary efforts from their early childhood, when they produced two magazines, the *Ivy Home Magazine* and the *Ivy Home Library*, from the garden of their Co. Laois family home, Lambert Park. Mary Sweetman became a prolific novelist. Her sister Elinor published four volumes and submitted a number of poems to the *Irish Monthly* during the period from October 1889 to May 1894. Agnes, a third sister, married Anthony Egerton Castle, and the couple co-authored forty-two volumes. Mary Sweetman married Francis Blundell whose two sisters were writers. Later, Madge Blundell became her mother, Mary's, biographer.

Three of the four Furlong sisters, Alice (*c.*1875–1948), Mary (1866–1898) and Katherine (1872–1894), were published poets. The Furlongs lived in Tallaght, near to the family home of Katharine Tynan. The physical proximity generated a literary friendship, particularly between Alice Furlong and Katharine Tynan, although Tynan did not hold Mary Furlong's work in high esteem, noting that 'From the age of fourteen Mary scribbled determinedly in spite of much good and unpalatable advice from editors'.[1]

Literary friendships are to be found throughout the mass of nineteenth-century Irish women writers. Katharine Tynan Hinkson was strongly influenced by her friend Rosa Mulholland Gilbert. The two women travelled together prior to Mulholland's marriage. Hinkson later suspected that Sir John Gilbert did not entirely approve of her liberal views, thus he tempered his wife's friendship with Hinkson.

Lady Dufferin, herself a member of the Sheridan literary dynasty, was a strong influence on her fellow writers. Among her Northern contemporaries, a number of single poems and volumes of poetry were dedicated to her. Religious causes or denominations also generated friendships among women writers. Sarah Geraldina Stock, a Protestant missionary, developed a friendship with Cecil Frances Humphreys Alexander, wife of William, Primate of Ireland. The editor of the *Irish Monthly*, Father Matthew Russell, introduced, one-to-another, a number of women who wrote for his magazine. Another cluster of women poets were affiliated with the *Nation*. Although writers tended to publish pseudonymously in the *Nation*, women writing for the same periodical undoubtedly held opinions of, and were, in turn, influenced by their contemporaries. A thorough study of women writers associated with the *Nation* has yet to be undertaken. Although Mary Eva Kelly O'Doherty ('Eva'), Ellen Mary Patrick Downing ('Kate', 'Ellen' and 'Mary') and Lady Jane Francesca Elgee Wilde ('Speranza') are frequently cited, lesser known women remain unexplored: Kate Culhane, Fanny Forrester, Olivia Knight, Katharine Mary Murphy, Ellen O'Leary, Marie M. Thompson, Jane Verner, Elizabeth Willoughby Treacy Varian, to name but a few.

A number of women writers were related to famous male political and literary figures of the nineteenth century: Ellen O'Connell Fitzsimon was the daughter of Daniel O'Connell, Mary Jane Irwin was the 'little poetess wife' of Jeremiah O'Donovan Rossa, Ellen O'Leary the sister of John O'Leary, Ely McCarthy the

---

1 Katharine Tynan Hinkson, *Cabinet of Irish Literature*, (4 vols; London, 1902–3), iv, p. 241.

sister of Justin McCarthy, and Charlotte Grace O'Brien the daughter of William Smith O'Brien. These literary women were overshadowed by the men in their families, but their strong genealogical connections provide evidence of a significant support network, and demonstrate an interesting link between family politics and the writings these women produced.

Genres

The nineteenth century was not a period of specialisation in terms of genre, so women writers were comfortable selecting the genre to suit the subject when they took pen in hand. Although Thomas MacDonagh called Alice Milligan 'the best living Irish poet' in the October–November 1914 issue of the *Irish Review*, Milligan wrote plays, essays, biography, children's literature, a novel, and co-authored a travel book in addition to the poetry MacDonagh praised. Such multiple-genre writing was the normal state of writing for nineteenth-century Irish women.

Women were also active in writing non-fiction during this period. The Clerke sisters, Agnes and Ellen, were noted scientists. Agnes (1842–1907) was a brilliant astronomer while Ellen (1840–1906) was a poet, mathematician and geologist. Agnes's first text on astronomy was begun when she was fifteen years of age. *A Popular History of Astronomy During the Nineteenth Century* was published in 1885, and it became a standard text throughout Europe for many years. Neither Agnes nor Ellen ever married, the two sisters preferring to live together life-long. They travelled extensively about Europe and as far as the Cape of Good Hope in pursuit of astronomical phenomenoan. Agnes published a further six volumes pertaining to astronomy and astrophysics, and a single non-scientific volume entitled *Familiar Studies in Homer* (London, 1892). Ellen Mary Clerke shared her sister's interest in astronomy, as *Jupiter and His System* (London, 1892) indicates, but she was best known for her poetry and published three volumes of poems from 1881 to 1902. Ellen was also a gifted linguist, publishing articles in Arabic and providing versified translations of Italian poetry for Dr Garnett's *History of Italian Literature* (London, 1898). In her biography of the sisters, *Agnes Mary Clerke and Ellen Mary Clerke; an Appreciation* (privately printed, 1907), Lady Huggins calls Ellen a particularly 'devoted and exemplary Catholic'. Ellen's poetry was largely devotional, with *The Flying Dutchman and Other Poems* (London, 1881) being perhaps her finest volume. The sisters died within one year of each other, at their home in London. Other scientific women of the nineteenth century and their chosen fields were: Katherine Bailey – botany, Margaret Stokes – archaeology, Mary King – astronomy and microscopy, and two notable historians, Alice Stopford Green and Eleanor Hull.

Travel writing was especially fashionable during the nineteenth century and women were eager participants in this genre. Among the most prolific and adventurous of the women travellers was Beatrice Grimshaw, born 1880 in

Cloona, Co. Antrim. Grimshaw moved first to Dublin about 1900, then to London where she worked out a trade arrangement with several shipping companies and exchanged her publicity writings for free travel. An initial voyage to Tahiti in 1906 began her career as a travel writer. She ran a coffee plantation in Papua, New Guinea for a time, and was the first Caucasian woman to visit certain parts of Borneo and New Guinea. In addition to contributing articles to the *National Geographic* and *World Wide Magazine*, she published a steady stream of travel books, novels and stories, totalling thirty-eight volumes from 1897 to 1943.

Among those writers whose subject-matter came from nearer home, writing in dialect is a trend to be found predominantly among Northern authors. Elizabeth Gertrude Heron Hine (1857–1951) was a resident of Carrickfergus, Co. Antrim, and wrote under the pseudonym of 'Elizabeth Shane'. *Piper's Tunes* (London, c.1920), *Tales of the Donegal Coast and Islands* (London, 1921), and *By Bog and Sea in Donegal* (London, 1923) were written as Hine believed the English language to be spoken in the coastal areas of Donegal. Another Northerner, Agnes Nesta Shakespeare Higginson, later Mrs Walter Skrine, published under the pseudonym of 'Moira O'Neill'. A resident of Rockport, Cushendall, Co. Antrim, Moira O'Neill's poetry was heavily anthologised during her lifetime. Her *Songs of the Glens of Antrim* (Edinburgh and London, 1900) and *More Songs of the Glens of Antrim* (Edinburgh and London, 1921) were very popular and captured the Glens of Antrim tales in dialect; their popularity continues to the present.

Writing verses as lyrics and hymns was also a popular endeavour of women writers during the nineteenth century. Lady Dufferin published a companion volume to her collected poems which gives the musical adaptations for some of the poems. Mary McDermott, of Killyleagh, Co. Down, occasionally composed music to accompany her poetry, as did Charlotte Cowan Jobling, a Belfast woman who published under the pseudonym of 'Irish Molly'. Mrs Jobling's unusual style of writing verse caught the attention of W.J. Paul, who noted in *Modern Irish Poets* (Belfast, 1894) that she wrote the last verse first, the first verse second, and filled in the middle verse last. Her unique method of writing generated a career total of more than 800 poems and 150 songs, all published as single submissions to periodicals. In 1850, Charlotte Canning wrote an entire opera in verse, and Miss Davis's verse operetta was performed at a London theatre in 1892.

Among the many women writers in need of further study are a number of authors from the earlier part of the nineteenth century. Little is known about the life of Mary Benn who published two volumes of poetry, *The Solitary; or a Lay from the West* (London, 1854) and *Lays of the Hebrews* (London, 1854). Mary Balfour (c.1775–c.1820) was probably born in Derry, but she operated schools in both Belfast and Limavady; her *Hope, a Poetical Essay; with Various Other Poems* (Belfast, 1810) was published anonymously. Margaret Graves published under the pseudonym of 'Derenzy'. *A Whisper to a Newly-Married Pair, from a Widowed Wife* was originally published in 1824, but editions continued to be published until 1886. Graves published another five volumes before her publishing activities ceased circa 1828. Better known is Charlotte Elizabeth Tonna (1790–1846), author of the historical novel, *Derry, a Tale of the Revolution*, published under her pseudonym of 'Charlotte Elizabeth'. She wrote another eleven volumes before her death in 1846, but *Derry* remained her most popular work, with editions continuing for another half-century after its original publication.

Translation was a common writing activity for nineteenth-century women, particularly during the latter part of the century. A variety of languages were translated, with several women notably proficient in multiple languages. Languages translated from, or translated into, included Arabic, Chinese, French, Greek, Hindustani, Irish, Italian, Japanese, Latin, Portuguese, Russian, Scandinavian languages, Welsh and Yoruban. Frances Sarah Johnston Hoey, Mrs Cashel Hoey, was an especially prolific translator. She published twenty-nine volumes of translations from French, in addition to eighteen volumes of original work in assorted genres. It may be noted that some of the geographic areas represented by languages listed above, particularly those associated with Africa and the Far East, were centres of missionary activity. Women who either worked as missionaries or who were married to missionaries frequently published translations of Christian literature into the local languages. In some cases the women were publishing native tales from their missionary areas translated into English for readers at home. Amy Beatrice Carmichael was a prolific writer with twenty-six volumes to her credit. She was proficient in Japanese and Hindustani as a result of her missionary assignments. A similar pattern of translation activities exists among women married to members of the British military and posted to foreign lands.

Finally, with regard to genre, one of the most successful of nineteenth-century women writers was Nannie Lambert O'Donoghue, a leading equestrian writer who produced six volumes from 1877 to 1895. Generally publishing under her married name, Mrs Power O'Donoghue, she was a journalist, novelist and poet. She wrote two non-fiction books pertaining to women equestrians which were instant best sellers. *Ladies on Horseback; Learning Park-Riding and Hunting with Hints Upon Costume and Numerous Anecdotes* (London, 1881) was translated into five languages and reportedly sold over 94,000 copies. *The Common Sense of Riding; Riding for Ladies with Hints on the Stable* (London, 1887) was not as popular as the original volume, but was regularly reprinted and a new edition was issued in 1905. Her three-volume novel, *Beggar on Horseback* (London, 1884) sold an estimated 23,000 copies.

Women's Religious and Social Writings

At least fifteen cloistered religious women, during the nineteenth century, were writing poetry for submission to magazines or publishing volumes of their poems. The verses produced by religious women were largely devotional, although secular themes do emerge in some of their work. Margaret Cusack, 'the Nun of Kenmare' or Sister Mary Francis Clare, was the most prolific of the group and the most unusual. While a cloistered member of the Poor Clares convent in Kenmare, Sister

Mary Francis Clare ran a successful publishing house, Kenmare Publication Agency. *Cloister Songs* (London, 1881) was her only volume of poetry. During the early part of her publishing career she specialised in hagiography and history. *A History of the Kingdom of Kerry* (London, 1871) and *A History of the City and County of Cork* (Cork and Dublin, 1875) are her best known works and prized by book collectors. Her concern with the status of women is revealed in *Women's Work in Modern Society* (Kenmare, 1874) and *A Nun's Advice to Her Girls* (Kenmare, 1877). In her later years, following a tempestuous life, she renounced her Catholic faith and wrote a series of anti-Catholic volumes: *The Black Pope; a History of the Jesuits* (London and Brighton, c.1896), *Is There a Roman Catholic Church?* (London and Brighton, 1897), and *Revolution and War; The Secret Conspiracy of the Jesuits in Great Britain* (London, 1910), among other volumes. Less colourful than Cusack were nuns like Sister Mary Stanislaus MacCarthy, the daughter of Denis Florence MacCarthy and a Dominican; Maria Gibbons, Mother Columba, a Loreto nun from Navan; and Mary Gertrude Reddin, of the Loreto convent in Dublin.

Evelyn Noble Armitage's anthology, *Quaker Poets of Great Britain and Ireland* (London, 1896), reveals that seven Quaker women were engaged in writing poetry during the nineteenth century. The biographical notes Armitage includes for each writer indicate that several of these Quaker women later resigned their membership in the Society of Friends. The reason for their departure generally centres on a conflict between nationalistic politics and pacifistic Quaker beliefs. Hannah L. Harvey, born in 1854 near Waterford, was one such woman unable to reconcile her Quaker faith with her militant nationalism. Debroah Webb, a Dubliner born in 1837, also left the Society of Friends, but politics did not play a part in her decision. Webb's family had been active in 'all reforms and good causes, especially that of the negro slave', their house a resort 'particularly of abolitionists and escaped slaves'.[2] When Webb renounced her Quaker faith it was to pursue spiritualism and lesser known religious alternatives. As a whole, Quaker women's poetry focuses on strong biblical or social themes. Eleanor Dickinson's *The Pleasures of Piety, with Other Poems* (1824), Mrs Neale's *Biblical Sketches and Hymns* (1854), and Sarah Greer's *The Chained Bible and Other Poems* (1857) reflect the general themes of Quaker women's devotional verses.

Women hymnists were prolific, with Cecil Frances Humphreys Alexander being the most active of the group. Mrs Alexander was the wife of William, Archbishop of Armagh and Primate of Ireland. One anecdote recalls her being sent a collection of musical scores by a minister who needed the lyrics as quickly as possible. He thought it would take her several months to complete the task, but he received the lyrics almost by return courier. The minister boasted about Cecil's abilities as a hymnist thereafter. Sarah Geraldina Stock, another hymnist, spent most of her life in Africa, most likely as a missionary. She was fluent in Welsh and Yoruban, writing in both languages, and probably spoke Swahili. One

---

2 Evelyn Noble Armitage (ed.), *The Quaker Poets of Great Britain and Ireland* (London, 1896), p. 289.

of her novels is set during the Zulu Wars, and she was associated with the Victoria Nyanza Mission in Uganda.

Charlotte Grace O'Brien, daughter of William Smith O'Brien, exemplifies the nineteenth-century woman concerned with social issues. Born in 1845, at Cahirmoyle, Co. Limerick, she showed little interest in politics prior to 1880. Thereafter she dedicated her life to the question of emigrant rights, and worked to ensure safe and civilised shipboard conditions, especially for unmarried women emigrants travelling on the coffin ships. She also operated a pre-emigration boarding house for emigrants in Cobh. O'Brien was a regularly published poet, with four volumes to her credit. Her nephew, Stephen Gwynn, edited a volume of selections from her writings and correspondence in 1910, adding his own memoir of his aunt to the volume.

Sarah Gaynor Atkinson was another woman of social conscience. Born in Athlone in 1823, she married George Atkinson when she was twenty-five years of age. In 1861 she presented a paper on the workhouses at the Social Science Congress of 1861, in Dublin. She was a close friend of Rosa Mulholland Gilbert and of Katharine Tynan Hinkson who described Atkinson as one 'with perfect womanly sweetness', having 'a masculine force and clearness of intellect'.[3] Mrs Atkinson published three volumes, largely with biographical and hagiographic content. A book of essays with a memoir by Rosa Mulholland Gilbert was posthumously published in 1895.

One of the period's most memorable 'oddities' was Martha Spence (1812–73), an Irish writer who emigrated to America in 1834. She was a Dubliner who converted to the Church of Jesus Christ of the Latter Day Saints following her arrival in Utah. She married a Mormon man, and became one of his three living wives. Spence kept a diary about her life in a polygamous marriage on the American frontier.

Women's Biographies

The lives of two individuals, Ellen Mary Patrick Downing and Alice Furlong, are worth exploring in some detail, since they provide vivid examples of the romanticised female biographies of the nineteenth century. Researchers should note that women connected to political movements are very frequently the subjects for fictionalised biography. Ellen Mary Patrick Downing was connected to the *Nation* and to the Young Ireland and United Irishmen political groups. Her life is one of the most interesting and tragic of the century, and one of the most heavily romanticised. Downing was born 19 March 1828, in Cork. She was the daughter of the resident medical officer at the Cork Fever Hospital, and began writing poetry while she was still in her teens. At seventeen years of age, her first poem appeared in the *Nation*, under the pseudonym of 'Kate'. Downing also used

3 Hinkson, *Cabinet*, iv, p. 36.

the pseudonyms of 'Mary', 'Ellen' and her initials, 'E.M.P.D.'. The romanticising of Downing's life centres on her brief romantic relationship with a young man, possibly Joseph Brennan, who was transported for his political activities. A.M. Sullivan states in his biographical sketch of Downing in *New Ireland* that Brennan forgot his youthful vow of marriage while he was in exile. Downing, according to Sullivan, was so heartbroken by Brennan's unfaithfulness that she stopped writing and died a short time later. Unfortunately Mr Sullivan's account of Downing's death is contradicted by her publishing record. Downing continued to write and publish for twenty-two years after Mr Sullivan reported her demise. Her death actually occurred in 1869.

Alice Furlong suffers the same fictionalised fate in the context of the 1916 Easter Rising. The romantic version of Furlong's life says that she retreated into isolation in Tallaght after the 1916 executions, never speaking or writing another word in the English language. The isolation shrouding Furlong's later years is challenged by her publishing record, which shows English-language articles by Furlong appearing as late as the 1930s.

Such attempts to fictionalise women's biographies traded heavily on the perception of women as the weaker vessels, overly sensitive and dedicated to the point of martyrdom whenever their emotions were heavily engaged, either through an excess of love or faith in a political ideology. The history of nineteenth-century women writers, long overdue a detailed examination, reveals a very different profile, with many accomplished and successful female authors, publishing in an often startling diversity of genre.[4]

4 For further information regarding the women featured in this article, see Anne Colman, *Dictionary of Nineteenth-Century Irish Women Poets* (Galway, 1996).

Romantic Revolutionary Irishwomen: Women, Young Ireland and 1848

JAN CANNAVAN

> You cannot kindle up a fire,
> Then bid it not to blaze;
> You cannot stop a woman's lyre,
> At woman's fitting lays –
>
> 'Mary' of the *Nation*.

The participation of women in Irish nationalist movements in the nineteenth century is an important, if still largely unexplored, arena for research in gender studies. Allied to it is the question of the extent to which a feminist agenda can be detected in the ideologies of Irish nationalism throughout the nineteenth century. This article will examine the participation of women in the movement in the 1840s which, after the example of such continental movements as 'Young Italy', came to be called 'Young Ireland' – a label first affixed to it derisively by its enemies, but later taken up proudly by its members.[1]

This article will examine prose pieces and some poems written by women, together with the responses to them by men, in the Young Ireland newspaper the *Nation*, published between 1843 and the paper's suppression in July 1848, as well as female contributions, published between February and May 1848, to John Mitchel's more militant paper, the *United Irishman*. Though primarily concerned with nationalism, these women writers were also concerned about gender issues. Indeed, as time went on, their call for proper citizenship rights for women increased. Their polemics draw on the rhetoric both of the Enlightenment and of Romanticism. They also implicitly engage with the key paradigms of 'equality' and 'difference' which have been at the heart of modern feminist debate.[2]

The notion of equality in the gender debate derives from Mary Wollstonecraft and considers women and men to be the same in all significant respects, apart from obvious physical dissimilarities.[3] Observed differences, such as women's

---

1 Richard Davis, *The Young Ireland Movement* (Totowa, NJ, 1987), pp. 56–7. The movement's links with continental Europe were significant to a degree. The revolutionary French government, for example, had designed the Irish national flag that is still in use today, the tri-color of green, white and orange modelled on the French flag. See P. Beresford Ellis, *A History of the Irish Working Class* (New York, 1972), p. 116. 2 For a concise discussion of these terms and a summary of the debate see Josephine Donovan, *Feminist Theory: The Intellectual Traditions of American Feminism* (New York, 1992). 3 Mary Wollstonecraft, *A Vindication of the Rights of Woman with Strictures on Political and Moral Subjects* (1792; New York, 1974).

tendency to be more nurturing than men, are seen by equality feminists as social constructs and as factors in women's oppression. So-called 'difference feminists', on the other hand, influenced by the work of Carol Gilligan and Nancy Chodorow as well as by some nineteenth-century feminists, acknowledge and value gender-based behavioural differences, though most of them see such differences as deriving from psychological conditioning rather than biology.[4] For difference feminists, women's nurturing tendency makes them morally superior to men. In recent times Joan Scott has attempted to reconcile these two paradigms by positing the existence of a multiplicity of differences, instead of the single division of gender.[5]

I

Young Ireland theorised its nation's rights using the two discourses of Enlightenment and Romanticism. It had inherited the former from the United Irishmen, who based their claims on the ideas of the American and especially the French revolutions. These ideas included the desire for a democratic state with strong individual liberties, although Young Ireland supported a stronger component of social welfare than the United States. Another Enlightenment idea cherished by Young Ireland was that of complete secularism; it adhered to the dictum of Theobald Wolfe Tone, the United Irish leader, who had aspired 'To unite the whole people of Ireland, to abolish the memory of past dissensions, and to substitute the common name of Irishman in place of the denominations of Protestant, Catholic, and Dissenter.'[6] From the wave of revolutionary fervour sweeping Europe in the 1840s came the new ideas of Romanticism to augment and modify the earlier Enlightenment ideals. Influenced by poetry and art, these ideas stressed the primacy of emotion over rationality.

A synthesis, or at least a co-existence, of Enlightenment and Romantic paradigms shaped the discussion of women's rights, as well as national rights, in Ireland. Debates about women's proper role in the national struggle took place in a large number of articles, letters to the editor, and even in a male/female poetry exchange in the columns of nationalist newspapers. It is possible to trace over the five-year period between 1843 and 1848 the development both of women's calls for rights and duties and men's ambivalent reactions to such calls.[7]

---

4 Carol Gilligan, *In a Different Voice: Psychological Theory and Women's Development* (Cambridge, MA, 1982); Nancy Chodorow, *The Reproduction of Mothering: Psychoanalysis and the Sociology of Gender* (Berkeley, 1978). For a discussion of nineteenth-century difference feminism, see Karen Offen, 'Defining Feminism: A Comparative Historical Approach' in *Signs*, xiv, 1 (1988), pp. 119–57.   **5** Joan W. Scott, 'Deconstructing Equality-versus-Difference: or the Uses of Post-structuralist Theory for Feminism' in *Feminist Studies*, xiv, 1 (1988), pp. 33–50.   **6** Quoted in T. A. Jackson, *Ireland Her Own* (New York, 1970), p. 117.   **7** I do not mean to imply here that nationalist women in Ireland moved in a linear progression from 'duties' arguments to those based on 'rights'. Discussions about

At least fifteen women writers contributed to the *Nation*, nearly all of them using pseudonyms. The three most important were 'Eva', 'Speranza' and 'Mary'. 'Eva' was Mary Anne (or Mary Eva) Kelly whose family had strong republican sympathies. When her fiancé, Kevin O'Doherty, was convicted of taking part in revolutionary activities and was offered a lenient sentence in exchange for an expression of remorse, she urged him to refuse. She waited six years to marry him until his sentence of transportation to Van Diemen's Land was commuted. 'Speranza' was Jane Francesca Elgee, later Lady Wilde, mother of Oscar Wilde. She came from an upper middle-class Protestant family which disapproved of her nationalism. She had a singular talent for languages and contributed translations to the *Nation* of poetry in Russian, Turkish, Spanish, German, Italian, Portuguese and Swedish, as well as Latin and Greek. 'Mary' was Ellen Mary Patrick Downing. A militant and prolific writer, she left the *Nation* for the *United Irishman* when it broke away in 1848 in order to pursue a more military strategy. She is believed to have been involved romantically with Joseph Brennan, a fellow Young Irelander, but entered a convent in 1849 and turned her literary talents to religious poetry.[8]

The earliest contribution on the subject of gender appeared in the *Nation* in December 1843 in an extract from *Mrs Reid's Plea for Women* entitled 'Domestic Duties of Woman'. This short piece, serving as a space filler at the end of a long report of a speech by Daniel O'Connell, confers only duties on women and no rights. Women, who are conflated with mothers in the piece, are said to hold as their highest duty the moral and intellectual education of their children.[9] The subject's next appearance is in October 1844, with an unsigned article called 'The Mission of Women'. This piece also stresses duties to the detriment of rights, but in the ten months since the first article was published the scope of these responsibilities has widened somewhat: now the Romantic 'ethic of care'[10] not only demands that women educate their children's moral and intellectual faculties but requires, in addition, the inculcation of patriotism. Furthermore, the article asserts that '*active* patriotism is a duty bearing equally upon man and woman'.[11] Of course, the author assures his audience that this equal duty will be expressed in each sex's separate sphere; the man will act in the public sphere, but 'the world says that "women are not to *meddle* in politics"; and if by this is meant meddling *publicly*, the world is right. This is not a woman's sphere ... a woman's sphere is her home.'[12]

By the time of the next article, January 1847, women's rights have finally entered the equation. This time 'A Limerick Girl' writes a letter to the editor asking whether women are eligible to join the Irish Confederation, a nationalist club. She says that she 'cannot feel too grateful to those who would give us *our*

women's duties in the home continued throughout the period studied; however, rights-based demands became more frequent and more strongly argued over time.   8 See Anne Colman's discussion of the myths surrounding the biography of Ellen Mary Patrick Downing, in her essay eralier in this volume.   9 *Nation*, 19 October 1844.   10 Anne K. Mellor, *Romanticism and Gender* (New York, 1993), p. 210.   11 *Nation*, 19 October 1844.   12 Ibid.

proper position in society'.[13] The 'Limerick Girl' is not yet demanding rights, but she is beginning to define a 'proper position' for herself in the public sphere. The editor answers, in a rather cavalier fashion, that 'of course, the ladies are admissible'.[14]

In subsequent years a number of the male Young Irelanders showed themselves to be decidedly nervous about a new assertiveness among nationalist women. 'Mary', the *Nation's* most martial poet, became involved in a poetic duet, or, more correctly perhaps, a poetic duel in April 1847 with 'Shamrock', a prolific male poet and medical student. He began by addressing her 'in a voice of such tender warning':[15]

> Since that hour the girl no longer played with childhood's simple toys,
> But each day, with impulse stronger, sought for high and holy joys;
> But thou knowest the woe that slumbers music's shining waves beneath,
> And how oft the poet's numbers from a bleeding bosom breathe ...
> Fly then, dear, from passion's pages, turn from proud and gloomy song.[16]

In the following issue 'Mary' replied:

> You cannot kindle up a fire,
>   Then bid it not to blaze:
> You cannot stop a woman's lyre,
>   At woman's fitting lays ...
> War! – 'tis eternal war below
>   With head, or heart, or sword –
> Too much of battle strife I know
>   To shudder at the word –
> Nor shall I hold that year the worst,
>   Whate'er its tools may be,
> Which rends in twain a chain accursed,
>   And sets a people free.[17]

The editor's judgement on this debate is instructive. Duffy comes down solidly on 'Mary''s side, writing that she has 'a pure and noble passion, worthy of her womanhood and her genius' and that 'Shamrock' should not be frightened or disgusted by a strong, militant woman.[18] In a later correspondence with the editor, 'Mary' reveals the Romantic nature of her poetic sensibility: 'I like poetry wild with war, or hot with love, or all glowing with scenery, but would rather write one little song that a child or peasant might sing and feel than a very miracle-poem of abstraction and profundity.'[19] This privileging of emotion and simplicity

13 Ibid., 30 January 1847. My emphasis. **14** Ibid. **15** Ibid., 10 April 1847. **16** Ibid.
17 Ibid., 17 April 1847. **18** Ibid. **19** T. F. O'Sullivan, *The Young Irelanders* (Tralee, 1944), p. 116.

over abstract reason made Romantic poetry a attractive vehicle for nationalist writers keen to rouse the people to commitment and action.

In June 1847, two months after this poetry exchange, 'An Irish Mother' finally combines an Enlightenment-inspired demand for rights with a Romantic appeal to the image of a maternal care for the child/nation. She laments the condition of 'our sex, or rather its shackled condition ... all tinged with that mistrust of their own powers, so natural in this country, where women rarely speak on politics, however much they may think on the subject'.[20] She calls women 'rational beings' and demands a promised essay from the paper on 'Female Education'.[21] At the same time as she is demanding rights, the 'Irish Mother' is also using a nurturing discourse for the beneficial effects of a hoped-for new national government which shall 'cherish and protect [its] children'.[22] And women, she goes on, have similarly maternal duties to perform in the public sphere: 'to encourage the hopeful, stimulate the lagging, reprove the indifferent, and heap scorn upon the treacherous'.[23] Her argument thus skilfully raises the question of how men can keep real women/mothers out of the public forum when they envisage the effects of a benevolent government as being akin to those of a surrogate mother.

During the months leading up to the brief and abortive rebellion in July 1848, female *Nation* writers were actively pursuing their newly-found collective demand for women's rights. They had now largely dropped the Romantic care-giver imagery and spoke almost entirely in a language of 'rights'. Thus 'Eva' argues vehemently for equality in her article, 'To the Women of Ireland': 'What is virtue in man is virtue also in woman. Virtue is of no sex. A coward woman is as base as a coward man. It is not unfeminine to take sword or gun, if sword and gun are required.'[24] She finishes on a defiant note, 'Circumstances have hitherto moulded us. We shall now mould circumstances.'[25]

Two months later, 'Mary', writing in the *United Irishman*, also titled an article 'To the Women of Ireland'. Her piece is an argument against the equation of feminine virtue with pacifism. She goes on to argue for rebellion on the basis of a just war stance; she reminds her readers that famine and landlord abuses are killing thousands and contends that far less suffering and death will result from a war to establish a just society. 'The woman who would seek to avert that war is a traitor to humanity and her sex ... Remember, I beseech you, that to preserve this peace which you prize so dearly, millions must perish by famine and disease.' She bemoans the fact that 'a horror of blood-letting appears to be regarded as the feminine virtue in Ireland'.[26]

Male writers in the *Nation* had mixed reactions to female militancy, reactions which, like women's contributions, tended to change with the political situation. Prior to mid 1847, when armed insurrection did not seem like an immediate possibility, women were editorially discouraged from composing martial verse,

20 *Nation*, 12 June 1847.   **21** Ibid.   **22** Ibid.   **23** Ibid.   **24** Ibid., 25 March 1848.
25 Ibid.   **26** *United Irishman*, Dublin, 13 May 1848.

though this did not always succeed; 'Speranza' and 'Eva', at least, had many warlike poems accepted and praised. More typical though was the case of a poem which was rejected with the sarcastic comment: 'We beg our fair correspondent, "An Irish Girl", will not bruise her tender fingers on the cords of the war-harp – leave it for rude masculine hands. She possesses fancy and wit; but she would do well to keep them to enliven her conversation and her correspondence.'[27] Sarcasm, as such, was not reserved for female writers: rejected efforts were regularly ridiculed in each issue's 'Answers to Correspondents' column. However, male poets were criticised for their writing itself, while the critique of women extended to their very suitability as writers. When a female poet whose work had been rejected because of its 'deficient rhymes' wrote pointing out that many other *Nation* poets did not rhyme well, she was told that she had forgotten 'that strong thoughts, noble, tender, natural or witty, whose truth is at once felt and acknowledged, may dispense with the niceties of rhyme, with a freedom that is not allowable in the pretty and graceful commonplaces of a lady'.[28]

As the political situation became more difficult, male leaders were forced to address the issue of women's revolutionary fervour. On the one hand, they wanted to encourage women's active participation at a time when every nationalist was needed while, on the other, they still wanted to keep women in their own sphere. An editorial in October 1847 thus declares: 'One woman, with the intellect and devotion of Madame Roland, might organise [women] into an unseen but irresistible league.'[29] 'Unseen' is the operative term here, of course. When women's ideas of their place in the national movement contradicted this notion, they were often chastised, as was a female correspondent in May 1848, in a reply which effectively sought to deny the possibility of collective political action to women:

> We have received, in a feminine hand, a most seditious proposal for the formation of a Ladies' Society, to talk treason, and defy the Gagging Act. The intention is excellent, but the plan is unnecessary. Every drawing-room should be a lady's society for 'advocating the case of the country, and putting to shame the slaves who are content with it;' and, as for talking sedition, and acting it, the men must do that.[30]

In spite of this, however, at least some of the male Young Ireland leaders did positively support women's militant activity. John Mitchel encouraged women in their manufacture of arms in a *United Irishman* editorial: 'No lady is too delicate for the culinary preparation of casting bullets. No hand is too white to make up cartridges.'[31] Through this 'culinary' image Mitchel sought to convince Irishwomen that aiding the war effort would be an extension of their domestic duties into the public sphere, rather than an alien activity. Thomas Devin Reilly, another

---

27 *Nation*, 8 April 1843.   **28** Ibid., 4 January 1845.   **29** Ibid., 9 October 1847.
30 Ibid., 13 May 1848.   **31** Quoted in Rebecca O'Conner, *Jenny Mitchel: Young Irelander* (Tucson, 1985), p. 67.

Young Ireland leader, devised a military plan for an insurrection in which he delegated to women the task of throwing 'bricks, pots, heavy furniture, and boiling water' from windows onto attacking British troops.[32]

II

As well as contributing militant prose and poetry to the *Nation* and the *United Irishman*, women also had some part in the sometimes violent public incidents which effectively ended the Young Ireland movement in 1848, though they came from a different position in society than the middle-class women writers of the nationalist papers. Margaret Ward has argued in her study of Irish nationalism and feminism that because women had no leadership roles in either constitutional or physical-force nationalism they had less to lose than men by being uncompromising.[33] How far such a view has a bearing on the events of 1848, however, is not clear. On 27 May 1848, the day of John Mitchel's penal transportation, the only disturbance came from 'a group of women on a prominence [who] threw stones and sticks at the sabred dragoons. They were directed by a leader of Amazon stature'.[34]

Militant action by women was also significant in the one small insurrection which actually took place in Ireland in 1848, on 26 July in the Co. Tipperary village of Ballingarry. According to the Reverend P. Fitzgerald, an eyewitness to the skirmish who published his recollections in 1861, the Young Irish leader William Smith O'Brien arrived at the village of Ballingarry, 'attended indeed by a considerable multitude, but consisting chiefly of women and children, and not having in the entire procession more than fifty men capable of carrying arms'.[35] Fitzgerald pointed out the preponderance of women and children in order to illustrate his view that the rebellion was futile from the start; the fact remained, nonetheless, that women were prepared to engage in armed activity. The insurgents were eventually routed by an R.I.C. force that was superior in numbers and weaponry and many fighters were arrested, among them at least one woman, Miss Eliza Power.[36]

The participation of women in the Ballingarry incident has not received the attention of historians until now. Silences like these are, of course, a common occurrence in the history of women – particularly when the erased women were acting in ways perceived as 'unfeminine'. A wealth of archival evidence on women's revolutionary activity throughout Irish history has barely begun to be studied by historians; this lack makes it impossible as yet to test the relevance to Irishwomen of theories about women and war which are being developed and

32 Ibid., p. 82.   33 Margaret Ward, *Unmanageable Revolutionaries: Women and Irish Nationalism* (London, 1983), p. 37.   34 O'Conner, *Jenny Mitchel*, p. 82.   35 P. Fitzgerald, *Personal Recollections of the Insurrection at Ballingarry in July, 1848* (Dublin, 1861), p. 14. 36 O'Sullivan, *The Young Irelanders*, p. 662.

debated by feminist theorists and historians. It is probable that hypotheses of female pacifism, which are largely based on secondary historical works that have excluded women, may have to be rethought as more revolutionary women are rediscovered. Finding these female 'missing pieces'[37] is such a vital prelude to relevant theory that feminist historians, such as Joan Scott, who argue that the usefulness of 'her-story', the recovery of as many missing women as possible, has run its course because enough women have been studied to make theorising possible, miss many possible theoretical building blocks.[38] This is not to argue against the need for theory, but to rescue the project of her-story from the status of a poor relation to theorising, especially in countries like Ireland where much basic research still needs to be done.[39]

Even though research into the lives of the Young Ireland women is in its infancy, some tentative conclusions may be drawn from this essay. It is clear that nationalist women posed a challenge to the prevailing gender norms when they demanded a public role in the revolutionary movement; and that, as time went by, more specifically feminist demands, for education, for example, or the right for their voices to be heard or for equality of opportunity, began to creep into their thought and writing. By 1850 'Speranza' was arguing for married women's right to employment and independence:

> The more independent of each other each member of the household is, the greater the chance of happiness. If every wife had a definite employment, she would be less given to those little jealousies and watchings and pryings that fill up the time of vacant minds ... The lifework should be the first; and the lifework need not hinder the beautiful ministrations of Love.[40]

Speranza sought not only economic opportunity for women but their right to prioritise career over family as well. Women's growing interest in gender-based rights during the course of the nationalist revival of the 1840s is not coincidental; rather, their increase in public activity on behalf of the nation empowered them to make other demands as well. Although women were certainly not treated as equals by the men of Young Ireland, the most politically radical male leaders began to take women's participation much more seriously over time.

The other major issue raised in this essay is the often sophisticated interplay of 'equality' and 'difference' arguments in the writings of Young Ireland women. Both types were utilised throughout the existence of the *Nation*, though female correspondents began to place more stress on equality in the later years. The perceived differences between middle-class nationalist Irish women and men in

37 I am indebted for this term to the women of Irish Feminist Information Publications in their book *Missing Pieces: Women in Irish History* (Dublin, 1983).   **38** Joan W. Scott, *Gender and the Politics of History* (New York, 1988), p. 20.   **39** Margaret MacCurtain and Mary O'Dowd, 'An Agenda for Women's History in Ireland, 1500–1900' in *Irish Historical Studies*, xxviii, 109 (1992), p. 2.   **40** Undated journal entry, quoted in Terence de Vere White, *The Parents of Oscar Wilde: Sir William and Lady Wilde* (London, 1967), p. 148.

the 1840s seemed to be less significant to the former when compared with their shared national identity with the latter. Thus for a time the Irish/British difference partially eclipsed the gender divide, allowing politicised middle-class Irishwomen to claim greater equality with men on the basis of the Irish component in their identity. In addition, Young Ireland also briefly provided an opportunity for rural peasant women to become engaged both politically and militarily, as at Ballingarry.[41] These peasant women appear to have been less conflicted about taking part in militant activity along with their men than middle-class women perhaps because rural peasant families had fewer gender-based labour distinctions in comparison with middle-class urban society.

Feminists who privilege sexual difference often fail to understand women's interest in nationalist or socialist causes, because they understand women's interests to be entirely gender-related. This can lead to sweeping generalisations about women without historical specificity. This essay reveals the existence of complex and intriguing debates about women's rights during a time of intense political agitation. As historians examine in more detail the writings and events of this period, differences, not only between women and men, but also among women over such issues as class, gender and nationalism will prove central to an understanding of women and men's political activities.

41 Ellis, *A History of the Irish Working Class*, pp. 98–9.

'Insouciant Rivals of Mrs Barton': Gender and Victorian Aspiration in George Moore and the Women Novelists of the *Irish Monthly*

JAMES H. MURPHY

Without doubt the *Irish Monthly*, which was founded in 1873 as a review of literature, the arts, current affairs and religion, was one of the more significant Irish literary journals of the late nineteenth century. It was one of the first journals to publish the poetry of Oscar Wilde and W.B. Yeats, for example. The publishing of fiction, however, was one of its priorities, as is witnessed by the fact that when its founding editor Matthew Russell, the Jesuit litterateur, came to review the successes of its first twenty-five years, his first thoughts were of the fiction it had published.[1] During those years the *Irish Monthly* serialised novels by nineteen writers, thirteen of them women. Russell was in no way condescending in his acknowledgement of the contribution of these women writers. Without the support of the prolific and highly-popular Rosa Mulholland, for example, the *Irish Monthly* 'could hardly have been carried on and would probably never have been begun'.

Mulholland herself, who was related to Russell through marriage, had hoped that, in the era immediately before the Anglo-Irish literary revival, initiatives such as Russell's Dublin-based journal would have acted as a counter to the effects of 'the ready English market for fiction [which] draws off our talent and employs it at remunerative images on the themes its daily supply requires'. Attacking Justin McCarthy, the Irish Party parliamentarian, for writing 'perfect English for the English', she concluded somewhat sarcastically:

> Yet how can we quarrel with any of these bright spirits if they prefer to live their lives pleasantly and in affluent circumstances in the busy, working, paying world of London, rather than content themselves with the ideally uncomfortable conditions of him who elects to chew the cud of sweet and bitter Irish fancies with his feet in an Irish bog and his head in a rainbow.[2]

Russell's own hopes for the fiction published in the *Irish Monthly*, much of which was subsequently reissued in book form, had been quite specific. In 1885 he wrote:

---

1 Matthew Russell, 'Silver Jubilee Retrospect' in *Irish Monthly*, 25 (1897), pp. 1–6. 2 Rosa Mulholland, 'Wanted an Irish Novelist' in *Irish Monthly*, 19 (1891), pp. 368–73.

The very highest aspiration we can make for our periodical is that it may be the forerunner of a Catholic literature in Ireland … a literature religious to the core which should reflect the majesty and eternal truth of our Faith, and its beauty and poetry as well; Irish, too, to the core – thrilling with our Celtic nature and coloured by our wonderful history.[3]

In such hopes he must have been disappointed, however. Few of the three dozen or so novels serialised in the *Irish Monthly* in its first quarter century had settings whose Irishness was an important feature of their construction. Fewer still were explicitly Catholic in their intent. Indeed, the handful of specifically Catholic novels published were mostly by English writers who were priests or nuns. By contrast around one third of the novels were apparently bland romantic comedies by women novelists from the Irish Catholic upper middle class.

In fact there was an ideological agenda at work in these novels but one in which concerns of class eclipsed not only those of Catholicism and Irishness but of gender as well. In late nineteenth-century Ireland the Catholic upper middle class aspired to metropolitanism and consequently feared provincialism. The British political connection with Ireland was not perceived as a necessarily negative factor by the class of Catholic doctors, lawyers, merchants and landlords. They were more nationally-minded than nationalists. They certainly subscribed to an Irish sense of national identity but were not separatists. For them participation in a distinctively Irish national and religious identity was compatible not only with metropolitan Victorian culture but also with an imperial, British identity. They therefore viewed the continuing political and social tensions which existed between Ireland and Britain as damaging to their interests. These tensions fed British stereotypes about the Irish and threatened hopes for full Irish participation in Victorian respectability.

Upper middle class Catholics saw their task as being to modify the adverse image which Ireland had been allotted in English cultural discourse. By enhancing the image their country enjoyed within Anglo-Saxon culture they sought to increase not only the esteem in which they were held but their own self-esteem. It was not simply that they wanted to please the English. They wanted to please the English so that they could feel pleased with themselves. Failing that, they aspired to prove, to their own satisfaction at least, that if the English did not feel pleased with them then at least they *ought* to do so.

Rosa Mulholland, the most important of the *Irish Monthly* writers, published a handful of novels in Russell's journal, including two of her more famous works, *The Wild Birds of Killeevy* (1878–80) and *Marcella Grace* (1885). Both are designedly Irish in their settings, in accordance with Mulholland's stated policy on the matter of writing fiction. *Marcella Grace*, indeed, is overtly political in its concerns. Nonetheless, Mulholland also shared in her class's anxiety to demonstrate the probity of Irish Victorian virtue. For the most part, however, instead of using the

3 Matthew Russell, 'Irish Literature and Our Twelfth Anniversary' in *Irish Monthly*, 13 (1885), pp 335–43.

opportunity which the *Irish Monthly* afforded of writing romantic comedies of middle and upper class life for such a demonstration, Mulholland chose to publish in book form stories of the respectability of what would have been known as peasant women. Since from a British perspective all Irish people were the same, a flaw in one class was attributed to all. Mulholland's novels of the moral dilemmas faced by the peasantry thus bolstered her class's case for Victorian acceptance. Reviewers credited Mulholland with a special expertise in describing the conditions of the poorer classes.[4]

Mulholland's peasant characters are pillars of conventional Victorian propriety. Their greatest virtue is that they know their place. Ultimately, therefore, neither gender roles nor the position of women in Victorian society are ever seriously challenged in Mulholland's novels. Thus in *Onora* (1900), the servant girl heroine leaves the family for whom she is working when she judges that the young head of the family would imperil his financial position if he were to marry her, as he wishes, rather than a rich girl who has returned from America.

If *Onora* is about a woman anxious to remain respectable, then *Nanno* (1898) and *The Tragedy of Chris* (1903) are about women coping with the loss of respectability. *The Tragedy of Chris* contrasts the experience of two young girls, Sheelia O'Ryan and Chris. Both begin as poor Dublin flower sellers. Chris disappears to London and becomes a 'wicked woman' while Sheelia rises to be the maid of a respectable lady. Loyally, she goes to London to rescue her friend, resists the advances of Chris's keeper and marries a man who has devoted himself to saving good Irish girls from the temptations of a London which, not unintentionally, is seen as having much that militates against Irish respectability.

As both girls begin at the same level it is clearly Mulholland's position that what happens to Chris is not inevitable but the result of her own weakness which, though pathetic, is also culpable. Chris can be pitied and Sheelia may rescue her, but she cannot be rehabilitated and is conveniently allowed to die, overcome with guilt. Mulholland's novel is thus a fable about the consequences for women of straying from the path of Victorian rectitude.

Unlike *The Tragedy of Chris* which charts a fall from respectability, *Nanno* recounts an inappropriate attempt to recover it. An unmarried mother, Nanno leaves her child in a workhouse in Dublin and moves to Youghal where, pretending to be a widow, she becomes engaged to a wealthy, young farmer. The most interesting parts of the book centre on Nanno's conversations about the correctness of her actions with the priest she consults about it. When he tells her that what she is doing is wrong, she quotes the case of Mary Magdalene and asks if she cannot be forgiven. He replies that of course Christ would forgive as he had forgiven Mary Magdalene but that it would be too much to expect any decent man to ignore her past and marry her without her deceiving him as she was deceiving her fiancé. Nanno is left in no doubt about the soundness of this judgement when on returning to Youghal she hears her fiancé criticise a woman whose husband had discovered she had kept the full story of her past life from him. Nanno calls off the engagement, allowing him think that she loves someone else.

In this novel, Mulholland, perhaps inadvertently, opens up a gap between a Victorian, puritan ethic in which respectability, once lost, can never be recovered and a Catholic ethic which allows room for forgiveness. The arrogant tone of Nanno's remarks at the beginning of the novel as she makes it clear that she is determined to forge a respectable future for herself, is already an indication of how the novelist views her quest. Though she tries to accommodate a Catholic view within it, Mulholland opts for the puritan ethic precisely because Victorianism could only view Catholic forgiveness as a form of moral looseness, the very thing of which Mulholland wishes to avoid giving an impression. Yet she has also to justify what happens in Catholic terms and only succeeds in doing so awkwardly, by portraying Nanno's planned marriage as an affront to honesty and truthfulness, because she does not plan to reveal her past. In *Nanno* ideological tensions and contradictions are very close to the surface.

In general, Rosa Mulholland's novels of life among the peasantry present themselves as moral fables, teaching the necessity of the Victorian social code. From the point of view of writers like Mulholland this was an opportunity to demonstrate a loyal adherence to Victorian standards, both in the sort of novels written and in the sort of code for life advocated in them, rather than an opportunity to question or challenge the position allotted to women within the Victorian ethic. For Mulholland, class concerns came first and precluded any serious analysis of gender or of the patriarchal structures of Victorian society.

For the most part Mulholland's agenda was also the agenda of many of the other women novelists of the *Irish Monthly*. They showed themselves anxious to conform to perceived Victorian standards of action in such romantic comedies as *Molly's Fortune* (1889–90) by M.E. Francis, *The Monk's Prophecy* (1882) and *The Cardassan Family* (1888) by Attie O'Brien, *Eleanor's Story* (1878) by Katherine Roche, *Meg Blake* (1893) and *Bogwort* (1896) by M.E. Connolly, and *A Perplexing Contrast* (1887) and *A Striking Contrast* (1895) by Clara Mulholland. *A Girl's Ideal* (1905) by Clara's sister, Rosa, also falls into the category of romantic comedy, though it was not published in the *Irish Monthly*. All of these novels are works in which convention and stock plots replace realism, as is especially evident when they are contrasted with *A Drama in Muslin* (1886) written by the novelist George Moore, a contemporary of the *Irish Monthly* novelists and a writer they would no doubt have considered more notorious than famous. It is the contention of what follows here that *A Drama in Muslin* can and perhaps should be best read in the context of novels such as those of the *Irish Monthly*. If so, it can be recognised as a remarkable counter by Moore to the studied insouciance which produced these novels.

The romantic comedies published in the *Irish Monthly* concern themselves almost exclusively with the tension between the proprieties of Victorian romantic love and the politics and economics of marriage. Like *A Drama in Muslin*, which in fact antedates some of them, they evince an awareness of the cut-throat nature of competition middle class women faced for the social and financial security of a good marriage. Yet they continue to insist that fidelity to Victorian standards of romance and respectability will achieve the desired goal without the need for any further effort. They thus eschew any significant examination of the inter-relationship between culture, economics and gender on the one hand and the institution of marriage on the other.

These novels are full of characters like Moore's Mrs Barton. There are ambitious mothers, such as Lady Ashfield in *A Striking Contrast* and Mrs Hassett in *The Monk's Prophecy*, also greedy wives, such as Susan Cullinan in *Bogwort*, and callous lovers such as Captain Calvert in *The Carradassan Family*. And yet the difference is that Mrs Barton, with her ruthless ambition and unsentimental pragmatism, is at least credited with being in touch with the realities of a world where glamour and gaiety mask a struggle for survival. In the novels of Moore's contemporaries who published in the *Irish Monthly*, the world tends to operate under the laws of unsentimental pragmatic reality until, towards the end, there is a change of perspective, a gear shift into a world of fantasy-fulfilment which abides by naïve and sentimental norms. Ironically, it is the pragmatists who are seen, in the end, to be out of touch where fantasy and reality have become inverted. Thus both Lady Ashfield and Mrs Hassett end up having to eat their words about the matrimonial suitability of the heroines of their respective novels.

Several formalised themes and plot patterns are discernible. A very common narrative theme is that which begins with an atomising of duty and affection and then works towards their reconciliation. Stock plots commonly involve features such as difficulties over a disparity in social station, marriage promises, swopped children, unexpected inheritances and righting wrongs.

In the end, all these romantic comedies conform more or less to a pattern in which a figure of innocence and virtue, according to the Victorian perception of such matters, is faced with a dilemma. For example, Dora Neil in *A Striking Contrast* wants to marry Lord Ashfield but she is not of his social station. And Nesta Dillon in *A Perplexing Promise* wants to marry Frank Adair, but feels herself bound by a childhood love pact. At this point a figure representing manipulative prag-matism often proposes a solution, which the innocent figure rejects. The fictional world then shifts gear from realism to fantasy-fulfilment. The dilemma dissolves. Innocence triumphs and pragmatism is wrongfooted. Just as the initial dilemma is often provided by stock problems such as those posed by marriage promises or swopped children, so stock devices, such as unexpected inheritance or an apparent return from the dead, herald the shift of register. Thus Dora Neil discovers she is an heiress all along and Nesta Dillon that Frank Adair is the same person to whom she had pledged herself in her youth, only he has disguised himself.

None of these novels makes an attempt to transcend the clichéd blueprint out of which they operate or to challenge the conventions of a woman's place in Victorian society, with the possible exception of *Meg Blake*, whose main character remains an unrestored victim of the novel's conflicts. Some of the novels are better than others but that is not to flatter any of them. *A Perplexing Promise* may be marginally less incredible than *Molly's Fortune*, which flounders in a sea of inheritance conditions and appearing and disappearing heirs. Neither, however, amounts to a very convincing presentation of human experience.

At most this fiction had a certain social value in terms of the normalising function it performed for Irish Catholic upper middle class culture. The upper middle class acceptance of the Victorian version of reality in its fiction helped to promote its alliance with Victorian society – in its own eyes, at least. Thus in reviewing *A Striking Contrast*, the *Freeman's Journal* even managed to hint that the Irish saw themselves as being more properly Victorian than others, even the English: 'There is an atmosphere of goodness and affection in the book which is refreshing and which we dare swear is more true to nature than the … taint of vice by which so many modern novels are contaminated.'[5]

The low literary standard of the *Irish Monthly* novelists was no accident. Rather, it reflected the tragic dilemma of their own class which was caught in a colonial, vicious circle. Their aspiration to have their Irish culture recognised as a valid and valued culture within the parameters of metropolitan British culture was one which was beyond their power to achieve because they had no control over the vagaries of relations between Ireland and Britain. Those relations centred on the land war and agitation for home rule in which the main players were the members of the much more nationalistic lower middle class. The pursuit of realism in fiction thus held no attraction for upper middle class novelists. It could only remind them of the intractability of the dilemma they faced. Their only hope was to make themselves seem as acceptable as possible in British eyes. Nor did the pursuit of such an acceptance leave any room for the questioning of Victorian gender roles, even if they had wanted to do so. A literary output of bland Victorian fantasy was the result.

The economic and social constraints of middle class, Victorian marriage were not without an Irish novelist critic, however. Born into the Catholic gentry of Co. Mayo, George Moore had the ideal pedigree for the Irish upper middle class whose fiction he parodied and whose Victorian marriage values he attacked in *A Drama in Muslin* (1886).

A Drama in Muslin centres on the contrast between appearance and reality: the difference between the glamorous facade of Victorian society life and the frantic scramble for the economic and social security of a supposedly good marriage. This contrast is also evident in the difference between the veneer of romantic propriety the *Irish Monthly* writers took so seriously and the reality of the cut and thrust of what was in effect a marriage market whose supply of marriageable young girls exceeded the demand from wealthy bachelors.

Thus, Alice Barton, a diligent and respected convent schoolgirl, finds that in the outside world a different standard of values applies from that which obtained during her education. Her beautiful sister, Olive, is considered a much more marketable proposition by their mother than she is. Later, when Mrs Barton tries to deter Captain Hibbert, a suitor for Olive of whom she disapproves, their conversation is pointedly juxtaposed with that of the negotiations between Mr Barton and his tenants. And when the girls go with their mother to Dublin for the social season and Lord Lieutenant's ball, Olive's new clothes are described as being from 'the armouries of Venus'[6] and Mrs Barton reflects that, 'In the great matrimonial hunts women have to hunt in packs.'[7]

Mrs Barton tries to supplement the attractiveness of Olive's beauty by falsely hinting that she also has a fortune of £20,000. However, her efforts to induce Lord Kilcarney to propose to Olive backfire and he ends up engaged to Violet Scully, a school friend of Alice and Olive. Mrs Barton's humiliation results from her failure to triumph in the hunt. There is no doubting, however, that her cynicism is a justified response to the harsh realities of life, unlike her rivals in the novels of the *Irish Monthly*, who suffer because life turns out to be more civilised than they had imagined.

The critique of the configuration of Victorian marriage and gender roles presented by *A Drama in Muslin* extends to questioning the value of the marriages of even those apparently lucky few, like Violet, who manage to secure what is considered to be a suitable husband. Unlike the *Irish Monthly* heroines whose lives, up until their marriages at least, are full of activity, marriage in *A Drama in Muslin* heralds a life of pampered indolence, not of fulfilment. Mrs Barton's tragedy is that she regards such a life as the apogee of success and all her energy goes into trying to secure it for her daughters:

> 'Keep on trying, that is my advice to all young ladies: try to make yourself agreeable, try to learn how to amuse men. Flatter them; that is the great secret; nineteen out of twenty will believe you, and the one that doesn't can't but think it delightful ... A husband is better than talent, better even than fortune – without a husband a woman is nothing; with a husband she may rise to any height. Marriage gives a girl liberty, gives her admiration, gives her success; a woman's whole position depends upon it.'[8]

A Drama in Muslin was part of George Moore's advocacy of modernity. As with several of his novels with English settings, that advocacy took specific shape in *A Drama in Muslin* around the issue of gender. The novel is an attack against Victorian marriage conventions and their novelistic expression, and against the craven deference given to them by the Catholic upper middle class. Whether or not Moore read all the *Irish Monthly* novels himself, he was certainly well aware of the ambience which had produced them. *A Drama in Muslin* is thus an attack on Victorianism in a specifically Irish context. But it is equally an attempt on Moore's part to normalise the modern conventions and values with which he seeks to replace Victorianism. It skilfully deconstructs one mentality in order to

6 George Moore, *A Drama in Muslin* (1886; Gerrards Cross, 1981), p. 162.   7 Ibid., p. 157.
8 Ibid., p. 137.

replace it with another. It is an irony then that Moore did not even manage to eradicate all the conventions of the Victorian romantic comedy from his own narrative technique, as is evidenced by his use of a stock device found both in *A Drama in Muslin* and in Attie O'Brien's *Won by Worth*.

In *Won by Worth* the forty-year old Captain Arthur Crosbie is in love with Mary Desmond, who is much younger than he is. It is only when Crosbie nurses her brother through a bout of smallpox that she notices him. And her attention turns to love when Crosbie himself is badly wounded and she has to nurse him back to health. And yet this stock bedside romance plot is the very one to which Moore resorts at the end of *A Drama in Muslin* in order to provide Alice with a happy future as a married woman in the relatively free atmosphere of London. For it is at the bedside of a seriously-ill Olive that Alice and Edward Reed, the local doctor, come to know and love each other. In at least one respect then Moore's novel retreats from parody to reliance on the fictional forms he so obviously despised. This aspect of Moore's feminist novel thus offers proof in microcosm of the ironies, ambiguities and complexities which attended the issue of gender in nineteenth-century Ireland.

Notes on Contributors

GRÁINNE M. BLAIR is Administrator of the Women's Research and Resource Centre in University College, Dublin. A feminist historian, she is continuing research on the development of the Salvation Army in Ireland and has published a number of articles on the Salvation Army rescue network. She is also currently writing a multiography of Lola Montez.

JAN CANNAVAN is an independent scholar living in Boston, Massachusetts. She has an M.A. in European Women's History from Binghamton University in New York. Her main research interest is the intersection of gender, class and national identification, particularly as these are manifested in Irish history.

ANNE COLMAN received her B.A. degree from the University of the Pacific, M.A. from Sonoma State University, and Ph.D. from the National University of Ireland. She was formerly Research Fellow at the Institute of Irish Studies, Queen's University, Belfast, and is currently preparing a volume of Florence Mary Wilson's selected writings. She is the author of *A Dictionary of Nineteenth-century Irish Women Poets* (1996) and is particularly interested in the recovery of pre-1950 Irish women writers.

MARY CULLEN was formerly Senior Lecturer in Modern History and is currently an academic associate at St Patrick's College, Maynooth. She also contributes to the Women's Studies M. Phil. programme at Trinity College, Dublin. Her most recent publication is *Women, Power and Consciousness in Nineteenth-Century Ireland: Eight Biographical Studies*, co-edited with Maria Luddy.

MARY ELLEN DOONA is a psychiatric nurse and Associate Professor at Boston College. She is historian of the Massachusetts Nurse Association and chairs the executive committee of its Lucy Lincoln Drown Nursing History Society.

DAVID FITZPATRICK is the author of *Irish Emigration, 1801–1921* (1984) and *Oceans of Consolation: Personal Accounts of Irish Migration to Australia* (1995). He is Associate Professor of Modern History at Trinity College, Dublin.

ANNE FOGARTY lectures in the Department of English at University College, Dublin. She has published essays on Renaissance literature and on twentieth-century Irish writers including Mary Dorcey, Eavan Boland, Medbh McGuckian and Kate O'Brien. She is currently working on a study of Spenser and early modern colonial writings about Ireland.

TIMOTHY P. FOLEY teaches in the Department of English at University College, Galway. He is a graduate of University College, Galway and of the University of Oxford. He is the author (with Thomas Boylan) of *Political Economy and Colonial Ireland: the Propagation and Ideological Function of Economic Discourse in the Nineteenth Century* (1992).

COLIN GRAHAM lectures in English literature at the University of Huddersfield. He was formerly Junior Research Fellow at the Institute of Irish Studies, Queen's University of Belfast. He has published a number of articles on post-colonial theory and Ireland and has edited Robert Browning's *Men and Women and Other Poems and the Selected Poems of Elizabeth Barrett Browning*. He is currently working on an introduction to Irish Studies to be published by Routledge.

BRIAN GRIFFIN is a lecturer in Irish Studies in the History Department of Bath College of Higher Education. His research interests include Fenianism, the history of police in nineteenth-century Ireland and the Irish in the British army.

GLENN HOOPER lectures in the Department of English at St Mary's College, Belfast. He is a graduate of Trinity College, Dublin and University College, Dublin and has published a number of articles on travel literature and Ireland.

TOBY JOYCE lives and works in Galway. He is preparing his M.A. thesis for University College, Galway on Irish Nationalism in the period of the American Civil War.

MARGARET KELLEHER lectures in English in St Patrick's College, Maynooth. She is the author of *The Feminization of Famine* (1997) and has published a number of articles on famine literature and on Irish women's writings.

SIOBHÁN KILFEATHER is a lecturer in the School of English and American Studies at the University of Sussex. Her research interests include Irish women's writing since the seventeenth century and sexuality in modern Ireland.

JOHN LOGAN lectures in History in the University of Limerick and is the author of *Literacy and Schooling in Nineteenth-Century Ireland*, to be published by Cork University Press in 1997.

JOHN MCAULIFFE tutors in the English department at University College Galway where he is completing a M.A. on mid-nineteenth century travel writing in Ireland. He has also taught in Southern Illinois University at Carbondale. He edits *ROPES* (Review of Postgraduate Studies), a UCG production whose Spring 1996 issue concentrated on de Valera and representations of rural Ireland.

CHRISTINA HUNT MAHONY, a graduate of University College Dublin, is Associate Director of the Center of Irish Studies at the Catholic University of America in Washington, DC. She is preparing an introduction to contemporary Irish literature for St Martin's Press.

JAMES H. MURPHY lectures in English at All Hallows College, Drumcondra, Dublin. Among his recent publications are *Catholic Fiction and Social Reality in Ireland, 1873–1922* (1997) and *Nos Autem: Castleknock College and its Contribution* (1996).

CLÍONA Ó GALLCHOIR received her B.A. and M.A. degrees from University College, Dublin and is currently a doctoral student in the Faculty of English at Trinity College, Cambridge.

OONAGH WALSH is a lecturer in History and Director of Women's Studies at the University of Aberdeen. She has published a number of articles on women in nineteenth and twentieth-century Ireland, and is currently conducting research on the expansion of the asylum system in the West of Ireland.

Index